国际商务单证操作实训

GUOJISHANGWUDANZHENG CAOZUO SHIXUN

杨金玲　张建华 ◎ 主编

首都经济贸易大学出版社
·北京·

前言

PREFACE

在对外经贸企业单证员岗位典型工作任务和职业能力分析的基础上,借助虚拟的泰佛贸易公司(TIFERT TRADING CO., LTD),本教材的编写从新员工到公司"招聘室"应聘面试所进行的单证基础知识的【岗前测试】开始,面试通过后再到"经理室"接受有关单证缮制规范的【岗前培训】,最后被公司录用为员工受领任务后到"工作室"【上岗操作】,教材始终围绕这一就业流程展开,使整个学习过程融于单证岗的工作过程之中,做到学习过程与工作过程相一致。

为更好地实现课程教学目标,本教材的编写彻底打破了按照知识系统性组织教学的传统模式,采取以单证员岗位工作任务的相关性组织教学内容,以真实工作任务为情境,以贯穿国际贸易始终的"单据"为载体,在专门构建的职业情境中进行单证岗从业资格的知识传授、技能培养、职业素质养成教育,做到"做中学、做中教",培养学生具有由专业能力、方法能力和社会能力构成的关键能力。

本教材共分走进单证部、接触信用证、缮制单证、综合训练、审核单证五个学习情境及认知单证、缮制发票、缮制全套单据、审核单据等13个典型工作任务,每个任务中又分为【岗前测试】、【岗前培训】和【上岗操作】。其中:岗前测试部分依据单证岗典型工作任务的需要来选取单证相关基础知识,采用单选题、多选题和判断题的形式解决有关单证显性知识的获取问题;岗前培训部分主要针对各种单证各个栏目如何填制,每种单证都详列了操作规范和操作范例(以一笔女童夹克进料加工贸易所涉及的全部进出口单证贯穿教材始终),以此解决了单证操作隐性知识的获取问题;上岗操作部分就每种单证全部布置了初级、中级、高级不同难易度的典型工作任务,学生通过完成渐次复杂的工作任务,强化学生单证操作技能,满足不同层次学生求知、求技的需要。

本教材由《进出口单证实务》国家级精品课负责人杨金玲和第一主讲教师张建华

主编,天津对外经济贸易职业学院信息中心的宗路广、张鑫两位老师参与了部分内容的编写,并负责收集了大量的网络信息资源。在编写过程中,同时也得到了北方国际集团天津金纺进出口有限公司副总经理付斌和天津光大银行国际结算部刘斌的鼎力相助,他们提出了许多好的建议,在此一并表示感谢。由于编者水平有限,错误在所难免,恳请专家和同行不吝赐教。

编者

2009 年 8 月

目 录

CONTENTS

新员工致辞

欢迎您来到泰佛贸易公司!

Welcome to Tifert Trading Co., Ltd!

首先到招聘室接受岗前测试

然后到经理室接受培训
受领任务

再到工作室完成相关操作

欢迎您来到“泰佛贸易公司”,请首先到“招聘室”接受两位主考官就单证基础知识所进行的【岗前测试】,通过后再到“经理室”接受单证缮制规范的【岗前培训】,被公司录用为员工受领任务后到“工作室”【上岗操作】。工作室按照往来贸易区域进行设置,分别主管韩日地区(初级训练)业务、美加地区(中级训练)业务和中东地区(高级训练)业务,公司承诺给您提供充分施展业务才能的发展空间。

预祝您在泰佛贸易公司工作顺利,事业有成!

学习情境一　走进单证部

任务一　认知单证

岗前测试

一、单选题

> 温馨提示：
>
> 国际贸易买卖双方相距甚远不能做到一手交钱，一手交货，卖方往往以交单代替交货，买方也是见单付款，从某种程度上说，国际贸易就是典型的单据买卖，因此单证在国际贸易中处于一个非常重要的地位。

1. 金融（资金）单证不包括（　）。

A. 汇票　　B. 发票

C. 支票　　D. 本票

2. 外贸单证工作通常包括五个环节，下列排序正确的是（　）。

A. 制单—审证—审单—交单—归档

B. 审证—制单—审单—交单—归档

C. 审单—审证—制单—交单—归档

D. 审证—审单—制单—交单—归档

3. 公务单证不包括（　）。

A. 产地证　　B. 保险单　　C. 商检证书　　D. 许可证

4. 下列单据中可以由民间机构签发的单证是（　）。

A. 提单　　B. 保险单　　C. 一般原产地证　　D. 许可证

5. 下列单据中不属于出口商签发的单据是（　）。

A. 发票　　B. 提单　　C. 重量单　　D. 装箱单

6. 下列单据中既可以由官方机构也可由民间机构签发的证书是（　）。

A. 许可证　　B. 一般原产地证　　C. 提单　　D. 普惠制原产地证

7. “单证一致”是指进出口单据与（　）保持一致。

A. 许可证　　B. 原产地证　　C. 商检证　　D. 信用证

8. 信用证付款方式下，下列关于单据缮制的依据正确的排序是（　）。

A. 合同—信用证—供货厂家的码单—业务上的特殊要求—有关国际惯例

B. 供货厂家的码单—信用证—合同—业务上的特殊要求—有关国际惯例

C. 有关国际惯例—信用证—供货厂家的码单—业务上的特殊要求—合同

D. 信用证—合同—供货厂家的码单—业务上的特殊要求—有关国际惯例

9. 下列单据中属于公务单据的是(　)。

A. 发票　B. 提单　C. 许可证　D. 装箱单

10. 下列单据中不属于运输单据的是(　)。

A. 空运单　B. 提单　C. 铁路运单　D. 装运通知

二、多选题

1. 单据可以从不同的角度进行分类,通常可以(　)进行划分。

A. 从单证的性质上　B. 从单证的用途上

C. 从商品的流向上　D. 从单证的签发单位上

2. 单证的作用主要表现为(　)。

A. 履行买卖合同的证明　B. 结汇的必要工具

C. 解决争端的依据　D. 企业经营管理水平的重要标志

3. 下列单证中,既可以是出口单证,也可以是进口单证的是(　)。

A. 进境货物报检单　B. 信用证

C. 包装单据　D. 保险单

4. 其他单据通常包括(　)。

A. 寄单(样)证明　B. 装运通知　C. 磅码单　D. 受益人证明函

5. 出口商自行签发的单证通常有(　)。

A. 发票　B. 汇票　C. 提单　D. 装箱单

相关链接:

①全国国际商务单证员培训认证考试中心(单证员)

http://www.icd.net.cn/

②全国外贸跟单员培训认证考试中心(跟单员)

http://www.gdy.net.cn/

③全国外贸业务员培训认证考试中心(业务员)

http://www.chinawmks.com/

④中国国际货运代理协会考试中心(货代员)

http://ftp.coscoqmc.com.cn/hdks/

⑤报检员资格考试网(报检员)

http://www.baojianyuan.net.cn/

⑥中国报关员考试网(报关员)

http://www.bgyks.com/

三、判断题

1. 金融单据以外所有单证都称为商业单据。( )

2. 单证的完整是指单据内容完整和单据种类完整。( )

3. 及时出单包括两个方面的内容:一方面是指各种单据的出单日期必须合理可行;另一方面,还反映在交单议付上。( )

4. 银行提倡在信用证或其修改书中加注过多的细节内容,并且要反映到相应的单据中。( )

5. 在某种意义上说国际贸易就是单据买卖,几乎所有贸易环节的具体操作都与单据的交换密切相关。( )

6. 单证工作总体的要求是:"证同一致、单证一致、单单一致"。( )

7. 单证制作应做到正确、完整、及时、简明、整洁。( )

8. "单单一致"是指各种单据之间保持一致,不同单据中共有的信息可以略有不同。( )

9. 单据份数完整即要求出口商提供的各种单据的份数要按信用证、买卖合同和惯例的要求如数交齐,不能短缺。( )

10. 单据的内容应按合同、信用证要求和国际惯例要求填写,越烦琐越好。( )

岗前培训

一、单据缮制依据

表 1-1 单据缮制依据

买卖合同	在非信用证支付方式下,买卖合同是制单和审单的首要依据,从商品名称、数量、规格、价格条件到运输方式、支付方式等均应符合买卖合同的规定;而在信用证支付方式下,虽然单据的缮制应该以信用证条款为准,但有些项目如商品的品名、规格、单价、佣金等如果信用证没有明确规定,也须参照合同条款制单。在托收支付方式下,单据的缮制更是需要以合同为基础。
信用证	在信用证支付方式下,信用证取代买卖合同而成为主要的缮制进出口单证的主要依据,凡是信用证项下的单据,必须严格按照信用证的条款缮制。因为银行付款原则是"只凭信用证而不问合同",各种单据必须完全符合信用证的规定,银行才能承担付款责任。如果信用证条款与买卖合同相互矛盾,要么修改信用证,以求得"证同一致",否则应以信用证为准才能达到安全收汇的目的。
仓库的出库单/供货厂家的码单	有关商品的实际出运数量,一般以仓库的出库单载明的具体数量、重量、规格、尺码等为准,或以供货厂家提供的码单为准。有些商品的包装不是规格划一,如棉花一般采用机压包,每包的重量很难做到完全一样,包装单的缮制应该以供货厂家提供的磅码单为准;再如服装、鞋帽一般采用混色混码装,实际业务中,很难做到所有的货物都能严格按照搭配要求装箱,往往最后有些是混箱的,包装单的缮制应该以供货厂家提供的装箱单为准。

续表

业务上的特殊要求	由于每个行业都有其特定的要求，外经贸企业应按规定的格式和要求缮制单据。例如：出口纺织品时经常会遇到国外要求我们提供 AZO free Certificate（无偶氮证明，这是与人类健康有关的一种特殊单据）；出口到信仰伊斯兰教国家的禽类产品，进口商会提出由出口地伊斯兰教协会出具有关证明；AMS 舱单由美国开始，现已扩展到加拿大、澳大利亚、欧洲各国等；农药产品出口到美国、欧盟等国家和地区时，买方通常会要求卖方提供所出口的农药产品的 MSDS（危险数据资料卡）等。
有关国际惯例	国际贸易中的有关国际惯例，如国际商会的《UCP600》以及《托收统一规则》和《INCOTERMS 2000》等出版物，也是正确缮制进出口单证的依据。

二、单证范例

商业发票
COMMERCIAL INVOICE

Issuer
TIANJIN GARMENT I/E INC
NO.1 YOU YI ROAD, HE XI DISTRICT,
TIANJIN, CHINA

To
H&M TRADING SWEDEN AB
KORSGATAN 15 SE 412 18 SWEDEN

No. G2008S/A16001　Date OCT 18, 2008
S/C No. YD16008　L/C No. FM0809378

Trans Detail
SHIPMENT FROM TIANJIN, CHINA TO GOTHENBURG SWEDEN BY SEA

Terms of payment
BY L/C AT SIGHT

Marks & numbers	Number and kind of packages; description of goods	Quantity	Unit Price	Amount
H&M YD16008 GOTHERNBURG CTN NO.1-180	180 CARTONS = 5400PCS LAUNDRYBAG 100% POLYESTER SIZE 72 x 110CM			
	30CTNS ORDER NO.080816	900PCS	USD1.95/PC	USD1755.00
	120CTNS ORDER NO.080817	3600PCS	USD2.05/PC	USD7380.00
	30CTNS ORDER NO.080818	900PCS	USD2.00/PC	USD1800.00
	180CTNS	5400PCS		USD10935.00

TOTAL: GROSS WEIGHT 4500.00KGS
NET WEIGHT4320.00KGS
MEASUREMENT 4.726M3

TIANJIN GARMENTS IMPORT & EXPORT

样例1-1　商业发票

Issuer:

TIANJIN GARMENT I/E INC
NO.1 YOU YI ROAD, HE XI DISTRICT,
TIANJIN, CHINA

To

H&M TRADING SWEDEN AB
KORSGATAN 15 SE 412 18 SWEDEN

装 箱 单

PACKING LIST

Invoice No. G2008S/A16001 **Date** OCT 18, 2008

Marks and numbers | **Number and kind of packages Description of goods**

H&M
YD16008
GOTHERNBURG
CTN NO.1-180

LAUNDRYBAG
100% POLYESTER
SIZE 72 x 110CM

ORDER NO.	QTY	CTN NO.	G.W.	N.W.	MEAS
ORDER NO.080816	900PCS	30CTNS	750KGS	720KGS	0.788M3
ORDER NO.080817	3600PCS	120CTNS	3000KGS	2880KGS	3.150M3
ORDER NO.080818	900PCS	30CTNS	750KGS	720KGS	0.788M3
TOTAL:	5400PCS	180CTNS	4500KGS	4320KGS	4.726M3

L/C NO. FM0809378

TOTAL: GROSS WEIGHT 4500KGS
NET WEIGHT 4320KGS
MEASUREMENT 4.726M3

天津服装进出口股份有限公司(20)
TIANJIN GARMENTS IMPORT & EXPORT INCORPORATION

样例 1－2 装箱单

中华人民共和国出入境检验检疫　　　　正　本

ENTRY-EXIT INSPECTION AND QUARANTITE　　ORIGINAL
OF THE PEOPLE`S REPUBLIC OF CHINA

编号 No.: 120600209026897

QUALITY CERTIFICATE

发货人
Consignor　TIANJIN GARMENT I/E INC

收货人
Cosignee　* * * *

品名 Description of Goods　LAUNDRYBAG 报检数量/重量 Quantity/Weight Declared　5400PCS 包装种类及数量 Number and Type of Packages　180 CARTONS 运输工具 Means of Conveyance　HENGHE RIVER V.385	标记及号码 Mark & No. H & M YD16008 GOTHERNBURG CTN NO. 1-180

检验结果
Result of inspection

SAMPLES WERE DRAWN AT RANDOM FROM THE WHOLE LOT OF GOODS AND INSPECTED STRICTLY ACCORDING TO THE S/C NO. YD16008

ORDER NO. 080816　900PCS　30CARTONS
ORDER NO. 080817　3600PCS　120CARTONS
ORDER NO.080818　900PCS　30CARTONS

THE ABOVE RESULTS OF INSPCTION ARE IN CONFORMITY WITH THE REQUIREMENTS IN THE SAID CONTRACT.　　L/C NO. FM0809378

印章：　签证地点 Place of Issue　天津　签证日期 Date of Issue　OCT 26, 2008

Official Stamp

授权签字人 Authorized Officer　ZHANG MING　签名 Signature　张明

我们已尽所知和最大能力实施上述检验，不能因我们签发本证书而免除卖方或其他方面根据合同和法律所承担的产品质量责任和其他责任。

All inspection are carried out conscientiously to the best of our knowledge and ability. This certificate dose not in any respect absolve the seller and other related parties from his contractual and legal obligations especially when product quality is concerned.

样例 1－3　检验证书

ORIGINAL

1. Goods consigned from (Exporter's business name, address, country) TIANJIN GARMENT I/E INC NO.1 YOU YI ROAD, HE XI DISTRICT, TIANJIN, CHINA	Reference No. G091206100070200 **GENERALIZED SYSTEM OF PREFERENCES** **CERTIFICATE OF ORIGIN** **(Combined declaration and certificate)** **FORM A** Issued in THE PEOPLE'S REPUBLIC OF CHINA (country) See Notes. overleaf
2. Goods consigned to (Consignee's name, address, country) H&M TRADING SWEDEN AB KORSGATAN 15 SE 412 18 SWEDEN	
3. Means of transport and route (as far as known) SHIPMENT FROM TIANJIN, CHINA TO GOTHENBURG SWEDEN BY SEA	4. For official use

5. Item number	6. Marks and numbers of packages	7. Number and kind of packages; description of goods	8. Origin criterion (see Notes overleaf)	9. Gross weight or other quantity	10. Number and date of invoices
1	H&M YD16008 GOTHERNBURG CTN NO. 1-180	180 (ONE HUNDERD AND EIGHTY) CARTONS OF LAUNDRYBAG L/C NO. FM0809378 * * * * *	"P"	4500KGS	INV NO. G2008S/ A16001 OCT 18, 2008

11. Certification It is hereby certified, on the basis of control carried out, that the declaration by the exporter is correct. TIANJIN [illegible] 18, 2008 Place and date, signature and stamp of certifying authority	12. Declaration by the exporter The undersigned hereby declares that the above details and statements are correct; that all the goods were produced in CHINA (country) and that they comply with the origin requirements specified for those goods in the Generalized System of Preferences for goods exported to SWEDEN (importing country) TIANJIN GARMENTS IMP & EXP INC TIANJIN CHINA, OCT 18, 2008 Place and date, signature of authorized signatory

S065500265

样例 1-4 普惠制原产地证书

ORIGINAL

1. Exporter TIANJIN GARMENT I/E INC NO.1 YOU YI ROAD, HE XI DISTRICT, TIAJIN, CHINA	Certificate No. CCPIT 083711879 08C1200A0018/00175 CERTIFICATE OF ORIGIN OF THE PEOPLE' S REPUBLIC OF CHINA
2. Consignee H&M TRADING SWEDEN AB KORSGATAN 15 SE 412 18 SWEDEN	
3. Means of transport and route SHIPMENT FROM TIANJIN, CHINA TO GOTHENBURG SWEDEN BY SEA	5. For certifying authority use only
4. Country / region of destination SWEDEN	

6. Marks and numbers	7. Number and kind of packages; description of goods	8. H.S.Code	9. Quantity	10. Number and date of invoices
H&M YD16008 GOTHERNBURG CTN NO.1-180	180(ONE HUNDERD AND EIGHTY) CARTONS OF LAUNDRYBAG L/C NO. FM0809378 * * * * *	6305	4500.00KGS	INV NO. G2008S/ A16001 OCT 18, 2008

11. Declaration by the exporter	12. Certification
The undersigned hereby declares that the above details and statements are correct, that all the goods were produced in China and that they comply with the Rules of Origin of the People's Republic of China.	It is hereby certified that the declaration by the exporter is correct
TIANJIN OCT 18, 2008 陈晓宏	中国国际贸易促进委员会 单据证明专用章 (津) CHINA COUNCIL FOR THE PROMOTION OF INTERNATIONAL TRADE (TIANJIN) TIANJIN OCT 18, 2008
Place and date, signature and stamp of authorized signatory	Place and date, signature and stamp of certifying authority

样例1－5 一般原产地证书

Shipper 托運人	EAS **B/L No.** EASL089021186
TIANJIN GARMENT I/E INC NO.1 YOU YI ROAD, HE XI DISTRICT, TIAJIN, CHINA	**EAS LINE** 大通航運有限公司 **EAS EXPRESS SHIPPING LTD.** 联运提单 **COMBINED TRANSPORT BILL OF LADING**
Consignee or order 收貨人或指示 TO ORDER	RECEIVED the goods in apparent good order and condition as specified below unless otherwise stated herein. The carrier in accordance with the provisions contained in this document, 1) undertakes to perform or to procure the performance of the entire transport from the place at which the goods are taken in charge to the place designated for delivery in this document, and 2) assumes liability as prescribed in this document for such transport. One of the Bills of Lading must be surrendered duly indorsed in exchange for the goods or delivery order.
Notify party 通知地址 H&M TRADING SWEDEN AB KORSGATAN 15 SE 412 18 SWEDEN	

Pre-carriage by 前段運輸	Place of receipt 收貨地點		
Ocean vessel 海運船隻 HENCHE RIVER V.385	Port of loading 裝貨港 TIANJIN, CHINA		
Port of discharge 卸貨港 GOTHENBURG, SWEDEN	Place of delivery 交貨地點	Freight payable at 運費支付地	Number of original Bs/L 正本提單份數 THREE

Marks and Nos. 標志和號碼	Number and Kind of packages 件數和包裝種類	Description of goods 貨名	Gross weight (kgs) 毛重(公斤)	Measurement (m³) 尺碼(立方米)
H&M YD16008 GOTHERNBURG CTN NO.1-180	180CARTONS	LAUNDRYBAG	4500.00KGS	4.726M3

FREIGHT PREPAID

SHIPPER'S LOAD, COUNT AND SEAL

Original

ON BOARD

L/C NO. FM0809378

OCT 28, 2008

EASL4789321/11568/180/CPS/CPS

TOTAL: ONE HUNDRED AND EIGHTY CARTONS ONLY

以上細目由托運人提供
ABOVE PARTICULARS FURNISHED BY SHIPPER

Freight and charges 運費和費用	IN WITNESS whereof the number of original Bills of Lading stated above have been signed, one of which being accomplished, the other (s) to be void.
	Place and date of issue 簽單地點和日期 TIANJIN OCT 28, 2008
	Signed for or on behalf of the carrier 代表承運人簽字 **EAS EXPRESS SHIPPING LTD.** 韩 伟 As agent

样例1-6 海运提单

中国人民财产保险股份有限公司
PICC Property and Casualty Company Limited

货物运输保险单 CARGO TRANSPORTATION INSURANCE POLICY

印刷号 (Printed Number) № 001572　　保险单号(Policy No.) TT08/120107119840454２
合同号 (Contract No.) YD16008
发票号 (Invoice No.) G2008S/A16001
信用证号(L/C No.) FM0809378
被保险人(Insured): TIANJIN GARMENT I/E INC

中国人民财产保险股份有限公司（以下简称本公司）根据被保险人要求，以被保险人向本公司缴付约定的保险费为对价，按照本保险单列明条款承保下述货物运输保险，特订立本保险单。
THIS POLICY OF INSURANCE WITNESSES THAT PICC PROPERTY AND CASUALTY COMPANY LIMITED (HEREINAFTER CALLED "THE COMPANY") AT THE REQUEST OF THE INSURED AND IN CONSIDERATION OF THE AGREED PREMIUM PAID TO THE COMPANY BY THE INSURED, UNDERTAKES TO INSURE THE UNDERMENTIONED GOODS IN TRANSPORTATION SUBJECT TO THE CONDITIONS OF THIS POLICY AS PER THE CLAUSES PRINTED BELOW.

标记 MARKS & NOS.	包装及数量 QUANTITY	保险货物项目 GOODS	保险金额 AMOUNT INSURED
AS PER INV. NO. G2008S/A16001	180 CARTONS	LAUNDRYBAG L/C NO. FM0809378	USD12029.00

ORIGINAL

总保险金额：
Total Amount Insured: TWELVEN THOUSAND AND TWENY-NINE ONLY

保费(Premium): AS ARRANGED　　启运日期(Date of Commencement): AS PER B/L

装载运输工具(Per Conveyance): HENGHE RIVER V.385

自：From TIANJIN, CHINA　　经：Via　　至：To GOTHENBURG, SWEDEN

承保险别(Conditions):

COVERING ALL RISKS AND WAR RISK AS PER OCEAN MARINE CARGO CLAUSES OF PICC DATED 1/1/1981 INCLUDING WAREHOUSE TO WAREHOUSE

所保货物如发生保险单项下可能引起索赔的损失，应立即通知本公司或下述代理人查勘。如有索赔，应向本公司提交正本保险单（本保险单共有 2 份正本）及有关文件。如一份正本已用于索赔，其余正本自动失效。
IN THE EVENT OF LOSS OR DAMAGE WHICH MAY RESULT IN A CLAIM UNDER THIS POLICY, IMMEDIATE NOTICE MUST BE GIVEN TO THE COMPANY OR AGENT AS MENTIONED. CLAIMS, IF ANY, ONE OF THE ORIGINAL POLICY WHICH HAS BEEN ISSUED IN TWO ORIGINAL(S) TOGETHER WITH THE RELEVANT DOCUMENTS SHALL BE SURRENDERED TO THE COMPANY. IF ONE OF THE ORIGINAL POLICY HAS BEEN ACCOMPLISHED, THE OTHERS TO BE VOID.

THE INSURANCE COMPANY OF SWEDEN, LTD
KORSGATAN 18, SE 416 12 GOTHENBURG, SWEDEN
TEL: 0046 3 8756354

保险人：
Underwriter: PICC Property and Casualty Company Limited
Tianjin Branch
电话(TEL): (022)23317855 23315367
传真(FAX): (022)23301297
地址(ADD): No.2 Qu Fu Road, Heping District, Tianjin China 300042

赔款偿付地点
Claim Payable at GOTHENBURG IN USD
签单日期(Issuing Date) OCT 25, 2008
授权人签字：
Authorized Signature
核保人：　　制单人：　　经办人：

www.piccnet.com.cn

样例 1－7　保险单

TIANJIN GARMENT IMPORT AND EXPORT INC

NO.1 YOU YI ROAD, HE XI DISTRICT, TIAJIN, CHINA

CERTIFICATE

INV. NO. G2008S/A16001
DATE: OCT 30, 2008

WE HEREBY CERTIFY THAT ONE ORIGINAL GSP FORM A AND ONE SET OF NON-NEGOTIABLE OF SHIPPING DOCUMENTS INCLUDING COMMCERICAL INVOICE, PACKING LIST, INSPECTION CERTIFICATE, INSURANCE POLICY AND BILL OF LADING HAVE BEEN SENT TO H&M TRADING SWEDEN AB DIRECTLY WITHIN 3 DAYS AFTER SHIPMENT.

TIANJIN GARMENTS IMPORT & EXPORT INCORPORATIO

样例 1－8　证明函

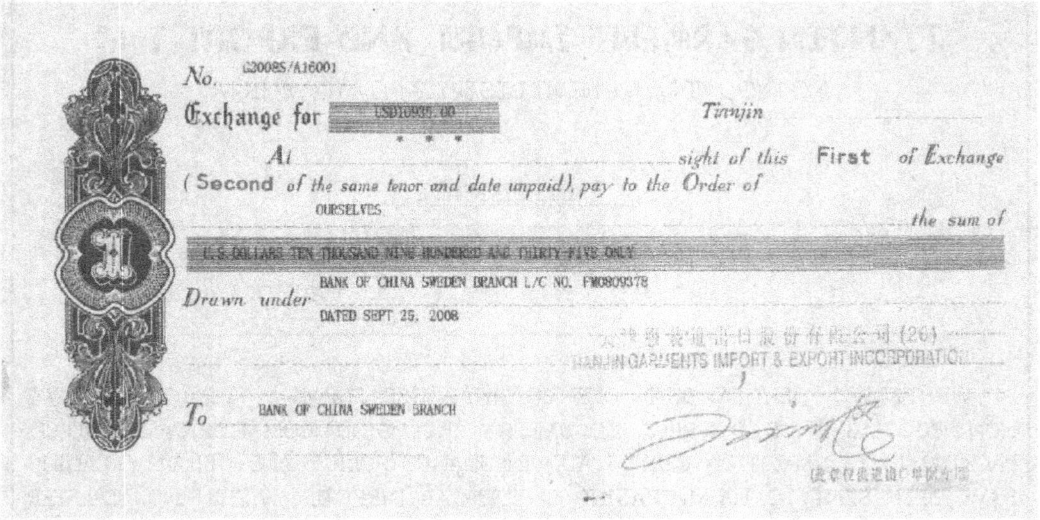
No. G20085/A16001

Exchange for USD10935.00　　　　Tianjin

At *** sight of this First of Exchange (Second of the same tenor and date unpaid), pay to the Order of OURSELVES the sum of

U.S.DOLLARS TEN THOUSAND NINE HUNDRED AND THIRTY-FIVE ONLY

Drawn under BANK OF CHINA SWEDEN BRANCH L/C NO. FM0809378 DATED SEPT 25, 2008

TIANJIN GARMENTS IMPORT & EXPORT INCORPORATION

To BANK OF CHINA SWEDEN BRANCH

样例 1－9　汇票

三、单证缮制的具体要求

单证缮制应做到正确、完整、及时、简明、整洁。

1. 正确(Correctness)。正确是进出口单证工作的前提,单证不正确就不能安全结汇。这里所说的正确,至少包括两方面的内容:一方面是要求各种单据必须做到“三相符”(即单据与信用证相符、单据与单据相符、单据与贸易合同相符);另一方面则要求各种单据必须符合有关国际惯例和进口国的有关法令和规定。通常从银行来说,他们只控制“单证相符”和“单单相符”;从进出口企业来说,除以上三个“相符”外,还要做到“单货相符”,这样单证才能真实代表出运的货物,确保履约正常,安全收汇。跟单托收业务虽然不像信用证那样严格,但如果不符合买卖合同的规定,也可能被进口商找到借口,拒付货款或延付货款。

2. 完整(Completeness)。单证的完整性是构成单证合法性的重要条件之一,是单证成为有价证券的基础。凭单据买卖的合同/信用证都会明确要求出口方需提交哪些单据、提交几份、有无正副本要求、需否背书及应在单据上标明的内容,所有这些都必须得到满足。单证的完整一般包括下列三层含义:

(1)单据内容完整。单据内容完整即每一种单据本身的内容(包括单据本身的格式、项目、文字和签章、背书等)必须完备齐全,否则不能构成有效文件。

(2)单据种类完整。单证在通过银行议付或托收时,一般都是成套、齐全而不是单一的。遗漏一种单据,就是单据不完整。例如在 CIF 交易中,出口商向进口商提供的单证至少应有发票、提单和保险单。出口商只有按信用证或合同规定备齐所需单据，银行（或进口商）才能履行议付、付款或承兑的责任。

（3）单据份数完整。单据份数完整即要求出口商提供的各种单据的份数要按信用证或买卖合同和惯例的要求如数交齐，不能短缺。目前，国外有些地区开来的信用证所列条款日趋繁复，所需单证类别甚多，除发票、提单、保险单等主要单据外，还有各种附属证明，如检验证书、重量单、装箱单、产地证、航行证、邮政收据、电报副本等，这些单证都需要经过一定手续和事先联系才能取得。因此，在单证制作和审核过程中，必须密切注意，及时催办，防止遗漏和误期，以保证全套单证的完整无缺。

3. 及时（Promptness）。进出口单证工作的时间性很强，各种单证都要有一个适当的出单日期。及时出单包括两个方面的内容：一方面是指各种单据的出单日期必须合理可行。就是说每一种单据的出单日期不能超过信用证规定的有效期限或按商业习惯的合理日期。例如，保险单的日期必须早于或同于提单的签发日期，提单日期不得迟于装运期限，装运通知书必须在货物装运后立即发出等。这些日期如果搞错了，同样会造成出单不符。另一方面，还反映在交单议付上。这里主要是指向银行交单的日期不能超过信用证规定的交单期和有效期。过期交单将会遭到拒付或造成利息损失。

总之，及时是指及时制单、及时审单、及时交单、及时收汇。制作单据是个复杂的工程，多数单据由出口方完成，有些需要相关部门配合完成；审核应齐抓共管，这样就可以保证在规定的时间内把全部合格单据向有关方面提交，及时交单肯定意味着能及时收汇，及时收汇意味着又一个良性业务环节的开始。

4. 简明（Conciseness）。单据的内容应按合同或信用证要求和国际惯例缮制，力求简明，切勿加列不必要的内容，以免弄巧成拙。

简化单证不仅可以减少工作量和提高工作效率，而且也有利于提高单证的质量和减少单证的差错。

《UCP600》第4条b款规定："开证行应劝阻申请人试图将基础合同、形式发票等文件作为信用证组成部分的做法。"因此为了防止混淆和误解，银行应劝阻在信用证或其任何修改书中加注过多的细节内容，单据中不应出现与单据本身无关的内容。

5. 整洁（Clearness）。所谓整洁是指单证表面的清洁、美观、大方，单证内容的清楚易认，单证内容记述的简洁明了。如果说正确和完整是单证的内在质量，那么整洁则是单证的外观质量。单证的外观质量在一定程度上反映单证员的业务水平。

单证的整洁要求单证格式的设计和缮制力求标准化和规范化，单证内容的排列要行次整齐、主次有序，重点项目突出醒目，字迹清晰，语法通顺，文句流畅，用词简明扼要、恰如其分。各种单证的更改都要有一个限止点，不允许在一份单证上多处涂改。更改处一定要盖校对章或简签。如涂改过多，应重新缮制单证。

上岗操作

任务栏

1. 通知:公司将有以下合同项下的货物装运出口,请根据有关要求配齐各种纸质空白单证或从制单软件中找到各种空白单证的电子模板。

2. 目的:本项任务的目的是认知并熟悉各种单证,为缮制单证做好准备。

3. 要求:下班前将各种纸质空白单证放入一个文件夹或将空白单证的电子模板存入一个文件夹交给师傅审核。

一、动脑思考

1. 我某进出口公司出口德国一批涤棉漂白棉床单,信用证规定面料的纱支密度为30s×30s 78×65,该公司实际交付的床单符合该规格,但缮制商业发票时,该公司的单证员误将每平方英寸密度78×65打成78×56,单据到国外后遭到开证行拒付。因为进口商在收到该批船前样时,认为床单面料的手感较硬,白度不好,不易销售,早有毁约意图,正苦于没有借口,恰巧发现发票上的一字之差,所以拒付货款。最后几经周折我进出口公司不得不以低价转卖其他客户,损失惨重。你作为公司的单证员从中应吸取什么教训?

2. 我某大型生产企业出口一批机床到埃及,机床型号为"BIZ-12",数量10台,每台单价为5500美元CIF亚历山大港,合同总金额为55000美元。货物出口后,我企业顺利地制单结汇。可一个月后我企业突然收到进口商的传真,告知该批货物已经抵达亚历山大港,在报关时被海关查出我方单据上的机床型号与机床上实际的型号不符,海关已扣留该批货物。若要提货则每台机床要被罚款500美元,要求我企业立即电汇该笔罚款否则向我方提出更大的索赔。后来经过多次交涉,最后由我企业电汇4000美元罚款才了结此案。你作为公司的单证员从中体会到什么?

3. 我某公司生产的产品商标为"黄河牌",习惯意译为"Yellow River Brand",而日本客户开来的信用证却音译为"Huang He Brand",单证员在缮制单据时仍按习惯打成"Yellow River Brand",单据缮制完毕后审单时发现了信用证音译为"Huang He Brand",由于临近交单期匆匆修改单据,但遗漏产地证中货物描述部分的"Yellow River Brand"没有更改,最后单据到日本开证行因单单不符遭拒付。鉴于该产品当时市场销路很好,最后进口商要求降价10%结束此案。你作为公司的单证员从中悟出了什么?今后工作又该如何改进?

二、动手操作

1. 初级训练

泰佛贸易公司从 Alibaba 网站获悉澳大利亚 Johnson 贸易公司正在询购一次性的口布,该商品正好属于泰佛贸易公司的经营范围且有可靠的供货渠道,随后泰佛贸易公司的李小姐主动发函与澳大利亚 Johnson 贸易公司建立业务关系,经过几个回合的磋商,Johnson 贸易公司给泰佛贸易公司下一个试订单,数量为 5000 打,金额为 USD2500,鉴于双方是第一次合作且合同金额较少,故双方最后同意采用 100% T/T 预付的付款方式,要求的结汇单证有发票、装箱单和提单。请你帮助泰佛贸易公司的李小姐备齐上述纸质的空白单证或电子单证模板,为单据缮制做好准备。在此笔业务中澳大利亚 Johnson 贸易公司为什么没有要求提供汇票作为结汇单证之一?

2. 中级训练

泰佛贸易公司与其老客户日本丸红株式会社就出口拉舍尔毛毯达成交易,数量为 15000 条,单价为 USD8.85/PC CFR 横滨,交货期为 7/8 月,为了保证拉舍尔毯子的质量符合合同约定的品质要求,日本丸红株式会社要求出运前委托 SGS 公司对毯子实施检验,同时为享受最低的进口关税税率,日本丸红株式会社要求对拉舍尔毯子的原产地进行认定,鉴于双方长期的业务关系,泰佛贸易公司接受了日本丸红株式会社采用 D/P 付款的请求。根据双方的约定和一般贸易惯例,泰佛贸易公司通过银行应向日本丸红株式会社至少提供哪些结汇单证?请将上述纸质的空白单证或电子单证模板备齐,为单据缮制做好准备,争取早交单、早结汇。

3. 高级训练

泰佛贸易公司与英国 C & A 纺织品公司就全棉台布达成一出口合同,英国 C & A 纺织品公司通过 MIDLAND BANK PLC LONDON 银行将信用证如期开出(见样例 1 - 10)。信用证付款属于银行信用,银行付款的前提条件是相符交单,为了能保证如期收回货款,泰佛贸易公司应向议付行提交哪些结汇单证?哪些单证有特殊要求?具体是什么?

FROM MIDLAND BANK PLC LONDON

TO BANK OF CHINA TIANJIN BRANCH

SEQUENCE OF TOTAL	*27:1/1
FORM OF DOC. CREDIT	*40A:IRREVOCABLE TRANSFERABLE
APPLICABLE RULES	*40E:UCP LATEST VERSION
DOC. CREDIT NUMBER	*20:044/3075989
DATE OF ISSUE	31C:081115
EXPIRY	*31D:DATE 090110 PLACE CHINA
APPLICANT	*50:C & A TEXTILES MORDERY ROAD PUDSET WEST LS28 7XD U. K.

BENEFICIARY *59:TIFERT TRADING CO., LTD
NO. 86, ZHUJIANG ROAD, TIANJIN, CHINA

AMOUNT *32B:CURRENCY GBP AMONT 32500,00

MAX. CREDIT AMOUNT 39B:MAXIMUM

AVAILABLE WITH/BY 41D:FREELY NEGOTIABLE AT ANY BANK
BY NEGOTIATION

DRAFT 42C:AT 60DAYS SIGHT

DRAWEE 42A:DRAWN ON MIDLAND BANK PLC LONDON FOR INVOICE VALUE

DESCRIPTION OF GOODS 45A:50000PCS OF 100% COTTON TABLE CLOTH SIZE 130 × 130CM AT GBP0. 65/PC CIFC2 SOUTHAMPTON COLOUR ASSORTMENT AS PER S/C. NO. 081131 PACKING IN STRONG CARTONS OF 10PCS EACH CARTONS BEARING THE SHIPPING MARKS AS FOLLOWS: C&A/081131/SOUTHAMPTON/CARONT NO 1 – UP

DOCUMENTS REQUIRED 46A:

+SIGNED COMMERCIAL INVOICE IN TRIPLICATE INDICATING S/C NO. AND BREAKDOWN THE VALUE OF FOB AND FREIGHT CHARGES AND INSURANCE
PREMIUM

+PACKING LIST IN DUPILCATE INDICATING THE CONTENTS OF EACH PACKAGE, AND TOTAL GROSS WEIGHT, NET WEIGHT AND MEASUREMENT

+INSURANCE POLICY OR CERTIFICATE IN DUPLICATE FOR 110% OF INVOICE VALUE COVERING ALL RISKS AND WAR RISK INCLUDING W/W CLAUSE SUBJECT TO OCEAN MARINE CARGO CLAUSES OF PICC DATED 1/1/1981

+ 3/3 SET OF CLEAN SHIPPED ON BOARD BILL OF LADING MADE OUT TO ORDER OF SHIPPER AND BLANK ENDORSED NOTIFY APPLICANT AND MARKED FREIGHT PREPAID

+ CERTICATE OF ORIGIN IN DUPLICATE ISSUED BY CCPIT

+ BENEFICARIY'S CERTIFICATE CERTIFYING THAT ONE SET OF NON – NEGOTIABLE OF SHIPPING DOCUMENTS TO BE SENT TO APPLICANT WITHIN 3DAYS AFTER SHIPMENT

ADDITIONAL CONDITION 47A:

+ ALL DOCUMENTS MUST BE MADE IN ENGLISH

+ ALL DOCUMENTS MUST BEAR L/C NO.

+ THIRD PARTY BILL OF LADING NOT ACCEPTABLE

78:INSTRUCTIONS TO PAY/ACCOUNT/NEG BK:

+ THE AMOUNT OF EACH DRAFT MUST BE ENDORSED ON THE REVERSE OF THIS CREDIT

+ ALL DOCUMENTS MUST BE FORWARDED TO US BY COURIER SERVICE IN ONE LOT ADDRESSED TO MIDLAND BANK PLC 456, EASTCHEP TST., LONDON, UK.

样例 1–10 信用证

学习情境二　接触信用证

任务二　开立信用证

岗前测试

一、单选题

> 温馨提示：
>
> 信用证是国际贸易中常用的付款方式之一，特别是对新客户的业务中，买卖双方通常会考虑采用此付款方式。买方及时正确开立信用证是卖方履行合同的前提条件。

1. 进口商填写开证申请书的主要依据是(　)。

A. 发票　　B. 进出口合同

C. 订单　　D. 进口许可证

2. 信用证开立后，应由一家通知行进行通知。以下关于通知行正确的选择是(　)。

A. 由开证申请人指定

B. 由开证行指定

C. 由受益人指定

D. 由进口商和出口商在订立合同时约定

3. 合同中要求货物装运前必须经过买方的指定代表检验，如果开证申请人希望在信用证中体现这一要求，则开证申请书恰当的填写方式是(　)。

A. DOCUMENTS REOUIRED: APPLICANT MUST INSPECT THE GOODS BEFORE SHIPMENT.

B. DOCUMENTS REOUIRED: THE APPOINTED REPRESENTATIVE OF THE BUYER SHALL INSPECT THE GOODS AND SIGN ON THE INSPECTION REPORT IF THE GOODS HAVE PASSED INSPECTION.

C. DOCUMENTS REOUIRED: GOODS MUST BE INSPECTED BY THE APPOINTED REPRESENTATIVE OF THE APPLICANT.

D. DOCUMENTS REOUIRED: INSPECTION REPORT SIGNED BY THE APPOINTED REPRESENTATIVE OF THE APPLICANT EVIDENCING THAT GOODS HAVE BEEN INSPECTED BEFORE SHIPMENT AND HAVE PASSED INSPECTION.

4. 下面关于信用证开立程序正确的说法是(　)。

A. 填写开证申请书—开证申请人向开证行支付开证费用—开证申请人提交保证

金或抵押品—开证行开立信用证

B. 开证申请人提交保证金或抵押品—填写开证申请书—开证申请人向开证行支付开证费用—开证行开立信用证

C. 填写开证申请书—开证申请人提交保证金或抵押品—开证申请人向开证行支付开证费用—开证行开立信用证

D. 开证申请人向开证行支付开证费用—填写开证申请书—开证申请人提交保证金或抵押品—开证行开立信用证

5. 开证申请书体现的是(　)契约关系。

A. 受益人和开证申请人　　B. 开证申请人和开证行

C. 开证行和受益人　　D. 付款行和开证申请人

6. 跟单信用证交易是一种(　)。

A. 货物交易　　B. 既是货物交易也是单据交易

C. 单据交易　　D. 或者是货物交易或者单据交易

7. 银行是凭单付款,不管货物质量如何,也不受合同约束,所以为使货物质量符合规定,开证申请人可在开证时规定要求对方提供(　)。

A. 许可证　　B. 普惠制原产地证　　C. 提单　　D. 商检证书

8. 如果采用空运,申请书中可以要求受益人提交(　)正本空运单据。

A. 一张　　B. 二张　　C. 三张　　D. 四张

9. 除非有特殊要求和规定,信用证申请书原则上应以(　)开立。

A. 中文　　B. 英文　　C. 法文　　D. 西班牙文

10. 我国银行一般不接受开立(　)。

A. 付款信用证　　B. 背对背信用证　　C. 保兑信用证　　D. 议付信用证

11. 信用证的到期地点一般为(　)。

A. 进口商所在地　　B. 受益人所在地　　C. 第三国　　D. 任何一个国家

二、多选题

1. 常用的信用证开立方式有(　)。

A. Full Teletransmission　　B. Airmail

C. With A Preliminary Advice by Teletransmission　　D. Swift

2. 开证申请人提交保证金可以为(　)。

A. 现金　　B. 其他银行或金融机构开立的保函

C. 抵押品　　D. 股票

3. 开证行在选择通知行时,通常会考虑(　)办理。

A. 通过其在出口商所在地的分支机构　　B. 任何一家银行

C. 通过其在出口商所在地的代理行　　D. 开证申请人指定银行

4. 通知行辨别信用证真伪,主要是核对(　)。

A. 信用证条款是否与合同条款相符　　B. 密押是否相符

C. 信用证是否与开证申请书相符　　D. 印鉴是否相符

5. 单据条款要明确,开证时必须列明需要出口商提供的各项单据的(　)。

A. 表述的内容　　B. 种类

C. 份数　　D. 签发机构

相关链接:

1. 中国银行http://www.boc.cn/cbservice/
2. 建设银行http://www.ccb.com/cn/corporate/international/productintro.html
3. 农业银行http://www.abchina.com/cn/hq/abc/qyfw/index.jsp/index.html
4. 招商银行http://www.cmbchina.com/corporate+business/international
5. 中信银行http://bank.ecitic.com/public/international/tool.html
6. 渣打银行http://www.standardchartered.com.cn/sme-banking/trade-services/zh/

三、判断题

1. 开证申请书依买卖双方签订的合同开立,因此其内容应与合同内容完全相同。(　)

2. 开证申请书中的开证人声明是开证人申请开立信用证应承担义务和责任的书面承诺。(　)

3. 买方在申请开立信用证时,须将合同中卖方应履行的各种义务转化为单据,具体体现在信用证中。(　)

4. 开证申请书是银行开立信用证的依据,是受益人与开证行之间明确彼此权利义务关系的契约。(　)

5. 开证申请书包括两个部分:第一部分是请求银行开出信用证的内容;第二部分是进口企业对开证行的承诺书,以明确双方的责任。(　)

6. 信用证金额是开证行履行付款义务的最高限额。(　)

7. 如果开证申请人申请开证的金额小于其授信额度,也必须交付保证金或抵押品。(　)

8. 在进口贸易中,我方对外开证时,一般不主动开出"可转让信用证",以免使我方被动。(　)

9. 如果单据与信用证条款相一致而申请人拒绝"赎单",则其作为抵押的存款或账户上已被冻结的资金将归银行所有。(　)

10. 开证行一旦接受开证申请,就必须严格按照申请人的指示行事并尽早开出信用证。(　)

岗前培训

一、开证申请书填写规范

表 2－1　开证申请书填写规范

项目顺序号	填写内容	要点提示
(1)申请日期 Date	进口商申请开立信用证的日期	按英文习惯填写
(2)开立方式 Credit to be issued by	可选择空邮、简电、特快专递和电传等形式	尽量选择贸易双方可接受的方式
(3)有效期及到期地点 Date and place of expiry	根据业务情况如实填写	有效期一般较最迟装运期晚 10～15 天，到期地点一般在受益人所在国
(4)通知行 Advising bank	通知行名称	由开证行填写
(5)受益人 Beneficiary	填写受益人名称及地址	应与合同中的卖方名称地址一致
(6)开证申请人 Applicant	填写开证申请人名称及地址	应与合同中的买方名称地址一致
(7)总值 Currency code and amount	根据合同填写小写金额和大写金额	应保持大小写的一致
(8)分批装运和转船 Partial shipments & transshipment	是否允许	应与合同约定一致
(9)装运港、目的港和装运期 From... to... latest date of shipment	填写装运港、目的港名称及装运期	根据合同约定填写
(10)具体付款方式及付款时间 Credit available with	需选择即期付款、承兑付款、议付或延期付款，是否使用受益人汇票，填写汇票金额、付款期和付款人	此部分应按照信用证付款惯例填写
(11)贸易术语 Trade term	选择贸易术语	根据合同约定进行选择
(12)信用证种类 Form of L/C	选择是否可转让	根据合同约定进行选择，一般我们不主动开出可转让信用证
(13)保兑 Confirmation	选择是否加保兑	根据合同约定进行选择，一般我们不接受开具保兑信用证的请求
(14)单据条款 Documents required	选择并填写所需要的单据种类、份数、具体要求等	根据实际进口要求，填写并选择需要由出口商提供的单据

续表

项目顺序号	填写内容	要点提示
(15)货描 Description of the goods	填写商品名称、规格、数量、单价、包装等内容	根据合同约定进行填写
(16)额外指示 Additional conditions	填写其他需要的条款或指示	可根据贸易惯例和业务情况合理填写
(17)开证人签字盖章 Signature and seal of the applicant	开证人签字	
(18)银行使用 For bank user only	银行填写栏	

二、开证申请书范例

PURCHASE CONTRACT

Contract No. :08MC1568　　Date:FEB 5, 2008　　Signed at:TIANJIN

1. The Buyers:TIFERT TRADING CO. , LTD

   Address:NO. 86, ZHUJIANG ROAD, TIANJIN,CHINA

2. The Sellers:MARUBENI CORP

   Address:5 -7, HOMMACHI, 2 - CHOME, CHUO - KU, OSAKA, JAPANA

The undersigned Sellers and Buyers have confirmed this contract in accordance with the terms and conditions stipulated below:

3. Commodity & Specification	4. Quantity	5. Unit Price	6. Amount
WOVEN TWILL 100% COTTON	10000METERS	USD2. 80/METER FOB TOKYO	USD28000. 00

7. Total Value (in words):U. S. DOLLARS TWENTY - EIGHT THOUSAND ONLY.

8. 10% more or less in quantity and value allowed.

9. Price Terms: ☒ FOB　　☐CFR　　☐CIF　　☐DDU

11. Packing:IN ROLLS OF 50METERS EACH

12. Shipping Mark:

TIFERT/08MC1568/TIANJIN/NO. 1 - UP

13. Shipment from TOKYO (Port of Shipment) to TIANJIN (Port of Destination).

14. Transshipment: ☒allowed　　☐not allowed

    Partial shipment: ☒allowed　　☐not allowed

    Shipment Time:WITHIN 20DAYS AFTER RECEIPT OF IRREVOCABLE SIGHT L/C.

15. ☒ Insurance to be covered by the buyer.

16. Terms of Payment:

☒ The buyers shall issue an irrevocable L/C at * * * sight through BANK OF CHINA in favor of the sellers prior to FEB 10, 2008 indicating L/C shall be valid in JAPAN through negotiation within 15 days after the shipment effected, the L/C must mention the Contract Number.

17. Shipping advice: The sellers shall immediately, upon the completion of the loading of the goods advise the buyers of the Contract No. ,names of commodity, loaded quantity, invoice value, gross weight, name of vessel and shipment date by FAX/MAIL.

18. Inspection and Claims:

The claims, if any regarding to the quality of the goods, shall be lodged within 30 days after arrival of the goods at the destination, if any regarding to the quantities of the goods, shall be lodged within 60 days after arrival of the goods at the destination. The sellers shall not take any responsibility if any claims concerning the shipping goods in up to the responsibility of Insurance Company/Transportation Company.

19. Force Majeure: The sellers shall not hold any responsibility for partial or total non – performance of this contract due to Force Majeure. But the sellers shall advise the buyers on time of such occurrence.

20. Disputes settlement: All disputes arising out of the contract or in connection with the contract shall be submitted to the China International Economic and Trade Arbitration Commission for arbitration in accordance with its Rules of Arbitration. The arbitral award is final and binding upon both parties.

TIFERT TRADING CO. , LTD	MARUBENI CORP
王宏	小泉太郎

样例 2 – 1　女童夹克面料进口合同

IRREVOCABLE DOCUMENTARY CREDIT APPLICATION

(Please mark x in appropriate boxes)

TO: Bank of China　Tianjin Branch　　　(1) Date: FEB 8, 2008

(2) Credit to be issued by ☒ Full Teletransmission ☐ Airmail ☐ With A Preliminary Advice by Teletransmission	Irrevocable Documentary Credit No. (3) Date and Place of Expiry　Date: MAR 30, 2009 Place: IN JAPAN
(4) Advising Bank	(5) Beneficiary (Name and Address) MARUBENI CORP 5 – 7, HOMMACHI, 2 – CHOME, CHUO – KU, OSAKA, JAPAN
(6) Applicant (Name and Address) TIFERT TRADING CO. , LTD NO. 86, ZHUJIANG ROAD, TIANJIN, CHINA	(7) Currency Code and Amount In Figures: USD28000. 00 In Words: SAY US DOLLARS TWENTY EIGHT THOUSAND ONLY

(8) Partial Shipments ☒ allowed ☐not allowed	Transshipment ☒ allowed ☐not allowed	(10) Credit available with ☒ any bank ☐Issuing Bank ☐by sight payment ☐by acceptance ☒ by negotiation ☐by deferred payment Against presentation of the documents detailed herein and ☒ beneficiary's draft for 100 % of invoice value at ☒ sight ☐days sight ☐days after date of shipment drawn on ☒ Issuing Bank
(9) Loading on board/dispatch/taking in charge at/from TOKYO For transportation to TIANJIN Latest Date of Shipment MAR 15, 2008		

(11) Trade Term: ☒FOB ☐CFR ☐CIF ☐other term (please specify):	(12) Form of L/C ☐Transferable ☒Not Transferable	(13) Confirmation ☐Confirm ☒Without

(14) Documents Required: (marked with x)

1. ☒Signed Commercial Invoice in 2 originals and 2 copies indicating L/C No. and Contract No. 08MC1568
2. ☒Full set ☐2/3 set (including 3 originals and 3 non-negotiable copies) of clean on board ocean Bills of Lading made out to order and blank endorsed, marked Freight ☒Collect ☐Prepaid ☐ , notifying ☒Applicant with full name and address☐
3. ☐Airway Bill consigned to ☐Applicant ☐Issuing Bank and notify ☐Applicant ☐Issuing Bank, marked Freight ☐Collect ☐Prepaid and indicating actual flight date
4. ☐Railway Bill showing Freight ☐Collect ☐Prepaid and consigned to
5. ☐Full set (including originals and copies) of Insurance Policy/Certificate for at least 110% of the invoice value showing claims payable in China in currency of the draft, blank endorsed, covering ☐ocean marine transportation ☐air transportation ☐overland transportation all risks, war risks and
6. ☒Packing List/Weight Memo in 2 originals and 1 copies indicating GROSS/NET WEIGHT AND MEASUREMENT OF EACH CARTON.
7. ☐Certificate of Quantity in originals and copies issued by indicating
8. ☒Certificate of Origin in 1 original and 2 copies issued by CHAMBER OF INTERNATIONAL COMMERCE.
9. ☐Certificate of Quality in originals and copies issued by indicating
10. ☒Beneficiary's Certified Copy of Fax/E-mail dispatched to the applicant within 24 hours after shipment advising name of vessel, B/L No., loading port/airport of departure, date of shipment, contract No., L/C No., commodity, quantity, weight and value of shipment
11. ☐Beneficiary's Certificate certifying that extra copies of all documents required in this Credit have been sent to the Applicant within days after shipment.
12. ☐Other documents:

(15) Description of the goods:

10000METERS OF WOVEN TWILL 100% COTTON

@USD2.80/METER FOB TOKYO

PACKING: IN ROLL OF 50METER EACH

(16) Additional Conditions 1. ☒All Banking charges and interest, if any, outside issuing bank and our reimbursement charge are for account of the beneficiary. 2. ☒Documents to be presented within 15 days after the date of shipment but within the validity of the Credit. 3. ☐Third party as shipper/consignor in transport documents not acceptable. 4. ☒Short form/blank back B/L not acceptable. 5. ☒Both quantity and amount 10 % more or less are allowed. 6. ☒All documents should be forwarded to the Issuing Bank in one lot by courier. 7. ☒All documents must be issued in English. 8. ☐Other terms:	
(17) Signature and Seal of the Applicant Contact Person: Tel. No. Fax No.	(18) For bank user only

样例2-2 女童夹克面料开证申请书

三、开立信用证应注意的问题

1. 申请开立信用证前,对于国家管制商品、限制商品一定要落实进口批准手续及做好购汇准备。

2. 开证时间的掌握应在出口商收到信用证后能在合同约定的装运期内出运为原则。

3. 开证申请书填写完毕,为节省费用避免日后改证,最好把开证申请书先传真给出口商,与其事先进行沟通,待双方对开证申请书中的所有条款达成一致以后,再开立信用证。

4. 开证要求"证同一致",必须以对外签订的正本合同为依据。若货物描述过多、过长,可以注明"详情参照××合同"的字样,但不能将有关合同附件附在信用证后,因信用证是一个独立的文件,不依附于任何买卖合同。

5. 汇票的付款期限要与买卖合同的付款期限相吻合,如为远期,要明确汇票期限以及起算日期,价格条款必须与相应的单据要求、费用负担及表示方法相吻合。

6. 由于银行是凭单付款,不管货物质量如何,也不受合同约束,所以为使货物质量符合规定,可在开证时规定要求出口商提供检验检疫证书,明确货物的规格品质,指定检验检疫机构。

7. 单据条款要明确。开证时必须列明需要出口商提供的各种单据的种类、份数,规定各单据表述的内容及签发机构。特别是开立运输单据、保险单据、商业发票以外的单据时,开证申请中更应表明出单人及单据措辞等内容。

8. 合同约定的条款应转化在相应的信用证条款中并应单据化，因为在信用证支付方式下，只要单据表面与信用证条款相符合，开证行就必须按规定付款。如信用证申请书中含有某些条件而未列明应提交与之相应的单据，银行将认为未列此条件，而不予理睬。

9. 国外通知行由开证行指定。如果进出口商在订立合同时，坚持指定通知行，可供开证行在选择通知行时作参考。

10. 在信用证中规定是否允许分批装运、转运，是否接受第三者装运单据等条款。

11. 如果采用空运，不应在申请书中要求受益人提交一张以上的正本空运单据，更不能要求提供全套的正本空运单据，因为只有第三张正本空运单是给发货人。

12. 各银行事先印制的固定格式申请书中凡涉及选择的项目，一律在有关项目前打“×”表示选中。

13. 除非有特殊要求和规定，信用证申请书原则上应以英文开立。

14. 我国银行一般不接受开立他行保兑的信用证及带电索条款的信用证，对可转让信用证也持谨慎态度。

15. 开证申请书文字应力求规范、完整、明确。进口商要求银行在信用证上载明的事项，必须完整、明确，不能使用含混不清的文字。应避免使用“约”、“近似”或类似的词语，这样，一方面可使银行处理信用证或出口商履行信用证的条款时有所遵循，另一方面也可以此保护自己的权益。

上岗操作

任务栏

1. 通知：公司将有以下合同项下的货物装运进口，请根据有关合同及相关信息填写开证申请书。

2. 目的：本项任务的目的是熟悉开证申请书的基本要求，做到正确及时开立信用证。

3. 要求：下班前将填写好的开证申请书交给师傅审核。

一、动脑思考

1. 英国某大型采购商每月从泰佛贸易公司进口两个40尺高柜的玻璃器皿，客户要求礼品包装，货到后直接上架出售，为了免去进口商开证手续和节省开证的费用，作为业务员你建议进口商采用哪种信用证付款比较合适？为什么？这样做对你公司有何便利？

2. 天津针织品进出口公司与香港中间商HM公司有长期业务关系，双方一直采用背对背信用证结算货款，但最近 HM 公司提议改用可转让信用证结算货款，你作为公司的业务员，接受 HM 公司的建议吗？如果接受该建议，对你公司安全收汇是否有隐患？

3. 通过双方友好洽商，泰佛贸易公司最近与非洲一新客户就印花棉布达成一出口合同，金额 USD56000 美金，为了保证能安全及时收汇，你作为业务员在签订合同时最好采用哪种信用证？并阐明你的理由。

二、动手操作

1. 初级训练

2008 年 5 月，主要从事包装产品、造纸原材料等产品进出口业务的泰佛贸易公司与德国哈罗德有限公司签订了购买 150 吨废纸的进口合同，并于 6 月 3 日向天津中信银行提出开立信用证的申请，请根据下列信息及相关合同（见样例 2－3），填写信用证开立申请书（见样例 2－4）。

PURCHASE CONTRACT

No. TIFERT080515

Date: MAY 15TH 2008

THE BUYER: TIFERT TRADING COMPANY LTD.
NO. 86, ZHUJIANG ROAD, TIANJIN, CHINA
FAX: 02285665678　TELE: 02285665679　EMAIL: TIFERT@trade.com

THE SELLER: HAROLD COMPANY LIMITED, GERMANY
NO. 28, HAROLD STREET, HAMBURG, GERMANY
FAX: 004924245656　TELE: 004924245658　EMAIL: HAROLD@trade.net

1. COMMODITY: WASTE PAPER
2. QUALITY: PROHIBITIVE MATERIALS≤2%
   MOISTURE≤12%
   OUT－THROWS≤1%
3. QUANTIY: 150MTS(＋/－10%)
4. UNIT PRICE: USD70/MT CFR XINGANG, CHINA
5. TATAL VALUE: USD10500.00 (SAY US DOLLARS TEN THOUSAND FIVE HUNDRED ONLY)
6. PACKING: EXPORT STANDARD PACKING IN CONTAINER SHIPMENT
7. TIME OF SHIPMENT: BEFORE JUNE 20, 2008
8. PORT OF SHIPMENT: EUROPEAN MAIN PORT
9. PORT OF DESTINATION: XINGANG, CHINA
10. INSURANCE: TO BE COVERED BY THE BUYER
11. PAYMENT: BY L/C 90 DAYS AFTER SIGHT

SELLERS	BUYERS
RONALD	王宏

样例 2－3　购货合同

IRREVOCABLE DOCUMENTARY CREDIT APPLICATION

(Please mark x in appropriate boxes)

TO: China CITIC Bank Tianjin Branch　　　　　　　　　　　　　　　　Date:

<table>
<tr><td colspan="2">Credit to be issued by
☐Full Teletransmission
☐Airmail
☐With A Preliminary Advice by Teletransmission</td><td colspan="2">Irrevocable Documentary Credit No.
Date and Place of Expiry　Date:
Place:</td></tr>
<tr><td colspan="2">Advising Bank</td><td colspan="2">Beneficiary (Name and Address)</td></tr>
<tr><td colspan="2">Applicant (Name and Address)</td><td colspan="2">Currency Code and Amount
In Figures:
In Words:</td></tr>
<tr><td>Partial Shipments
☐allowed
☐not allowed</td><td>Transshipment
☐allowed
☐not allowed</td><td colspan="2" rowspan="2">Credit available with
☐any bank　☐Issuing Bank　☐
☐by sight payment　☐by acceptance
☐by negotiation　☐by deferred payment
Against presentation of the documents detailed herein and ☐beneficiary's draft for ___% of invoice value at ☐sight ☐days sight ☐days after date of shipment ☐drawn on ☐Issuing Bank☐</td></tr>
<tr><td colspan="2">Loading on board/dispatch/taking in charge at/from
For transportation to
Latest Date of Shipment</td></tr>
<tr><td colspan="2">Trade Term: ☐FOB　☐CFR　☐CIF
☐other term (please specify):</td><td>Form of L/C
☐Transferable
☐Not Transferable</td><td>Confirmation
☐Confirm
☐Without</td></tr>
<tr><td colspan="4">Documents Required: (marked with x)
1. ☐Signed Commercial Invoice in ___originals and ___copies indicating L/C No. and Contract No.
2. ☐Full set ☐2/3 set (including ___originals and ___non-negotiable copies) of clean on board ocean Bills of Lading made out to order and blank endorsed, marked Freight ☐Collect ☐Prepaid ☐ , notifying ☐Applicant with full name and address ☐
3. ☐Full set (including ___originals and ___copies) of Insurance Policy/Certificate for at least 110% of the invoice value showing claims payable in China in currency of the draft, blank endorsed, covering ☐ocean marine transportation ☐air transportation ☐overland transportation all risks, war risks and
4. ☐Packing List/Weight Memo in ___originals and ___copies indicating ___________
5. ☐Beneficiary's Certified Copy of Fax /E - mail dispatched to the applicant within hours after shipment advising name of vessel /flight No. /wagon No. , B/L No. , loading port /airport of departure, date of shipment, contract No. , L/C No. , commodity, quantity, weight and value of shipment
6. ☐Other documents:
Description of the goods:</td></tr>
</table>

Additional Conditions 1. □All Banking charges and interest, if any, outside Issuing Bank and our reimbursement charge are for account of the Beneficiary. □Documents to be presented within ____days after the date of shipment but within the validity of the Credit. □Both quantity and amount ____% more or less are allowed. □Other terms:

Signature and Seal of the Applicant Contact Person: Tel. No. Fax No.	For bank user only

样例 2-4 空白开证申请书

2. 中级训练

泰佛贸易公司与英国 J. C. B 公司就进口针织机械设备达成一订购合同,你作为公司的单证员请依据下面的订购合同(见样例 2-5)填写开证申请书(见样例 2-6)并与招商银行联系开立信用证事宜。

泰 佛 贸 易 公 司 TIFERT TRADING CO., LTD. NO. 86, ZHUJIANG ROAD, TIANJIN, CHINA 订 购 合 同 **PURCHASE CONTRACT**

THE SELLERS: J. C. B Sales Limited Rocester, Staffordshire, England ST 14 5JP	CONTRACT NO.:08TJ198 PLACE:TIANJIN DATE:2008-5-18

THE SELLER AGREES TO SELL AND THE BUYER AGREES TO BUY THE UNDERMENTIONED COMMODITY ACCORDING TO THE TERMS AND CONDITIONS STATED BELOW:
1. NAME OF COMMODITY, SPECIFICATION: 1000sets Knitting machines No. KM-205 at GBP349.17/set FOB London 2. TOTAL VALUE: GBP349,170.00 3. PACKING: In strong wooden cases of one set each 4. COUNTRY OR ORIGIN AND/OR MANUFACTURED: England 5. TERMS OF PAYMENT: 90% of total value will be by L/C at 60days sight, the balance will be paid after the machines well adjusted at the factory. 6. INSURANCE: To be covered by the buyer 7. TIME OF SHIPMENT: within 60days after receipt of the relative L/C

8. SHIPPING MARK: TIFERT/KM－205/TIANJIN/CTN NO 1－1000 9. PORT OF LOADING: London 10. PORT OF DESTINATION: Tianjin Remarks: * The goods should be inspected by SGS before shipment and the inspection certificate issued by SGS will be one kind of documents to be presented for negotiation. * The seller shall immediately, upon the completion of the loading of the goods advise the buyer of the Contract No. names of commodity, loaded quantity, invoice value, gross weight, names of vessel and shipment date by FAX/MAIL. * The claims, if any regarding to the quality of the goods, shall be lodged within 30 days after arrival of the goods at the destination, if any regarding to the quantities of the goods, shall be lodged within 60 days after arrival of the goods at the destination. The sellers shall not take any responsibility if any claims concerning the shipping goods in up to the responsibility of Insurance Company/Transportation Company.

THE SELLERS J. C. B Sales Limited John Smith	THE BUYERS TIFERT TRADING CO., LTD 王宏

样例 2－5　购货合同

APPLICATION FOR DOCUMENTARY CREDIT

Mark "×" in appropriate boxes

致：招商银行

To: China Merchants Bank

Please issue by □Teletransmission □Brief teletransmission □Airmail an IRREVOCABLE CREDIT as follows:	Expiry date: Place for presentation:
Applicant (name and address)	Beneficiary (name and address)
Advising Bank	Amount in figures: Amount in words:
Credit available with Nominated Bank: □by payment at sight □by deferred payment at: □by acceptance of drafts at: □by negotiation against the following documents □and beneficiary's drafts drawn on for % invoice value accompanied by the following documents.	

Partial shipments □allowed □not allowed	Transshipments □allowed □not allowed	Transferable □transferable □not transferable	Confirmation of credit requested authorized if requested by beneficiary
Shipment from for transportation to via not later than .			
Goods description in brief Price Terms: □CIF □FOB □CFR □CIP □others as per INCOTERMS			
– All banking charges including relative reimbursement/payment charges, outside/inside issuing bank are for account of beneficiary. – Documents to be presented within days after shipment date but within the validity of the credit. – Please debit our account for your commission, charges and usance interest (the interest rate is LIBOR +[ ]BPs), if any. Our account No.:			

This page is an integral part of the application which consists of the first page, the second page and attachment(s), if any.

CONTRACT NO.: CONTRACT AMT:

To be continued on the second page

APPLICATION FOR DOCUMENTARY CREDIT

致:招商银行

To: China Merchants Bank

Documents required:

□Signed commercial invoice in original (s) and copy (ies) indicating this L/C No. and Contract No.

□Packing list in original(s) and copy(ies).

□Full set of clean on board marine Bill of Lading marked "Freight Prepaid" made out to order and blank endorsed notifying the applicant with full name and address.

□2/3 set of clean on board marine Bill of Lading marked "Freight Prepaid" made out to order and blank endorsed notifying the applicant with full name and address.

□Full set of clean on board multimodal transport document marked "Freight Prepaid" made out to order and blank endorsed notifying the applicant with full name and address.

□2/3 set of clean on board multimodal transport document marked "Freight Prepaid" made out to order and blank endorsed notifying the applicant with full name and address.

☐Clean Air Waybill indicating actual flight date consigned to ______ and notifying ______ marked "Freight Prepaid".

☐Clean Rail Waybill indicating actual departure date consigned to ______ and notifying ______ marked "Freight Prepaid".

☐Forwarding agent cargo receipt consigned to ______ and notifying ______ marked "Freight Prepaid".

☐Full set of insurance policy /certificate blank endorsed for full CIF value plus 10pct with claims if any, payable at destination in the currency of this credit covering . Institute Cargo Clauses A Institute War Clauses Institute Strikes Clause from warehouse to warehouse included.

☐Certificate of origin in original(s) and copy(ies) issued by chamber of commerce in .

☐Certificate of quality in original(s) and copy(ies) issued by chamber of commerce in .

☐Certificate of quantity in original(s) and copy(ies) issued by chamber of commerce in .

☐Beneficiary's certificate certifying that one set of non-negotiable documents including 1/3 set of original B/L has been sent to the applicant directly by courier/speed post and the postal receipt is required for negotiation.

Special terms and conditions:

☐percent more or less are allowed on both credit amount and quantity.

☐Third party as shipper is acceptable.

☐Third party as shipper is not acceptable.

We hereby instruct you or any third party authorized by you to pay the usance draft(s) on sight basis ,the relevant interest and charges will be for account of us.（申请开立假远期信用证时，需选择此项）

This page is an integral part of the application which consists of the first page, the second page and attachment(s), if any.

样例 2－6　空白开证申请书

3. 高级训练

泰佛贸易公司欲从中东阿联酋进口一批纯手工波斯地毯，经双方友好洽商最后每条地毯以 USD25. 50 美元 FOB 迪拜成交，数量为 1800 条，尺寸 150x200cm，交货期 7/8 月，付款方式 20% T/T 预付，80% 见票后 30 天付款信用证，具体合同(见样例 2－7)，请按照合同要求填写开证申请书(见样例 2－8)。

泰佛贸易公司 正本

TIFERT TRADING CO.，LTD (ORIGINAL)

天津市珠江道 86 号

NO. 86, ZHUJIANG ROAD, TIANJIN, CHINA

购货合同 编号 NO. TF-SC0611

PURCHASE CONTRACT 日期 DATE:2008/11/8

买方

Sellers：DUBAI CARPET CO., LTD

地址

Address: 5-18 ISUKI-BUILDING, DUBAI, SAUDI ARABIA

电话 传真

Tel: 971-04-282828 Fax: 971-04-282829

兹经买卖双方同意成交下列商品订立条款如下：

The undersigned Sellers and Buyers have agreed to close the following transaction according to the terms and conditions stipulated below:

货物名称及规格 NAME OF COMMODITY AND SPECIFICATTION	数量 QUANTITY	单价 UNIT PRICE	金额 AMOUNT
PERSIAN CARPET QUALITY: 100% SILK SIZE: 150×200CM	1800PCS	FOB DUBAI USD25.50/PC	USD45900.00
	总值 TOTAL AMOUNT: USD45900.00 Say US Dollars forty-five Thousand Nine Hundred Only		

PACKING: 1pc in a plastic roll and 1pc to a carton.

SHIPMENT: To be effected during July/Aug 2008 from Dubai to Tianjin with partial shipments allowed transshipment not allowed.

INSURANCHE: To be covered by the buyer.

PAYMENT: The buyer shall open an L/C for 80% of contract value at 30days sight to reach the seller before June 15, 2008 and valid for negotiation in Dubai until the 15th day after the date of shipment.

REMARKS: With 5% more or less both in amount and quantity at the Seller's Option

卖方 SELLERS 买方 BUYERS

DUBAI CARPET CO., LTD TIFERT TRADING CO.，LTD.

样例 2－7 购货合同

IRREVOCABLE DOCUMENTARY CREDIT APPLICATION

TO: BANK OF CHINA TIANJIN BRANCH		Date:
□Issue by airmail □With brief advice by teletransmission □Issue by express delivery □ (which shall be the operative instrument)		Credit No. Date and place of expiry
Applicant		Beneficiary (Full name and address)
Advising Bank		Amount
Partial shipments □allowed □not allowed	Transshipment □allowed □not allowed	Credit available with By □payment □acceptance □negotiation against the documents detailed herein □and beneficiary's draft(s) for ____ % of invoice value At_______ sight drawn on
Loading on board/dispatch/taking in charge at/from not later than For transportation to:		
□FOB □CFR □CIF □or other terms		

Documents required: (marked with X)

1. ( ) Signed commercial invoice in _____ copies

2. ( ) Full set of clean on board Bills of Lading made out to order and blank endorsed, marked "freight [ ] to collect / [ ] prepaid [ ] showing freight amount" notifying ________________________________.

( ) Airway bills/cargo receipt/copy of railway bills issued by ________________________ showing "freight [ ] to collect/[ ] prepaid [ ] indicating freight amount" and consigned to______________________.

3. ( ) Insurance Policy/Certificate in _____ copies for _____ % of the invoice value showing claims payable in _________ in currency of the draft, blank endorsed, covering All Risks, War Risks and____

4. ( ) Packing List/Weight Memo in _____ copies

5. ( ) Certificate of Quantity/Weight in _______ copies issued by ________________.

6. ( ) Certificate of Quality in ______ copies issued by [ ] manufacturer/[ ] public recognized surveyor______________.

7. ( ) Certificate of Origin in _____ copies .

8. ( ) Beneficiary's certified copy of fax / telex dispatched to the applicant within _____ days after shipment advising L/C No., name of vessel, date of shipment, name, quantity, weight and value of goods.

Other documents, if any

Description of goods:

QUANTITY

PRICE TERM:

Additional instructions:

1. ( ) All banking charges outside the opening bank are for beneficiary's account.

2. ( ) Documents must be presented within ______ days after date of issuance of the transport documents but within the validity of this credit.

3. ( ) Third party as shipper is not acceptable, Short Form/Blank back B/L is not acceptable.

4. ( ) Both quantity and credit amount _____ % more or less are allowed.

5. ( ) All documents must be sent to issuing bank by courier/speed post in one lot.

( ) Other terms, if any

样例 2－8　空白开证申请书

任务三　审核信用证

岗前测试

一、单选题

> 温馨提示：
>
> 信用证依据合同条款开立，对照合同条款逐条仔细地审核信用证，是出口商安全收汇的重要保障。

1. 信用证付款方式属于(　)。

A. 银行信用、顺汇　B. 商业信用、逆汇

C. 银行信用、逆汇　D. 商业信用、顺汇

2. 可转让信用证必须要注明“TRANSFERABLE”字样，根据国际商会《跟单信用证统一惯例 UCP600》的规定，一般可以转让(　)。

A. 一次　B. 两次　C. 三次　D. 四次

3. 根据《跟单信用证统一惯例 UCP600》的规定，信用证的第一付款人是(　)。

A. 进口商　B. 开证行　C. 议付行　D. 通知行

4. 承兑是(　)对远期汇票表示承担到期付款责任的行为。

A. 收款人　B. 出口商　C. 付款人　D. 议付银行

5. 信用证保兑后，首先对受益人负责的银行是(　)。

A. 保兑行　B. 开证行　C. 付款行　D. 通知行

6. 一张有效的信用证必须规定一个(　)。

A. 有效期　B. 装运期　C. 交单期　D. 议付期

7. 受益人开立远期汇票但可通过贴现即期足额收款的信用证是(　)。

A. 即期信用证　B. 远期信用证　C. 假远期信用证　D. 预支信用证

8. 信用证规定有效期为 2004 年 11 月 30 日，而未规定装运期，则可理解最迟装运期为(　)。

A. 2004 年 11 月 1 日　B. 2004 年 12 月 15 日

C. 2004 年 12 月 21 日　D. 2004 年 11 月 30 日

9. 某公司与外商签订出口合同，数量为 12000 公吨，来证规定 7/8/9/10 月份分批等量装运。7 月份装出 3000 公吨，8 月份因货未备妥，没有装运。则(　)。

A. 9 月份可装两批，共 6000 公吨

B. 8 月份落空不补，9，10 月份照装

C. 8 月份及以后各月均不得凭以装运支款

D. 8 月份的货物延至 11 月份

10. 收到国外来证两份:①棉布 10 万码,每码 0.40 美元,信用证总金额 42000 美元;②服装 1000 套,每套 20 美元,信用证总金额 21000 美元。据此,两证出运的最高数量和金额可分别掌握为(　)。

A. 棉布 100000 码,40000 美元;服装 1000 套,20000 美元

B. 棉布 105000 码,42000 美元;服装 1000 套,20000 美元

C. 棉布 105000 码,42000 美元;服装 1050 套,21000 美元

D. 棉布 100000 码,40000 美元;服装 1050 套,21000 美元

二、多选题

1. 在国际贸易中,常用于中间商转售货物交易的信用证是(　)。

A. 对背信用证　B. 对开信用证　C. 可撤销信用证　D. 可转让信用证

2. 下列关于可转让信用证表述正确的是(　)。

A. 只有信用证上明确注明可转让字样,受益人才有权要求银行将信用证的全部和一部分一次转让给一个或者数个本国或者外国的第三者,由第二受益人在其所在地交单议付

B. 信用证转让时,只能按原条款转让,但其中的金额、单价可以减低,有效期和装货期可以缩短,保险加保比例可以增加

C. 信用证转让后,第一受益人仍应对交货承担合同义务

D. 信用证的修改必须得到第一受益人与第二受益人的同意

3. 对背信用证主要用于(　)。

A. 中间商转售他人货物　B. 转口贸易

C. 一般贸易　D. 进料加工

4. 某公司分别以 D/P at 90 days after sight 和 D/A at 90 days after sight 两种支付条件对外出口了两批货物,这两笔业务具有的特点是(　)。

A. 前者是进口商在到期日付清货款才可以取得装运单据,后者是进口商在见票时承兑后即可取得装运单据

B. 前者没有遭进口商拒付的风险,而后者存在这种风险

C. 前者的风险比后者大

D. 后者的风险比前者大

5. 下列说法正确的是(　)。

A. 根据《跟单信用证统一惯例 UCP600》的规定,信用证如未规定有效期,则该证可视为无效

B. 国外开来信用证规定货物数量为 3000 箱,6/7/8 月,每月平均装运。我出口公司于 6 月份装运 1000 箱,并收妥款项。7 月份由于货未备妥,未能装运。8

月份装运 2000 箱。根据《跟单信用证统一惯例 UCP600》的规定，银行不得拒付

C. 在信用证支付方式下，受益人只要在信用证规定的有效期内向银行提交符合信用证规定的全部单据，银行就必须履行付款义务

D. 如果受益人要求开证申请人将信用证的有效期延长一个月，在信用证未规定装运期的情况下，同一信用证上的装运期也可顺延一个月

三、判断题

小贴士：

凡是通过 SWIFT 系统开立的信用证称为 SWIFT 信用证，也称"全银电协信用证"。其特点是：SWIFT 需要会员资格、SWIFT 的费用较低、SWIFT 的安全性较高、SWIFT 的格式标准化。

1. 在信用证业务中，信用证的开立是以买卖合同为基础，因此信用证条款与买卖合同条款严格相符是开证行向受益人承担付款责任的前提条件。(　)

2. 根据《跟单信用证统一惯例 UCP600》的规定，信用证金额前有"大约"字样，表明金额有 10% 的增减幅度。(　)

3. 可转让信用证办理转让后，买卖合同也随之由第一受益人转让第二受益人。(　)

4. 在信用证业务中，有关各方处理的不仅仅是单据而且还涉及出运的货物。(　)

5. 可转让信用证只能转让一次，因此，可转让的第二受益人只有一个。(　)

6. 在信用证业务中，出口散装货物，若信用证数量前没有规定机动幅度的，根据《跟单信用证统一惯例 UCP600》的规定，卖方交货的数量不能多也不能少。(　)

7. 对于保兑信用证，保兑行与开证行所处的地位不同，保兑行负第二性付款责任。(　)

8. 跟单信用证与备用信用证的区别之一在于，前者在受益人履约时使用，后者在申请人违约时才能使用。(　)

9. 采用 SWIFT 信用证，必须遵守 SWIFT 使用手册的规定，受《跟单信用证统一惯例 UCP600》的约束，反映在信用证中 40 区域的内容为"UCP LATEST VERSION"。(　)

10. 循环信用证是指两张信用证的开证申请人互以对方的受益人而开立的信用证。(　)

岗前培训

一、审核信用证规范

表 3－1　信用证的审核规范

	信用证具体内容	信用证条款及与之对应的合同条款	审核的重点
信用证本身说明	(1)信用证页次 Pages/Sequence of total		①页码是否齐全 ②信用证所涉及的附件是否锁好
	(2)信用证种类 Kinds of credit		《UCP600》已取消可撤销信用证
	(3)信用证证号 Credit No.		每份证应该有唯一证号
	(4)金额 Amount	对应合同的总金额	①金额与合同是否相符 ②币种与合同是否相同 ③如有大小写是否一致 ④佣金、折扣是否包含在总金额中 ⑤溢短装是否适用金额中
	(5)开证日期和地点 Date and place of issue		是否按照合同约定的期限开出信用证
	(6)装运期 Latest shipment date	对应合同中的装运期	①装运期是否与合同规定相符 ②如提前视具体情况考虑接受否 ③如推迟(最晚……)无须改证
	(7)有效期和到期地点 Place and date of expiry	对照合同中的装运期	①一般比装运期晚 10～15 天为宜 ②原则上不接受在国外到期
	(8)交单期 Period of presentation		一般装船后 10～15 天为宜
	(9)兑用方式 Available with	对应合同中的支付条款	①最好是议付信用证 ②最好不是付款信用证
	(10)有效性 Effectiveness		①是否有有效期 ②是否有条件生效 ③是否有软条款 ④信开/电开证是否印鉴/密押相符

续表

	信用证具体内容	信用证条款及与之对应的合同条款	审核的重点
信用证当事人	(11)开证申请人 Applicant	对应合同中的买方	公司名称和地址都要核对
	(12)受益人 Beneficiary	对应合同中的卖方	公司名称和地址都要核对
	(13)通知行 Advising bank		通知行最好与受益人在同一地点
	(14)议付行 Negotiating bank		如议付行与受益人不在同一城市又限制议付，需考虑时间上的可行性
汇票条款	(15)出票人 Drawer	对应合同中的卖方	
	(16)受款人 Payee	对应合同中的卖方或议付行	
	(17)付款人 Drawee	对应信用证中的开证行或指定的付款行	付款人不能是开证申请人
	(18)付款期限 Tenor	对应合同中的支付条款	汇票的付款期限是否与合同中的付款期限相符
	(19)出票依据 Drawn under		通常包括开证行、证号和开证日期
货物描述	(20)商品名称 Commodity name	对应合同中的品名条款	品名是否有拼写错误
	(21)规格/货号 Specification/Art No.	对应合同品质条款	须仔细审核，特别是规格中最高、最多、最低、最少等描述是否与合同相符，货号是否完全正确
	(22)数量 Quantity	对应合同中的数量条款	①数量是否与合同相符 ②是否有溢短装
	(23)单价 Unit price	对应合同的价格条款	①单价是否正确 ②币别是否相同 ③计量单位是否相符 ④贸易术语是否一致
	(24)唛头 Shipping marks	对应合同中的唛头	①若不一致视具体情况考虑接受否 ②若已经备妥货物，原则上应要求改证 ③若没有备妥货物，按证中唛头刷唛
	(25)详细资料参照 Details as per...	对应合同号和合同日期	①引用的合同号是否与买卖双方签订的合同相符 ②引用的合同日期是否与实际合同相同

续表

	信用证具体内容	信用证条款及与之对应的合同条款	审核的重点
装运条款	(26)装运港 Port of loading	对应合同中的装运条款	①装运港是否与合同相同 ②如不同,不增加费用且能做到无需改证 ③来证笼统规定"CHINA MAIN PORTS"无须改证
	(27)目的港 Port of destination	对应合同中的装运条款	①目的港是否与合同相同 ②如不同,不增加费用且能做到无需改证 ③注意世界上重名港问题,其后应加国别
	(28)分批 Partial shipments	对应合同中的装运条款	若合同中规定禁分而来证允许,无需改证
	(29)转运 Transshipment	对应合同中的装运条款	若合同中规定禁转而来证允许,无需改证
单据条款	(30)发票 Commercial invoice		若要求开证人会签需删除
	(31)装箱单 Packing list		若要求开证人会签需删除
	(32)提单 Bill of lading		①1/3 正本提单自寄需修改 ②运费支付情况与贸易术语矛盾需修改
	(33)保险单/凭证 Insurance policy/certificate	对应合同保险条款	①投保加成是否与合同规定相符 ②投保险别是否与合同相符 ③依据的保险条款及其版本年份是否一致 ④ICC 中的险别是否与 CIC 中的险别同时出现在保险条款中
	(34)原产地证 Certificate of origin		①签发单位是否可接受 ②是否需要使领馆认证
	(35)检验证书 Inspection certificate	对应合同中的检验条款	①检验机构是否是对我友好的独立的第三方 ②是否是客检证,若是需修改
	(36)其他证明 Other certificate		所要求证明是否能够自行出具,如需第三方能否保证及时签发
	(37)特殊条款 Special terms	对应合同的备注	①特殊条款是否已单据化,若是,是否能够保证及时签发 ②重点审核是否含有软条款

续表

	信用证具体内容	信用证条款及与之对应的合同条款	审核的重点
付款承诺	(38)开证行保证付款责任文句 Undertaking clause of opening bank		信开/电开证必须有银行保证付款的责任文句，否则信用证无效
适用惯例	(39)信用证所适用惯例 Credit is subject to . . .	THID CREDIT IS SUBJECT TO . . . UCP 600	①信开/电开证必须适用于《UCP600》，否则信用证无效 ②升级后的 SWIFT 报文格式也增加了所适用的惯例

二、审核信用证范例

销 售 合 同

SALES CONTRACT

编号 No.: 08TF0858　　日期 Date: MAR 5, 2008

The sellers: TIFERT TRADING CO., LTD

Add: NO. 86, ZHUJIANG ROAD, TIANJIN, CHINA　　POST CODE: 300221

The buyers: MARUBENI CORP

Add: 5 - 7, HOMMACHI, 2 - CHOME, CHUO - KU, OSAKA, JAPAN

TEL: 81 - 1 - 2124046　　FAX: 81 - 1 - 2124055

兹确认售予你方下列货品，其成交条款如下：

We hereby confirm having sold to you the following goods on the terms and conditions as specified below:

(1)货物名称及规格 Name of Commodity and Specifications	(2)数量 Quantity	(3)单价 Unit price	(4)总值 Total Amount
GIRL JACKET SYTLE NO. GJ234 SHELL: WOVEN TWILL 100% COTTON LINING: WOVEN 100% POLYESTER	5000PCS 10% MORE OR LESS ALLOWED	USD10. 50/PC CIF TOKYO	USD52500. 00

(5)包装：

Packing: 20PCS/CARTON, EACH CARTON SHOULD BE INDCIATED COMMODITY NAME, COLOR NO AND STYLE NO AND CARTON SIZE

(6)装运唛头:

Shipping Mark: MARUBENI

S/C 08TF0858

TOKYO

CTN NO. 1 - UP

(7)装运期限:

Time of Shipment: APR 30, 2008

(8)装运口岸: 目的地:

Port of Shipment: TIANJIN Destination: TOKYO

WITH PARTIAL SHIPMENTS AND TRANSSHIPMENT ALLOWD

(9)付款条件:

Payment Terms: BY SIGHT L/C WHICH REMAINS VALID IN CHINA FOR NEGOTIATION UNTIL 15DAYS AFTER SHIPMENT.

(10)保险:卖方负责投保海运险按照 CIF 金额的 110% 投保一切险和战争险,如果发生索赔,在日本用美元赔偿。

Insurance:THE SELLER SHALL ARRANGE MARINE INSURANCE COVERING ALL RISKS AND WAR RISK FOR 110% OF CIF VALUE. CLAIM, IF ANY, PAYABLE IN JAPAN, IN CURRENCY OF USD.

(11)检验:货物出运前应该由出入境检验检疫局进行施检,其签发的检验证书作为向银行议付货款的单据之一。

Inspection:THE GOODS SHOULD BE INSPECTED BY CIQ BEFORE SHIPMENT AND THE INSPECTION CERTIFICATE ISSUED BY CIQ WILL BE ONE KIND OF DOCUMENTS TO BE PRESENTED FOR NEGOTIATION.

(12)买方须于 2008 年 3 月 15 日前开出本批交易的信用证。否则,售方有权:不经通知取消本合同,或接受买方对本销售合同未执行的全部或部分,或对遭受的损失提出索赔。

THE BUYER SHALL ESTABLISH THE COVERING LETTER OF CREDIT BEFORE MAR15, 2008. FAILING WHICH THE SELLER RESERVES THE RIGHT TO RESCIND WITHOUT FURTHER NOTICE, OR TO ACCEPT WHOLE OR ANY PART OF THIS SALES CONTRACT UNFULFILLED BY THE BUYER, OR TO LODGE A CLAIM FOR DIRECT LOSSES SUSTAINED IF ANY.

(13)凡以 CIF 条件成效的业务,保额为发票价的 110%,投保险别以本销售合同中所开列的为限,买方如要求增加保额或保险范围应在装船前经售方同意,因此而增加的保险费由买方负责。

FOR TRANSACTIONS CONCLUDED ON CIF BASIS, IT IS UNDERSTOOD THAT THE INSURANCE AMOUNT WILL BE FOR 110% OF THE INVOICE VALUE AGAINST THE RISKS SPECIFIED IN THE SALES CONTRACT, IF ADDITIONAL INSURANCE AMOUNT OR COVERAGE IS REQUIRED, THE BUYER MUST HAVE THE CONSENT OF THE SELLER BEFORE SHIPMENT, AND THE ADDITIONAL PREMIUM IS TO BE BORNE BY THE BUYER.

(14)品质/数量异议:如买方提出索赔,凡属品质异议须于货到目的口岸之日起 2 个月内提出。凡属数量异议须于货到目的口岸之日起 15 天内提出,对所装货物所提任何异议属于保险公司、轮船公司及期货有关运输机构所负责者,售方不负任何责任。

QUALITY/QUANTITY DISCREPANCY:IN CASE OF QUALITY DISCREPANCY, CLAIM SHOULD BE FILED BY THE BUYER WITHIN 2 MONTHS AFTER THE ARRIVAL OF THE GOODS AT THE PORT OF DESTINATION WHILE FOR QUANTITY DISCREPANCY CLAIM SHOULD BY FILED BY THE BUYER WITHIN 15 DAYS AFTER THE ARRIVAL OF THE GOODS AT THE PORT OF DESTINATION. IT IS UNDERSTOOD THAT SELLER SHALL NOT BE LIABLE FOR ANY DISCREPANCY OF THE GOODS SHIPPED DUE TO CAUSES FOR WHICH THE INSURANCE COMPANY,

SHIPPING COMPANY OTHER TRANSPORTATION ORGANIZATION ARE LIABLE.

(15)本合同内所述全部或部分商品,如因人力不可抗拒的原因,以致不能履约或延迟交货,售方概不负责。

THE SELLER SHALL NOT BE HELD LIABLE FOR FAILURE OR DELAY IN DELIVERY OF THE ENTIRE LOT OR PORTION OF THE GOODS UNDER THIS SALES CONTRACT IN CONSEQUENCE OF ANY FORCE MAJEURE INCIDENTS.

确认签署

Confirmed by

MARUBENI CORP　　　　TIFERT TRADING CO., LTD

小泉太郎　　　　王宏

样例 3－1　女童夹克衫销售合同

中国银行 BANK OF CHINA 天津分行

信用证通知书

Notification of Documentary Credit

ADDRESS:80, JIEFANG BEI LU, TIANJIN, CHINA

CABLE:CHUNGKOU

TELEX:23233 TJBOC CN

FAX:0086 22 23128900　　　　DATE:MAR 19,2008

To:致 TIFERT TRADING CO., LTD NO. 86, ZHUJIANG ROAD, TIANJIN, CHINA	When corresponding please quote our Ref No.
Issuing Bank 开证行 BANK OF CHINA, TOKYO BRANCH	Transmitted to us through 转递行
L/C No. 证号　A－08－0058 Dated 开证日期　MAR 15, 2008	Amount 金额 USD52500.00
Expiry 效期　MAY 15, 2008 Tenor 远期	Charge 费用

Dear Sirs,

迳启者:

We have pleasure in advising you that we have received from the a/m bank a(n)

兹通知贵司,我行收自上述银行

( )telex issuing　电传开立　　( )ineffective　未生效

( )pre-advising of　预先通知　　( )mail confirmation of　证实书

(X)original　正本　　( )duplicate　副本

letter of credit, contents of which are as per attached sheet(s).

This advice and the attached sheet(s) must accompany the relative documents when presented for negotiation. 信用证一份,现随附通知,贵司交单时,请将本通知书及信用证一并提示。 (X) Please note that this advice does not constitute our confirmation of the above L/C nor does it convey any engagement or obligation on our part. 本通知书不构成我行对此信用证之保兑及其他任何责任。 (   ) Please note that we have added our confirmation to the above L/C, negotiation is restricted to ourselves only. 上述信用证已由我行加具保兑,并限向我行交单。
Remark

This L/C consists of 2 sheet(s), including the covering letter and attachment(s).

本信用证连同面函及附件共2纸。

If you find any terms and conditions in the L/C which you are unable to comply with and or any error(s), it is suggested that you contact applicant directly for necessary amendment(s) of as to avoid any difficulties which may arise when documents are presented

如本信用证中有无法办到的条款及/或错误，请迳与开证申请人联系进行必要的修改，以排除交单时可能发生的问题。

Yours faithfully

for BANK OF CHINA

样例3-2 女童夹克衫信用证通知函

中国银行 BANK OF CHINA 东京分行

PAGE:1/1(**1**)

	IRREVOCABLE DOCUMENTARY CREDIT(**2**) NO. A-08-0058(**3**)
DATE AND PLACE OF ISSUE 08/3/15 IN TOKYO (**5**)	DATE AND PLACE OF EXPIRY 08/5/15 JAPAN (**7**) + (**10**)
APPLICANT (**11**) MARUBENI CORP 5-7, HOMMACHI, 2-CHOME, CHUO-KU, OSAKA, JAPAN	BENEFICIARY (**12**) TIFERT TRADING CO., LTD NO. 86, ZHUJIANG STREET, TIANJIN, CHINA
ADVISING BANK (**13**) BANK OF CHINA, TIANJIN BRANCH	AMOUNT: USD52500.00 (**4**) SAY: U. S. DOLLARS FIFTY-TWO THOUSAND FIVE HUNDRED ONLY.

<table>
<tr>
<td>LATEST SHIPMENT DATE 08/4/30(6)
SHIPMENT FROM TIANJIN CHINA (26) TO TOKYO JAPAN(27)
PARTIAL SHIPMENT NOT ALLOWED (28)
TRANSHIPMENT NOT ALLOWED (29)</td>
<td>CREDIT AVAILABLE BY NEGOTIATION (9) AGAINST PRESENTATION OF THE DOC. DETAILED HEREIN AND OF YOUR (15) DRAFT AT 30 DAYS SIGHT (18) DRAWN ON APPLICANT (17) FOR FULL INVOICE VALUE (19) PAY TO TIFERT TRADING CO. , LTD ONLY (16) BEARING DRAWN UNDER L/C NO. A – 08 – 0058 ISSUED BY BANK OF CHINA TOKYO BRACH DATED 08/2/15 (19)</td>
</tr>
<tr>
<td colspan="2">LIST OF DOCUMENTS TO BE PRESENTED
1. SIGNED COMMERCIAL INVOICE IN TRIPLICATE CERTIFYING THE GOODS ARE OF CHINESE ORIGIN AND COUNTERSIGNED BY APPLICANT. (30)
2. 2/3 SET OF CLEAN ON BOARD OCEAN BILL OF LADING MADE OUT TO ORDER AND BLANK ENDORSED NOTIFY APPLICANT WITH FULL NAME, ADDRESS AND TEL NO. 8745 9986 AND INDICATING THE NAME OF CARRYING VESSEL'S NAME AND TEL NO. AT THE PORT OF DESTINATION MARKED FREIGHT TO COLLECT. (32)
3. PACKING LIST IN DUPLICATE SHOWING THE GOODS HAVE BEEN PACKED CARTONS OF 20PCS EACH AND CERTIFYING EACH ITEM HAS BEEN MARKED THE LABEL "MADE IN CHINA". (31)
4. INSURANCE POLICY OR CERTIFICATE IN THE NAME OF APPLICANT FOR 120% OF INVOICE VALUE AGAINST ALL RISKS AND WAR RISK AS PER ICC DATED 1/1/1982 CLAIM IF ANY PAYABLE AT PORT OF DESTINATION. (33)
5. GSP CERTIFICATE OF ORIGIN FORM A ISSED BY CIQ INDICATING THE L/C NO AND SHOWING THE NAME OF MANUFACTURER. (34)
6. BENEFICARY'S CERTIFICATE CERTIFYING THAT 1/3 ORIGINAL B/L AND ONE SET OF NON – NEGOTIABLE SHIPPING DOCUEMENTS TO BE SENT TO APPLICANT WITHIN 48 HOURS AFTER SHIPMENT. (36)
7. SHIPPING ADVICE SHOULD BE SENT TO APPLICANT WITHIN 2DAYS AFTER SHIPMENT NOTIFYING THE VESSEL NAME, B/L NO. QUNTITY SHIPPED, TOTAL AMOUNT AND SHIPMENT DATE. (36)
8. SHIPPING COMPANY'S CERTIFICATE CERTIFYING THAT THE CARRYING VESSEL IS NOT OVER 15YEARS OLD. (36)
9. INSPECITON CERTIFICATE IN DUPLICATE ISSUED AND SIGNED BY AUTHORIZED PERSON OF APPLICANT WHOSE SIGNATURE MUST COMPLY WITH THAT HELD IN OUR BANK'S RECORD. (10) + (35)</td>
</tr>
<tr>
<td colspan="2">COVERING SHIPMENT OF
5000PCS(22) OF GIRL JACKET(20) SYTLE NO. GJ234 SHELL: WOVEN TWILL 100% COTTON, LINING: WOVEN 100% POLYESTER(21) PACKING: 1PC TO A PLASTIC BAG, 20BAGS TO A CARTON
UNIT PRICE: USD10. 50/PC CIF TOKYO(23) DETAILS AS PER S/C 08TF0858 (25)</td>
</tr>
<tr>
<td colspan="2">OTHER TERMS AND CONDITIONS</td>
</tr>
</table>

1. SHIPPING MARKS: MARUBENI

信用证通知费已收
津中行

S/C 08TF0858

TOKYO
CTN 1 – UP (24)

2. ALL BANKING CHARGES ARE FOR BENEFICIARY'S ACCOUNT.

3. DOCUMENTS MUST BE PRESENTED TO THE NEGOTIATING BANK WITHIN 7DAYS AFTER SHIPMENT BUT WITHIN THE VALIDITY OF THE CREDIT. (8)

4. SHIPMENT MUST BE EFFECTED BY CONTAINER ONLY AND B/L SHOWING THE SAME. (37)

5. NEGOTIATION AND PRESENTATION OF THE DOCUMENTS UNDER THIS CREDIT IS RESTRICTED TO BANK OF CHINA TIANJIN BRANCH. (14)

6. NEGOTATING BANK IS KINDLY FORWARD ALL DOCUMENTS IN ONE LOT BY REGISTERED AIRMAIL IMMEDIATELY AFTER NEGOTIATION.

7. 10% MORE OR LESS BOTH IN QUANTITY AND AMOUNT ALLOWED. (22)

8. THE CREDIT WILL BECOME EFFECTIVE AFTER RECEIPT OF APPROVAL OF PRE – SHIPMENT SAMPLE FROM THE APPLICANT. (10)

WE HEREBY ENGAGE WITH DRAWERS, ENDORSERS AND/OR BONA FIDE HOLDERS THAT DRAFTS DRAWN AND NEGOTIATED ON PRESENTATION AND THAT DRAFTS ACCEPTED WITHIN THE TERMS OF THIS CREDIT WILL BE DULY HONORED AT MATURITY. (38)

THIS CREDIT IS SUBJECT TO UNIFORM AND CUSTOMARY PRACTICE 2007 REVERSION PUBLICATION NO. UCP600. (39)

YOURS FAITHFULLY,
FOR BANK OF CHINA HONGKONG BRANCH
(10)周秀仪 麦德强 印鉴核符

样例 3 – 3 女童夹克衫信用证

信用证审核记录

收证日期 2008-3-20

信用证证号	A-08-0058	合同号	08TF0858	订单号	
开证行	Bank of China Tokyo branch			开证日期	08/3/15
开证人	Marubeni Corp				
受益人	Tifert Trading Co., Ltd				
货物名称	Girl Jacket	数量	5000pcs	金额	USD52500.00
装运期	08/4/30	有效期	08/5/15	交单期	
装运港	Tianjin	目的港	Tokyo	可否分批	Not allowed
贸易术语	CIF Tokyo	汇票期限	At 30 days sight	可否转运	Not allowed

特殊条款	1.Shipment must be effected by container only and B/L showing the same. 2.Negotiation and presentation of the documents under this Credit is restricted to Bank of China Tianjin Branch. 3.The credit will become effective after receipt of approval of pre-shipment sample from the applicant.

单据种类及份数	汇票	发票	装箱单	重量单	尺码单	保险单	提单正本	提单副本	原产地证	GSP产地证	品质证	重量证	植检证	船行证明	寄单证明	寄样证明	受益人证明	邮包收据	其他
	2	3	2			2	3			2	2				1				

需要修改内容	来证条款内容	应修改后条款内容
	1. 信用证到期地点由 JAPAN	应修改为 CHINA，原则上不接受国外到期
	2. 受益人地址由 ZHUJIANG STREET	应修改为 ZHUJIANG ROAD，地址不符
	3. 转运由 NOT ALLOWED	应修改为 ALLOWED，与合同不符
	4. 汇票付款期限由 AT 30 DAYS SIGHT	应修改为 AT SIGHT，与合同不符
	5. 汇票的付款人由 DRAWN ON APPLICANT	应修改为 DRAWN ON US，信用证为银行信用
	6. 发票中的 COUNTERSIGNED BY APPLICANT	应该删除，否则无法保证在交单期内交单
	7. 提单中的 2/3 SET	应修改为 3/3 SET，否则受益人无法控制物权
	8. 提单中的 FREIGHT TO COLLECT	应修改为 FREIGHT PREPAID，与贸易术语不符
	9. 保险单中的投保加成 120%	应修改为 110%，与合同不符
	10. 保险单中依据的保险条款和版本年份由 AS PER ICC DATED 1/1/1982	应修改为 AS PER CIC DATED 1/1/1981，保险险别与依据的保险条款混淆
	11. 受益人证明函中的 1/3 ORIGINAL B/L	应修改为 COPY OF B/L
	12. 检验证书的签发人由 ISSUED AND SIGNED BY AUTHORIZED PERSON OF APPLICANT WHOSE SIGNATURE MUST COMPLY WITH THAT HELD IN OUR BANK'S RECORD	应修改为 ISSUED BY CIQ，此系软条款
	13. 银行费用由 ALL BANKINGCHARGES ARE FOR BENEFICIARY'S ACCOUNT	应修改为 ALL BANKING CHARGES OUTSIDE JAPAN ARE FOR BENEFICIARY'S ACCOUNT，否则不合理
	14. 交单期由 WITHIN 7DAYS	应修改为 WITHIN 15DAYS，与合同不符
	15. 特殊条款中的第 8 条 THE CREDIT WILL BECOME EFFECTIVE AFTER RECEIPT OF APPROVAL OF PRE-SHIPMENT SAMPLE FROM THE APPLICANT	应该删除，属于暂不生效条款
外销员签字	陈 丽	部门经理签字 赵天明

样例 3－4　女童夹克衫信用证审核记录

中国银行 天津分行
BANK OF CHINA

修改通知书
Notification of Amendment

ADDRESS:80, JIEFANG BEI LU, TIANJIN, CHINA
CABLE:CHUNGKOU
TELEX:23233 TJBOC CN
FAX:0086 22 23128900

DATE:MAR 27, 2008

To:致 TIFERT TRADING CO., LTD NO. 86, ZHUJIANG ROAD, TIANJIN, CHINA	When corresponding please quote our Ref No.
Issuing Bank 开证行 BANK OF CHINA, TOKYO BRANCH	Transmitted to us through 转递行
L/C No. 信用证号 A-08-0058	Amendment No 修改次数 1
L/C advised 信用证通知日期 MAR 19, 2008	Amendment dated 修改日期 MAR 25, 2008

Dear Sirs,
迳启者:

We have pleasure in advising you that we have received from the a/m bank a(n)
兹通知贵司,我行收自上述银行

(×) telex of 电传开立　　( ) ineffective 未生效
( ) original 正本　　( ) duplicate 副本

amendment to the captioned L/C, contents of which are as per attached sheet(s).
内容见附件。

This amendment should be attached to the captioned L/C advised by us, otherwise, the beneficiary will be responsible for any consequences arising there from.
本修改须附于有关信用证,否则,贵公司须对因此产生的后果承担责任。

Remark 备注

This L/C consists of 2 sheet(s), including the covering letter and attachment(s).
本信用证连同面函及附件共 2 纸。

Yours faithfully
for BANK OF CHINA

样例 3-5 女童夹克衫信用证修改通知书

FROM: BANK OF CHINA TOKYO BRANCH

TO: BANK OF CHINA TIANJIN BRANCH

80 JIEFANG BEI LU, TIANJIN

PEOPLE'S REP. OF CHINA

TEST: FOR USD52500.00 ON DATE 15/03/2008

PLEASE ADVISE BENEFICIARY OF THE FOLLOWING AMENDMENT TO L/C NO. A-08-0058 ISSUED BY US DATED 25/03/2008

DATE & NUMBER OF AMENDMENT: FIRST AMENDMENT ON MAR 25, 2008 IN JAPAN

THE LETTER OF CREDIT BE AMENDED AS FOLLOWS:

1. THE PLACE OF EXPIRY SHOULD BE IN CHINA INSTEAD OF IN JAPAN
2. THE CORRECT ADDRESS OF BENEFICIARY IS NO. 86, ZHUJIANG ROAD, TIANJIN, CHINA.
3. TRANSHIPMENT SHOULD BE ALLOWED INSTEAD OF NOT ALLOWED
4. BENEFICIARY'S DRAFT SHOULD BE AT SIGHT INSTEAD OF AT 30DAYS SIGHT
5. DRAFT SHOULD BE DRAWN ON OPENING BANK INSTEAD OF ON APPLICANT
6. DELETE COMMERCIAL INVOICE COUNTERSIGNED BY APPLICANT
7. B/L SHOULD BE FULL SET OF CLEAN ON BOARD INSTEAD OF 2/3 SET AND MARKED FREIGHT PREPAID NOT FREIGHT TO COLLECT.
8. INSURANCE VALUE SHOULD BE INVOICE VALUE OF GOODS PLUS 10% NOT 20% AND AS PER CIC DATED 1/1/1981 INSTEAD OF AS PER ICC DATED 1/1/1982
9. BENEFICIARY'S CERTIFICATE SHOULD CERTITY THAT ONE COPY OF B/L INSTEAD OF 1/3 ORIGINAL B/L
10. DELETE INSPECITON CERTIFICATE IN DUPLICATE ISSUED AND SIGNED BY AUTHORIZED PERSON OF APPLICANT WHOSE SIGNATURE MUST COMPLY WITH THAT HELD IN OUR BANK'S RECORD. AND INSERT INSPECTION CERTIFICATE IN DUPLICATE ISSED BY CIQ
11. ALL BANKINGCHARGES ARE FOR BENEFICIARY'S ACCOUNT SHOULD CHANGE TO ALL BANKINGCHARGES OUTSIDE JAPAN ARE FOR BENEFICIARY'S ACCOUNT.
12. DOCUMENTS SHOULD BE PRESENTED FOR NEGOTIATION WITHIN 15DAYS AFTER SHIPMENT INSTEAD OF 7DAYS.
13. THE CREDIT WILL BECOME EFFECTIVE AFTER RECEIPT OF APPROVAL OF PRE-SHIPMENT SAMPLE FROM THE APPLICANT WHICH SHOULD BE DELETED.

OTHER TERMS AND CONDITIONS REMAIN UNCHANGED.

样例3-6　女童夹克衫信用证修改

三、审核信用证应注意问题

1. 首先要注意审核信用证的"四性",即有效性、真实性、完整性和风险性。

2. 其次对照合同条款做到逐个条款审核,检查信用证中的所有条款是否能够满足。

3. 注意区分单据化条款和非单据化条款,对于单据化条款不能做到的一定坚持让进口商修改。

4. 对于信开证中的软条款要睁大眼睛仔细识别,及早剔除安全收汇的隐患。

5. 掌握信用证的修改原则,分清"必须修改"、"可改可不改"及"无须修改"的界限。

上岗操作

任务栏

1. 通知:公司将有以下合同项下的货物装运出口,并且已经收到国外客户通过银行开立的信用证。

2. 目的:本项任务的目的是熟悉并掌握信用证审核的技巧,为安全收汇把好关。

3. 要求:下班前将填写好的信用证审核记录交给师傅审核。

一、动脑思考

1. 天津胜利制衣有限公司与法国家乐福采购商通过友好洽商达成一睡衣套出口合同,合同规定 2008 年 3 月 15 日前从天津新港运往马赛港,而家乐福采购商通过法国巴黎银行开立的信用证规定:"SHIPMENT FROM CHINESE MAIN PORTS",你作为公司单证员认为有必要修改信用证吗?为什么?

2. 天津棉纺进出口公司拟出口全棉印花布约 10000 米到南非的好望角港,待货物备妥出运前业务员发现信用证货物描述的数量前没有"About"字样,因为国内染整厂设备临时出现故障,最后仅备齐 9600 米面料,再推迟就要过装运期,要求客户修改信用证也为时已晚,此时业务员万分焦急,请你帮助他找出最好的解决方案?

3. 最近泰佛贸易公司收到一份美国花旗银行开来的信用证,单证员对该信用证进行了认真审核,没有发现与合同条款不符的内容,但整个信用证只有有效期,信用证开立日期、最迟装运日期、交单期等都没有,单证员不知道该证是否有效,打电话向中行天津分行国际结算部进行了咨询。如果你就是中行结算部的工作人员,你应该如何回答单证员的问题呢?

二、动手操作

1. 初级训练

泰佛贸易有限公司与日本通用贸易公司就出口印花细布达成一份出口合同(见样例3-7),日本通用贸易公司银行已将信用证开出(见样例3-8),请根据所提供的合同主要条款审核信用证并填写信用证审核记录(见样例3-9)。

销 售 合 同

合同号码:PS-1234

签订日期、地点:2008年10月11日于北京

卖方:泰佛贸易公司(Tifert Trading Co., Ltd)

买方:日本通用贸易公司(General Trading Company, Japan)

商品名称:"鸽牌"印花细布("Dove" Brand Printed Shirting)

规格:30s×36s 72×69 35/6′×42码

数量:67200码

单价:CIF大阪每码3.00日元

总值:210600.00日元

装运期:2008年11月30日前自中国港口至大阪,允许分批装运和转船。

付款条件:凭不可撤销即期信用证付款,于装运期前1个月开到卖方,并开上述装运期后15天内在中国议付有效。

保险:由卖方根据中国人民保险公司1981年1月1日中国保险条款按发票金额的110%投保一切和战争险。

样例3-7 销售合同

LETTER OF CREDIT

Date: Oct 15, 2008

We hereby open our Irrevocable Letter of Credit No. L－1437 in favour of Tifert Trading Co., Ltd. for account of General Trading Company, Japan, up to an aggregate amount of JPY201, 600.00 (Say Japanese Yuan Two Hundred and One Thousand Six Hundred Only) CIFC 2% Osaka for 100% of the invoice value relative to the shipment of: 67,200 Pieces of Dove Brand Printed Shirting 30s × 36s 72 × 69 35/6 × 42 yards as per Contract No. PS－1234 dated October 11, 2008 from China port to Osaka, Japan.

Drafts to be drawn at 30 days after sight on our bank and accompanied by the following documents, marked "X":

(X) Signed Commercial Invoice in triplicate;

(X) Full set of CLEAN ON BOARD BILLS of LADING made out to our order quoting L/C NO. L－1437, marked FREIGHT PAID;

(X) One original Marine Insurance Policy or Certificate for 130% of invoice value covering ALL Risks and War Risk with claims payable in Japan in the currency of draft(s).

Partial shipments are permitted.

Transshipment is prohibited.

Shipment must be effected not later than Nov 30, 2008.

Draft(s) drawn under this credit must be negotiated in Japan on or before Nov 30, 2008.

样例 3－8 信用证

审核后请将修改意见填入下表

合同号	
信用证号	
修改意见	

样例 3－9 信用证审核记录

2. 中级训练

泰佛贸易公司经过友好洽商与加拿大 NEO 贸易公司就出口陶瓷餐具达成合同一纸，现加拿大客户已通过皇家银行将信用证开抵泰佛贸易公司，请根据所提供的合同（见样例 3－10）审核信用证（见样例 3－11）并填写审证记录（见样例 3－12）。

销售合同

SALES CONTRACT

卖方 **SELLER:**	TIFERT TRADING CO., LTD NO. 86, ZHUJIANG ROAD, TIANJIN, CHINA	编号 NO.: 日期 DATE: 地点 **SIGNED IN:**	SHDS03027 APR.03, 2008 TIANJIN
买方 **BUYER:**	NEO GENERAL TRADING CO. #362 JALAN STREET, TORONTO, CANADA		

买卖双方同意以下条款达成交易：
This contract Is made by and agreed between the BUYER and SELLER , in accordance with the terms and conditions stipulated below.

1. 品名及规格 Commodity & Specification	2. 数量 Quantity	3. 单价及价格条款 Unit Price & Trade Terms	4. 金额 Amount
			CIFC5 TORONTO
CHINESE CERAMIC DINNERWARE			
DS1511 30-PIECE DINNERWARE AND TEA SET	542SETS	USD23.50	12737.00
DS2201 20-PIECE DINNERWARE SET	800SETS	USD20.40	16320.00
DS4504 45-PIECE DINNERWARE SET	443SETS	USD23.20	10277.60
DS5120 95-PIECE DINNERWARE SET	254SETS	USD30.10	7645.40
Total:	**2039SETS**		**46980.00**

允许 With 10% 溢短装，由卖方决定 MORE OR LESS OF SHIPMENT ALLOWED AT THE SELLER'S OPTION

5. 总值 **Total Value** SAY US DOLLARS FORTY SIX THOUSAND NINE HUNDRED AND EIGHTY ONLY.

6. 包装 **Packing** DS2201 IN CARTONS OF 2 SETS EACH AND DS1511, DS4504 AND DS5120 TO BE PACKED IN CARTONS OF 1 SET EACH ONLY.
TOTAL: 1639 CARTONS.

7. 唛头 **Shipping Marks** AT BUYER'S OPTION.

8. 装运期及运输方式 **Time of Shipment & means of Transportation** TO BE EFFECTED BEFORE THE END OF APRIL 2008 WITH PARTIAL SHIPMENT AND ALLOWED AND TRANSHIPMENT ALLOWED.

9. 装运港及目的地 **Port of Loading & Destination** FROM: TIANJIN
TO: TORONTO

10. 保险 **Insurance** THE SELLER SHALL COVER INSURANCE AGAINST WPA AND CLASH & BREAKAGE & WAR RISK FOR 110% OF THE TOTAL INVOICE VALUE AS PER THE RELEVANT OCEAN MARINE CARGO OF P.I.C.C. DATED 1/1/1981.

11. 付款方式 **Terms of Payment** THE BUYER SHALL OPEN AN IRREVOCABLE LETTER OF CREDIT THOUGH A BANK ACCEPTABLE TO THE SELLER TO REACH THE SELLER BEFORE APRIL 10, 2008 VALID FOR NEGOTIATION IN CHINA UNTIL THE 15TH DAY AFTER THE DATE OF SHIPMEDNT.

The Buyer	**The Seller**
NEO GENERAL TRADING CO.	TIFERT TRADING CO., LTD
(signature)	(signature)

样例 3－10 销售合同

THE ROYAL BANK OF CANADA

□CONFIRMATION OF TELEX/CABLE PER-ADVISED
TELEX NO. 4720688 CA

DATE: APR 8, 2008
PLACE: VANCOUVER

IRREVOCABLE DOCUMENTARY CREDIT | CREDIT NUMBER: 01/0501-FCT | ADVISING BANK'S REF. NO.

ADVISING BANK:
SHANGHAI A J FINANCE CORPORATION
59 HONGKONG ROAD SHANGHAI, CHINA

APPLICANT:
NEO GENERAL TRADING CO.
#362 JALAN STREET, TORONTO, CANADA

BENEFICIARY:
TIFERT TRADING CO., LTD
NO.86,ZHUJIANG ROAD, TIANJIN, CHINA

AMOUNT:
USD46,980.00
(US DOLLARS FORTY SIX THOUSAND NINE HUNDRED AND EIGHTEEN ONLY)

EXPIRY DATE: MAY 15, 2008 FOR NEGOTIATION IN APPLICANT'S COUNTRY

GENTLEMEN:
WE HEREBY OPEN OUR IRREVOCABLE LETTER OF CREDIT IN YOUR FAVOR WHICH IS AVAILABLE BY YOUR DRAFTS AT SIGHT FOR FULL INVOICE VALUE ON US ACCOMPANIED BY THE FOLLOWING DOCUMENTS:

\+ SIGNED COMMERCIAL INVOICE AND 3 COPIES.
\+ PACKING LIST AND 3 COPIES, SHOWING THE INDIVIDUAL WEIGHT AND MEASUREMENT OF EACH ITEM.
\+ ORIGINAL CERTIFICATE OF ORIGIN AND 3 COPIES ISSUED BY THE CHAMBER OF COMMERCE.
\+ FULL SET CLEAN ON BOARD OCEAN BILLS OF LADING SHOWING FREIGHT PREPAID CONSIGNED TO ORDER OF THE ROYAL BANK OF CANADA INDICATING THE ACTUAL DATE OF THE GOODS ON BOARD AND NOTIFY THE APPLICANT WITH FULL ADDRESS AND PHONE NO. 77009910.
\+ INSURANCE POLICY OR CERTIFICATE FOR 130 PERCENT OF INVOICE VALUE COVERING: INSURANCE CARGO CLAUSES(A) AS PER I.C.C. DATED 1/1/1982.
\+ BENEFICIARY'S CERTIFICATE CERTIFYING THAT EACH COPY OF SHIPPING DOCUMENTS HAS BEEN FAXED TO THE APPLICANT WITHIN 48 HOURS AFTER SHIPMENT.

COVERING SHIPMENT OF:
4 ITEMS TERMS OF CHINESE CERAMIC DINNERWARE INCLUDING:
DS1511 30-PIECE DINNERWARE AND TEA SET, 544SETS
DS2201 20-PIECE DINNERWARE SET, 800SETS,
DS4504 45-PIECE DINNERWARE SET, 443SETS
DS5120 95-PIECE DINNERWARE SET, 245SETS
DETAILS IN ACCORDANCE WITH SALES CONTRACT HSDS03027 DATED APR. 3, 2006.
[ ]FOB / [ ]CFR / [X] CIF/ [ ]FCA TORONTO CANADA.

SHIPMENT FROM	TO	LATEST	PARTIAL SHIPMENTS	TRANSSHIPMENT
TIANJIN	VANCOUVER	APRIL 30,2008	PROHIBITED	PROHIBITED

DRAFTS TO BE PRESENTED FOR NEGOTIATION WITHIN 15 DAYS AFTER SHIPMENT, BUT WITHIN THE VALIDITY OF CREDIT. ALL DOCUMENTS TO BE FORWARDED IN ONE COVER, BY AIRMAIL, UNLESS OTHERWISE STATED UNDER SPECIAL INSTRUCTION.

SPECIAL INSTRUCTION: + BANKING CHARGES OUTSIDE CANADA ARE FOR ACCOUNT OF BENEFICIARY.
\+ ALL GOODS MUST BE SHIPPED IN ONE 20' CONTAINER CY TO CY AND B/L SHOWING THE SAME.
\+ THE VALUE OF FREIGHT PREP AID HAS TO BE SHOWN ON BILLS OF LADING.

DRAFT MUST BE MARKED AS BEING DRAWN UNDER THIS CREDIT AND BEAR ITS NUMBER; THE AMOUNTS ARE TO BE ENDORSED ON THE REVERSE HERE OF BY NEG. BANK. WE HEREBY AGREE WITH THE DRAWERS, ENDORSERS AND FIDE HOLDER THAT ALL DRAFTS DRAWN UNDER AND IN COMPLIANCE WITH THE TERMS OF THIS CREDIT SHALL BE DULY HONORED UPON PRESENTATION.
THIS CREDIT IS SUBJECT TO THE UNIFORM CUSTOMS AND PRACTICE FOR DOCUMENTARY CREDITS (2007 REVISION) BY THE INTERNATIONAL CHAMBER OF COMMERCE PUBLICATION NO. 600.

Yours Very Truly,

David Jone
AUTHORIZED SIGNATURE

Joanne Hsan
AUTHORIZED SIGNATURE

样例 3－11　信用证

信用证审核记录

信用证证号		合同号		订单号	
开证行				开证日期	
开证人					
受益人					
货物名称		数量		金额	
装运期		有效期		交单期	
装运港		目的港		可否分批	
贸易术语		汇票期限		可否转运	

特殊条款	

单据种类及份数	汇票	发票	装箱单	重量单	尺码单	保险单	提单正本	提单副本	原产地证	GSP产地证	品质证	重量证	植检证	船行证明	寄单证明	寄样证明	受益人证明	邮包收据	

需要修改内容	来证条款内容	应修改后条款内容

单证员签字		部门经理签字	

样例 3－12　信用证审核记录

3. 高级训练

泰佛贸易有限公司向迪拜 GAZA 公司供应全棉围裙，迪拜的客户已将信用证开出，请你根据买卖双方签订的合同（见样例3－13）审核信用证（见样例3－14）并用英文草拟改证函（见样例3－15）。

SALES CONTRACT

NO. AH107　　　　DATE: JAN. 5,, 2008

THIS SALES CONFIRMATION IS MADE AND ENTERED INTO BY AND BETWEEN TIFERT TRADING CO., LTD (NO. 86, ZHUJIANG ROAD, TIANJIN, CHINA) HEREINAFTER REFERRED TO AS THE SELLERS AND GAZA PALESTINE CO., LTD (P. O. BOX 8961, DUBAI) HEREINAFTER REFERRED TO AS THE BUYERS. THE SELLERS AGREE TO SELL AND THE BUYERS AGREE TO BUY THE COMMODITY/IES MENTIONED IN THIS CONTRACT SUBJECT TO THE TERMS AND CONDITIONS STIPULATED AS FOLLOWS:

NAME OF COMMODITY & SPECIFICATION PACKING AND SHIPPING MARK	QUANTITY (PCS)	UNIT PRICE	AMOUNT
100% PURE COTTON APRON		CFRC3 DUBAI	
ART. NO. 49394(014428)	3216	USD1.00	USD3216.00
ART. NO. 49393(014429)	3960	USD1.00	USD3960.00
ART. NO. 55306(014430)	1560	USD1.25	USD1950.00
REMARKS: 1) EACH PC IN A PLASTIC BAG, 12 BAGS TO A CARTON		TOTAL:	USD9126.00
2) SHIPPING MARK: GAZA DUBAI NO. 1-728			
TOTAL VALUE: SAY US DOLLARS NINE THOUSAND ONE HUNDRED AND TWENTY SIX ONLY.			

TIME OF SHIPMENT: WITHIN 45 DAYS OF RECEIPT OF LETTER OF CREDIT AND NOT LATER THAN THE MONTH OF MAY 2008 WITH PARTIAL SHIPMENTS AND TRANSSHIPMENT ALLOWED.

PORT OF LOADING: TIANJIN　　PORT OF DESTINATION: DUBAI

TERMS OF PAYMENT: BY IRREVOCABLE SIGHT LETTER OF CREDIT OPENED BY THE BUYER TO REACH THE SELLER NOT LATER THAN APRIL 15TH, 2008 AND TO BE AVAILABLE FOR NEGOTIATION IN CHINA UNTIL THE 15TH DAY AFTER THE DATE OF SHIPMENT. IN CASE OF LATE ARRIVAL OF THE L/C, THE SELLER SHALL NOT BE LIABLE FOR ANY DELAY IN SHIPMENT AND SHALL HAVE THE RIGHT TO RESCIND THE CONTRACT AND OR CLAIM FOR DAMAGES.

INSURANCE: TO BE EFFECTED BY THE SELLER FOR 110% OF THE CIF INVOICE VALUE COVERING ALL RISKS AND WAR RISK ONLY AS PER CHINA INSURANCE CLAUSES.

CONFIRMED BY THE BUYER　　THE SELLER

GAZA PALESTINE CO., LTD　　TIFERT TRADING CO., LTD

样例3－13　销售合同

LETTER OF CREDIT

MTS700 ISSUE OF A DOCUMENTARY CREDIT

SEQUENCE OF TOTAL	*27:1/1
FORM OF DOC. CREDIT	*40:IRREVOCABLEABLE
APPLICABLE RULES	*40E:UCP LATEST VERSION
DOC CREDIT NUMBER	*20:ABL – AN107
DATE OF ISSUE	*31C:080405
EXPIRY	*31D:DATE 080605 IN DUBAI
APPLICANT	*50: GAZA PALESTINE MILL P. O. BOX 8961, DUBAI
BENEFICIARY	*59: TIFERT TRADING CO. LTD., NO. 86, ZHUJIANG ROAD, TIANJIN, CHINA
AMOUNT	*32B: CURRENCY USD AMOUNT 8852,22
MAX CREDIT AMOUNT	*39B: NOT EXCEEDING
AVAILABLE WITH/BY	*41D: ANY BANK BY NEGOTIATION IN DUBAI
DRAFTS AT...	*42C: DRAFTS AT 20 DAYS' SIGHT FOR FULL INVOICE VALUE
DRAWEE	*42A: BANK OF CHINA DUBAI
PARTIAL SHIPMENTS	*43P: ALLOWED
TRANSSHIPMENT	*43T: PROHIBITED
LOADING IN CHARGE	*44E: SHIPMENT FROM CHINESE PORT(S)
FOR TRANSPORT TO	*44F: DUBAI
LATEST DATE OF SHIP.	*44C: 080531
DESCRIPT. OF GOODS	*45A: 100% COTTON APRON AS PER S/C NO AN107 ART NO QUANTITY UNIT PRICE CFR DUBAI 49394(014428)3216 PIECES USD1.00/PC 49393(014429)3690 PIECES USD1.00/PC 55306(014430)1560 PIECES USD1.25/PC
DOCUMENTS REQUIRED	*46

+ 2/3 SET OF ORIGINAL CLEAN ON BOARD CLEAN BILLS OF LADING MADE OUT TO ORDER OF SHIPPER AND BLANK ENDORSED AND MARKED "FREIGHT PREPAID" NOTIFY APPLICANT (WITH FULL NAME AND ADDRESS)

+ ORIGINAL SIGNED COMMERCIAL INVOICE IN 5 FOLD INDICATING S/C NO.

+ INSURANCE FOLICY OR CERTIFICATE IN TWO FOLD ENDORSED IN BLANK, FOR 120PCT OF THE INVOICE VALUE INCLUDING: THE INSTITUTE CARGO CLAUSES(A), THE INSTITUTE WAR CLAUSES, INSURANCE CLAIMS TO BE PAYABLE AT DESTINATION IN THE CURRENCY OF THE DRAFT

+ PACKING LIST IN 3 FOLD

+ BENEFICIARY'S CERTIFICATE STATING THAT ONE SET OF ORIGINAL SHIPPING DOCUMENTS HAS BEEN SENT DIRECTLY TO THE APPLICANT

ADDITIONAL COND. *47

1. T. T. REIMBURSEMENT IS PRONIBITED.

2. THE GOODS TO BE PACKED IN EXPORT STRONG COLORED CARTONS

3. INSPECTION IS TO BE EFFECTED BEFORE SHIPMENT AND RELEVANT CERTIFICATES/REPORTS ARE REQUIRED FROM THE INSPECTING AGENCY OR INSPECTOR DESIGNATED BY THE BUYER.

DETAILS OF CHARGES　　　　*71B

ALL BANKING CHARGES OUTSIDE DUBAI INCLUDING REIMBURSEMENT COMMISSIONS, ARE FOR ACCOUNT OF BENEFICIARY.

PRSENTATION PERIOD　　　　*48

DOCUMENTS TO BE PRESENTED WITHIN 5 DAYS AFTER THE DATE OF SHIPMENT, BUT WITHIN THE VALIDITY OF THE CREDIT

CONFIRMATION　　　　*49: WITHOUT

INSTUCTIONS　　　　*78:

THE NEGOTIATION BANK MUST FORWARD THE DRAFTS AND ALL DOCUMENTS BY REGISTERED AIRMIL DIRECT TO US IN TWO CONSECUTIVE LOTS, UPON RECEIPT OF THE DRAFTS AND DOCUMENTS IN ORDER, WE WILL REMIT THE PROCEEDS AS INSTRUCTED BY THE NEGOTIATING BANK.

样例 3－14　信用证

请用英文草拟改证函

Tifert Trading Co., Ltd.

No. 86, Zhujiang Road, Tianjin, China

样例 3－15　信用证改证函

学习情境三　缮制单证

任务四　缮制商业发票

岗前测试

一、单选题

> 温馨提示：
>
> 商业发票是全套单据的核心，一般首先缮制商业发票，因此商业发票的出单日期在全套结汇单证中是最早的。

一、单选题

1. 发票上的货物数量应与信用证一致，如信用证在数量前使用“约、大约”字样时，根据《跟单信用证统一惯例 UCP600》的规定，应理解为（　）。

A. 货物数量有不超过 5% 的增减幅度　　B. 货物数量有不超过 10% 的增减幅度

C. 货物数量有不超过 3% 的增减幅度　　D. 货物数量不得增减

2. 根据《跟单信用证统一惯例 UCP600》的规定，以下关于正副本份数正确的选项是（　）。

A. 如信用证要求提交的发票份数为“3COPIES”，则应提交 3 份副本发票

B. 如信用证要求提交的发票份数为“3COPIES”，则应提交至少 1 份正本发票

C. 如信用证要求提交的发票份数为“2FOLDS”，则应提交 2 份副本发票

D. 如信用证要求提交的发票份数为“DUPLICATE”，则应提交 2 份副本发票

3. 如信用证未规定货物的数量不得增减且数量不是以包装单位或个数记数，在支取款项不超过信用证金额的情况下，发票上显示的货物数量允许增减的幅度为（　）。

A. 3%　　B. 5%　　C. 8%　　D. 10%

4. 根据作用不同，发票可分为商业发票、海关发票、形式发票、领事发票、厂商发票、联合发票和证实发票等，其中（　）是出口业务结汇中最重要的单据之一，是单证工作的核心。

A. 商业发票　　B. 形式发票　　C. 领事发票　　D. 证实发票

5. 在托收和汇付方式下，商业发票的抬头人一般是（　）。

A. 进口地银行　　B. 买方　　C. 出口地银行　　D. 卖方

6. 根据《跟单信用证统一惯例 UCP600》的规定，除非信用证另有规定，商业发票

的签发人必须是(　　)。

A. 开证申请人　　B. 受益人　　C. 开证行　　D. 合同的买方

7. 根据《跟单信用证统一惯例 UCP600》的规定,除非信用证另有规定,商业发票的抬头必须是(　　)。

A. 开证行　　B. 开证行指定的银行

C. 开证申请人　　D. 受益人

8. 信用证要求受益人提交发票作为议付的单据之一,银行将拒绝接受(　　)代替发票。

A. 海关发票　　B. 最终发票　　C. 商业发票　　D. 临时发票

9. 如果信用证禁止分批装运,只要货物全部装运,且单价没有减少,则发票金额允许有(　　)的减幅。

A. 10%　　B. 5%　　C. 3%　　D. 2%

10. 如果信用证给出的贸易术语包含了术语的来源,如 CIFC2 LONDON INCOTERMS 2000,填写发票货物描述部分正确的是(　　)。

A. CIFC2 LONDON INCOTERMS 2000　　B. CIFC2 LONDON

C. CIF LONDON INCOTERMS 2000　　D. CIF LONDON

二、多选题

小贴士:

商业发票中的货物描述要与信用证中货物描述一致,并不要求如同镜子反射那样一致,信用证中的货物描述细节可以在发票的若干地方反映出来,只要合并在一起时与信用证规定一致即可视为与信用证中货物描述一致。

1. 商业发票是卖方向买方签发的载明货物的品质、数量、包装和价格等内容,并凭以索取货款的凭证,其作用主要有(　　)。

A. 是买卖双方收付货款及记账依据　　B. 是货物运输的收据

C. 是买卖双方办理报关、纳税的依据　　D. 是缮制其他出口单据的依据

2. 除最常见的商业发票外,发票还包括(　　)。

A. 海关发票　　B. 形式发票　　C. 领事发票　　D. 证实发票

3. 以下单据中作为发票的附属单据,对发票起着补充说明作用的是(　　)。

A. 运输单据　　B. 保险单据　　C. 装箱单　　D. 重量单

4. 根据《跟单信用证统一惯例 UCP600》的规定,除非信用证另有规定,商业发票(　　)。

A. 必须由信用证中指定的受益人签发　　B. 必须做成开证申请人抬头

C. 必须签署　　D. 金额不得超过信用证金额

5. 发票的主要内容包括(　)。

A. 首文部分　　B. 自由处理区　　C. 正文部分　　D. 结尾部分

三、判断题

1. 信用证规定货物数量可有5%伸缩,虽对金额未作此规定,商业发票金额也允许有5%伸缩。(　)

2. 在信用证支付方式下,商业发票中的货物描述必须与信用证的描述一致,省略或增加任何内容都会造成单证不符。(　)

3. 如果信用证中没有特殊规定,其他单据中的货物描述只要不与信用证中的货物描述相矛盾即可。(　)

4. 商业发票总额不可以超过信用证总金额,对于佣金和折扣应按信用证规定的处理。(　)

5. 商业发票的抬头人一般指信用证中的受益人。(　)

6. 商业发票是由商会签发的,必须要签署。(　)

7. 在不用汇票的情况下,发票替代汇票作为付款的依据。(　)

8. 信用证要求商业发票作为议付的单据之一,银行可接受临时发票代替商业发票。(　)

9. 商业发票中允许包括免费的样品、广告材料。(　)

10. 商业发票是出口业务结汇中最重要的单据之一,是单证工作的核心单据。(　)

岗前培训

一、商业发票缮制规范

表4-1　商业发票缮制规范

项目顺序号	填写内容	要点提示
(1)单据名称 Name of doc	Commercial invoice 或 Invoice	与信用证上的规定完全一致
(2)出单人 Issuer	签发发票的人	①信用证项下为受益人 ②托收和电汇项下为合同卖方 ③有些公司可能已印就,无须填写
(3)受单人 To	抬头人	①信用证项下为开证申请人 ②托收和电汇项下为合同买方
(4)运输详情 Transport details	启运港(地)、目的港(地)和运输方式	启运港(地)应明确具体,目的港(地)如有重名港后面要加国别

续表

项目顺序号	填写内容	要点提示
(5)发票号码 Invoice No.	此笔业务的发票号码	由卖方自行编制
(6)日期 Date	发票的出票日期	一般在信用证开证日期后提单签发日前，且不能迟于信用证的交单期和有效期
(7)合同号 S/C No.	此笔业务的合同号码	应与信用证上引用的合同号保持一致
(8)信用证号 L/C No.	此笔业务的信用证号码	应与信用证上列明的证号保持一致，采用其他付款方式可留空
(9)付款方式 Terms of payment	此笔业务的付款方式	信用证方式填 By L/C，托收填 By D/P，电汇填 By T/T
(10)唛头 Marks and numbers	合同或信用证规定的唛头	信用证或合同有指定唛头必须严格按照规定制唛；信用证或合同没有规定唛头出口商可自行设计；没有唛头填 N/M
(11)货物描述 Number and kind of package, description of goods	包括货物的件数、货物名称、规格、包装情况等	必须与信用证上的货物描述完全一致，但无需照镜子式反射
(12)数量 Quantity	一般填写货物的实际出运数量	不要遗漏计量单位
(13)单价 Unit price	包括计价货币、计量单位、单位金额和贸易术语	填写要完整、正确，不能遗漏贸易术语
(14)总金额 Amount	单价与实际出运数量的乘积即发票总值	①一般不能超过信用证金额 ②有折扣或明佣的应在此扣除，计算出净值
(15)声明文句 Statement	来证要求的发票上加注各种费用金额、原产地、特定号码等声明文句	这些内容加注在发票货物描述栏以下的空白处
(16)签字 Signature	一般加盖签发人的英文名称加法人代表签字图章	①商业发票只能由 L/C 规定的受益人出具 ②无特殊规定，发票可以无需签署 ③若信用证要求手签，出单人要亲笔签署不能以盖章代替

二、商业发票缮制范例

Issuer (2) TIFERT TRADING CO., LTD. NO. 86, ZHUJIANG ROAD, TIANJIN, CHINA	商 业 发 票 (1) **COMMERCIAL INVOICE**	
To (3) MARUBENI CORP 5-7, HOMMACHI, 2-CHOME, CHUO-KU, OSAKA, JAPAN	No.: (5) INVOICE NO. 123456	Date: (6) APR 15, 2008
Transport Details (4) SHIPMENT FROM TIANJIN TO TOKYO BY SEA	S/C No. (7) 08TF0858	L/C No. (8) A-08-0058
	Terms of payment (9) L/C AT SIGHT	

Marks and numbers (10)	Number and kind of packages, Description of goods (11)		Quantity (12)	Unit price (13)	Amount (14)
					CIF TOKYO
MARUBENI	250 CARTONS	5000PCS		USD10.50/PC	USD52500.00
S/C 08TF0858		GIRL JACKET			
TOKYO		SYTLE NO.GJ234			
CTN 1-250		SHELL:WOVEN TWILL 100% COTTON			
		LINING: WOVEN 100% POLYESTER			

PACKED IN CARTONS OF 20PCS EACH

WE HEREBY CERTIFY THAT THE GOODS ARE OF CHINESE ORIGIN (15)

(16) 王 宏

样例 4－1 女童夹克衫商业发票

三、缮制商业发票应注意问题

1. 发票的种类。信用证要求“发票”但未做进一步的要求,则提交任何形式的发票都可以接受,如商业发票、海关发税务发票、最终发票、领事发票等。但是“临时发票”(Provisional Invoice)、“形式发票”(Proforma Invoice)或类似的发票是不可接受的,除非信用证另有授权。当信用证要求提交商业发票时,标为“发票”的单据是可以接受的。

2. 发票的签发人。除可转让信用证外,发票必须表面看来由信用证中具名的受益人出具。地址中的电传或传真号码等内容无需提供;如果提供,也可不必与信用证中的相同,但必须在同一国家内。

3. 发票抬头人。除信用证另有规定或可转让信用证外,发票必须以申请人为抬头。地址中的电传或传真号码等内容无需提供;如果提供,也可不必与信用证中的相同。如果信用证有指定其他抬头人的,按来证规定缮制发票。如果该信用证已被转让,则银行也可接受由第二受益人提交的以第一受益人为抬头的发票。

4. 发票的签署。除非信用证要求,发票无须签字或标注日期。但是如信用证要求的证明文句加注在未要求签字的发票上,则该发票必须要签署。

5. 发票的货物描述。发票上的货物描述部分是发票的中心内容,必须反映实际装运的货物,必须与信用证规定相符。如信用证规定了多种货物,应根据实际发货情况注明其中一种或几种,不可盲目照抄,发票也不能显示信用证未要求的货物(包括样品、广告材料等)即使注明免费。信用证规定的货名并非英文文字,如中文或法文,这时发票也应照原文显示出来。

如出运的货物较多,信用证上标有统称时,发票上可在具体品名上按来证显示统称。信用证只规定了货物的总称,发票应照样显示外,还可加列详细的货名,但不得与总称矛盾。如信用证未规定货物的总称,但列举的货物名称很详细,则发票除显示详细的货物名称外,还可加注统称。

6. 发票的数量。发票必须如实反映实际装运的货物的数量,特别允许分批装运和允许溢短装的情况下更应该注意。即使信用证没有溢短装条款,信用证要求的货物数量可以有5%的溢短装幅度,但如果信用证规定货物数量不得超额或减少,或信用证规定的货物数量是以包装单位或个数计算时,不适用此条。货物数量在5%幅度内的溢装并不意味着允许支取的金额超过信用证金额。

7. 发票的总金额不能超过信用证的最高限额。发票中显示的单价和币种必须与信用证中的一致,发票必须显示信用证要求的折扣或扣减,发票还可显示信用证未规定的与预付款或佣金、折扣等有关的扣减额。

8. 发票的总金额允许比信用证少支取5%。如果信用证禁止分批装运,只要货物全部装运,且单价(如信用证有规定的话)没有减少,则发票金额有5%的减幅是可接受的,如果信用证未规定货物数量,发票的货物数量即可视为全部货物数量。

9. 发票的格式要求。如在一张发票中有多种货号的货物内容,要求在缮制发票时,格式整齐,每一货号的货物内容和总数排列有序,应做到:横排是每一货号的货物内容,如货号、规格、数量、单价、该货号的金额;竖排应是各货号该列内容的总和,如数量、总金额。

10. 佣金和折扣。发票中对佣金、折扣等用词要正确。如果信用证或合同规定的单价含有"佣金",发票绝不可以"折扣"代替。如果信用证规定为"现金折扣"则也不能只写"折扣"或"贸易折扣"。总之,此类项目一个字不能错也不能省。如果信用证既有佣金也有折扣,一般是先扣除折扣,然后再计扣佣金,因为折扣部分是不应支付佣金的。

上岗操作

任务栏

1. 通知:公司将有以下合同项下的货物装运出口,加工厂已将货物备妥,请根据有关资料缮制商业发票,以便办理报检手续。

2. 目的:本项任务的目的是熟悉并掌握商业发票的缮制技巧。

3. 要求:下班前将缮制好的商业发票交给师傅审核。

一、动脑思考

1. 天津家纺进出口公司收到国外来信用证,货物描述为:"2000pcs of Ladies skirts at USD2.10/pc CIF London, including less 5% commission and 5% allowance (discount) total amount USD4200"。你作为单证员在缮制商业发票时如何处理才能满足信用证的要求?是首先扣减折扣还是首先扣减佣金?为什么?

2. 天津粮油进出口公司向非洲纳米比亚出口小麦20公吨,客户开来的信用证最大金额为4750美元,信用证的货物描述为"20M/T of Chinese Wheat at USD250.00/MT CIFC5% Walvis Pont",受益人实际发货20公吨。为保证安全收汇,你作为单证员在发票金额上如何处理才能不突破信用证的最大金额?

3. 天津隆盛米业有限公司与德国客户成交20公吨大米,客户通过银行开来的信用证金额为5000美元,信用证的货物描述为"20M/T of Chinese Rice in bulk at USD250.00/MT CIF Hamburg"。受益人实际出运20.5公吨大米,显然溢装0.5公吨,而信用证的金额只有5000美元,为了能安全收汇,你作为单证员对超出信用证部分的款项应该如何在商业发票上巧妙处理?

二、动手操作

1. 初级训练

泰佛贸易公司与日本 ITOCHU 公司经过友好洽商就出口女式针织衫达成一份出口合同，数量 1500 件，CIF KOBE，付款方式即期信用证（L/C at sight）。作为单证员，请你根据摘录的信用证有关条款和其他补充信息缮制商业发票（见样例 4－2）。

信用证中与发票相关的主要条款如下：

59：BENEFICIARY：　TIFERT TRADING CO.，LTD

NO. 86，ZHUJIANG ROAD，TIANJIN，CHINA

50：APPLICANT：　ITOCHU CORP

88，RED SUN BUILDING，TOKYO，JAPAN.

44E：PORT OF LOADING　TIANJIN

44F：PORT OF DISCHARGE　KOBE

45A：DESCRIPTION OF GOODS/SERVICE

LADY'S SWEATER　ART NO. 123　700PCS　USD10. 00/PC　CIF KOBE

ART NO. 456　800PCS　USD15. 00/PC

PACKING IN CARTONS OF 10PCS EACH

SHIPPING MARKS：　ITOCHU CORP

S/C NO. SC258

KOBE

NO. 1－150

46A：DOCUMENTS REQUIRED

＋SIGNED COMMERCIAL INVOICE IN 6 COPIES INDICATING S/C NO. SC258 AND L/C NO. LC369

其他补充信息如下：

发票号码为：INV. TF3489

发票日期为：2008 年 2 月 20 日

<table>
<tr><td>Issuer</td><td colspan="2" rowspan="2">商 业 发 票
COMMERCIAL INVOICE</td></tr>
<tr><td rowspan="2">To</td></tr>
<tr><td>No.:</td><td>Date:</td></tr>
<tr><td rowspan="2">Transport Details</td><td>S/C No.</td><td>L/C No.</td></tr>
<tr><td colspan="2">Terms of payment</td></tr>
</table>

Marks and numbers	Number and kind of packages, Description of goods	Quantity	Unit price	Amount

样例 4－2　空白商业发票

2. 中级训练

天津金星贸易公司与埃塞俄比亚 AMENLI 公司经过友好洽商就出口五金工具箱达成一份出口合同,数量 10000 套,CIF ASEB,付款方式为电汇加托收(T/T IN ADVANCE + D/P AT SIGHT)。作为单证员请你根据贸易合同有关条款(见样例 4 - 3)及其他补充信息缮制商业发票(见样例 4 - 4)。

销 售 合 同

SALES CONTRACT

编号 No.: SC080216 日期 Date: FEB 16, 2008

The sellers: TIANJIN GOLDEN STAR TRADING CO., LTD

Add: NO. 18 ZHUJIANG ROAD, TIANJIN, CHINA POST CODE: 300221

The buyers: AMENLI COMPANY, ETHIOPIA.

Add: #5054 - 7 KING STREET, ETHIOPIA

TEL: (+03)3434 7856

兹确认售予你方下列货品,其成交条款如下:

We hereby confirm having sold to you the following goods on the terms and conditions as specified below:

(1)货物名称及规格 Name of Commodity and Specifications	(2)数量 Quantity	(3)单价 Unit price	(4)总值 Total Amount
Hardware Tools Case	CIF ASEB		
TC110	6000SETS	USD5.00	USD30000.00
TC120	4000SETS	USD4.00	USD16000.00
TOTAL:	10000SETS		USD46000.00

(5)包装:

Packing: PACKED IN ONE CARTON OF 100 SETS EACH

(6)装运唛头:

Shipping Mark: AMENLI/SC080216/ASEB/NO. 1 - UP

(7)装运期限:

Time of Shipment: NOT LATER THAN APRIL 10, 2008

(8)装运口岸: 目的地:

Port of Shipment: TIANJIN Destination: ASEB

(9)付款条件:

Payment Terms: 20% T/T IN ADVANCE, THE OTHERS 80% D/P AT SIGHT.

(10)保险:卖方负责投保海运险按照 CIF 金额的 110% 投保一切险和战争险,如果发生索赔,在埃塞俄比亚用美元赔偿。

Insurance:

THE SELLER SHALL ARRANGE MARINE INSURANCE COVERING ALL RISKS AND WAR RISK FOR 110% OF CIF VALUE. CLAIM, IF ANY, PAYABLE IN ETHIOPIA, IN CURRENCY OF USD.

(11)品质/数量异议:如买方提出索赔,凡属品质异议须于货到目的口岸之日起 2 个月内提出。凡属数量异议须于货到目的口岸之日起15天内提出，对所装货物所提任何异议属于保险公司、轮船公司及期货有关运输机构所负责者，售方不负任何责任。

QUALITY/QUANTITY DISCREPANCY: IN CASE OF QUALITY DISCREPANCY, CLAIM SHOULD BE FILED BY THE BUYER WITHIN 2 MONTHS AFTER THE ARRIVAL OF THE GOODS AT THE PORT OF DESTINATION WHILE FOR QUANTITY DISCREPANCY CLAIM SHOULD BY FILED BY THE BUYER WITHIN 15 DAYS AFTER THE ARRIVAL OF THE GOODS AT THE PORT OF DESTINATION IT IS UNDERSTOOD THAT SELLER SHALL NOT BE LIABLE FOR ANY DISCREPANCY OF THE GOODS SHIPPED DUE TO CAUSES FOR WHICH THE INSURANCE COMPANY SHIPPING COMPANY AND OTHER TRANSPORTATION ORGANIZATION ARE LIABLE.

Confirmed by

AMENLI COMPANY, ETHIOPIA.	TIANJIN GOLDEN STAR TRADING CO., LTD
Jonnie	王义
买方 (the buyers)	卖方 (the sellers)

样例4-3　合同

其他补充信息如下：

(1)发票号码为：INV. TDP 0802

(2)发票日期为：2008年2月20日

天津金星贸易公司
TIANJIN GOLDEN STAR TRADING CO., LTD
商　业　发　票
COMMERCIAL INVOICE

TO:

INVOICE NO:

DATE: ____________

L/C NO: ____________

S/C NO: ____________

FROM: ____________　　TO: ____________

MARKS & NOS	DESCRIPTIONS OF GOODS	QUANTITIES	UNIT PRICE	AMOUNT

样例4-4　空白商业发票

3. 高级训练

天津纺织品进出口公司与科威特 SAMIEH TEXTLE & BLANKET CO. , LTD 客户成交一批涤棉粘胶面料,客户开来信用证(见样例4-5)要求发票以 KUWAIT GARMENT CO. , LTD 为抬头,并且手签,发票上分别注明运费和 FOB 金额,来证规定数量约 6000 码,天津纺织品进出口公司实际出运 6500 码面料,同时发票要求由商会或贸促会进行认证。作为单证员,请你按照要求正确、完整填制一份商业发票(见样例4-6)。

ALAHLI BANK OF KUWAIT

IRREVOCABLE LETTER OF CREDIT NO. 609/23262

KUWAIT, DATE:5 MAY 2008

BENEFICIARY:

TIANJIN TEXTILE IMPORT & EXPORT CORP.

7 ZHANSHAN ROAD, TIANJIN, CHINA

ADVISING BANK:

BANK OF CHINA, TIANJIN BRANCH

AMOUNT:

ABOUT USD7200. 00 (ABOUT SEVEN THOUSAND TWO HUNDRED US DOLLARS)

APPLICANT:

SAMIEH TEXTLE & BLANKET CO. LTD

P. O. BOX 299934, SAFAT, KUWAIT

VALID IN:CHINA UNTIL 15 AUG, 2008

PLEASE ADVISE OUR ABOVE IRREVOCABLE LETTER OF CREDIT AVAILABLE BY BENEFICIARIES DRAFT/S, WITHOUT RECOURSE DRAWN ON US FOR THE FULL INVOICE VALUE AND ACCOMPANIED BY THE FOLLOWING DOCUMENTS:

- MANUALLY SIGNED COMMERCIAL INVOICE IN QUINTUPLICATES SHOWING BREAKDOWN OF FREIGHT CHARGES AND FOB VALUE CERTIFYING THAT EACH PIECE CARTON/CASE OF THE GOODS CARRIES THE NAME OF COUNTRY OF ORIGIN IN NON - DETACHABLE OR NON - ALTERABLE WAY.

……

SHIPMENT FROM TIANJIN, CHINA TO KUWAIT NOT LATER THAN 30 JULY, 2008.

COVERING ABOUT 6000 YARDS ART 032, 65% POLYESTER 35% VISCOSE MIXED SUITING FABRICS WEIGHT: ABT. 250 GRAMS PER YARD SIZE:58" X ABT. 25 UNIT YARDS PRICE @ USD. 1. 20 PER YARD CFR KUWAIT

ALL OTHER DETAILS OF THE GOODS SHIPPED ARE AS PER INDENT NO. CTT/CH - 33/08 S/C NO. :08JUN30.

SPECIAL CONDITIONS:

- INVOICE SHOULD BE MADE OUT IN THE NAME OF KUWAIT GARMENT CO. , LTD
- INVOCIE SHOULD BE CERTIFIED BY CHAMBER OF COMMERCE OR CCPIT.

样例4-5 信用证

其他补充信息如下：

(1) SHIPPING MARKS:

ABUZIAD - KUWAIT

CTT/CH - 33/08

MADE IN CHINA

NO. 1 - 12

(2) INVOICE NO: 08MSF43

(3) INVOICE DATE: JULY 28, 2008

(4) PACKED IN CARTONS OF 22 PIECES EACH (NO. 1 - 10) 10 PIECE EACH (11 - 12)

TOTAL: 240 PIECES

TIANJIN TEXTILE IMPORT & EXPORT CORP.

7 ZHANSHAN ROAD, TIANJIN, CHINA

致 TO:

发票号码
Invoice No. ____________

日期
Date ____________

合同号
Contract No. ____________

起运港
port of departure ____________

目的港
port of destination

唛头及号数 Marks & Numbers	品名 Descriptions	数量单位 Quantities	单价 Unit Price	总价 Amount

样例 4 - 6　空白商业发票

任务五　缮制装箱单

岗前测试

一、单选题

> 温馨提示：
> 装箱单是对商业发票的补充，也是常用的结汇单证之一。因每笔业务买卖双方所交易的商品不同，故包装方式不同，装箱单的缮制方法也会有所不同。总之，装箱单的缮制比较灵活，需要反复训练才能掌握。

1. 装箱单是用以说明货物包装细节的清单，又称为（　）。

A. 包装纸　　B. 下货纸

C. 花色码单　　D. 关单

2. 在结汇单据中，（　）是对商业发票的补充。

A. 提单　　B. 汇票

C. 装箱单　　D. 保险单

3. 如果出口合同是通过中间商达成的，信用证有时会要求受益人提交（　）。

A. SIGNED PACKING LIST　　B. NATURAL PACKING LIST

C. MANUALLY SIGNED PACKING LIST　　D. THIRD PARTY PACKING LIST

4. 定牌中性包装是指（　）。

A. 在商品及其包装上不使用买方指定的商标/牌号，但标明产地

B. 在商品及其包装上使用买方指定的商标/牌号，也标明产地

C. 在商品及其包装上不使用买方指定的商标/牌号，也不标明产地

D. 在商品及其包装上使用买方指定的商标/牌号，但不标明产地

5. 运输包装俗称（　）。

A. 大包装、小包装　　B. 小包装、内包装

C. 大包装、外包装　　D. 外包装、内包装

6. 按照国际惯例，包装费用（　）。

A. 不应包括在货物价格之内，并在合同中列示

B. 包括在货物价格之内，一般不在合同中另外列示

C. 应包括在货物价格之内，但必须在合同中另外列示

D. 不应包括在货物价格之内，也不必在合同中列示

7. 除非另有约定，采用定牌中性包装时，在我出口商品和/或包装上（　）。

A. 必须标明“中国制造”字样

B. 不需标明“中国制造”字样

C. 是否标明“中国制造”字样,由买卖双方协商而定
D. 是否标明“中国制造”字样,由我方决定
8. “NUDE CARGO”是指(　)。
A. 小包装货　B. 大包装货　C. 散装货　D. 裸装货
9. 包装单通常显示(　)。
A. 运输标志　B. 指示性标志　C. 警告性标志　D. 识别性标志
10. 装箱单中“CONSIGNEE”指的是(　)。
A. 发货人　B. 受益人　C. 收货人　D. 以上都不是

二、多选题

1. 包装标志按其用途,可分为(　)。
A. 运输标志　B. 指示性标志　C. 警告性标志　D. 条形码标志
2. 国际标准化组织推荐的标准唛头应包括(　)。
A. 收货人名称的缩写或代号
B. 参考号(合同号、订单号码等)
C. 箱号或件号
D. 产地标志
3. 运输包装从方式上看,可以分为(　)。
A. 单件包装　B. 集合运输包装　C. 中性包装　D. 标牌包装
4. 运输标志的作用是(　)。
A. 便于识别货物　B. 方便运输　C. 防止错发错运　D. 促进销售
5. 常见的集合包装一般包括(　)。
A. 集装袋　B. 编织袋　C. 集装箱　D. 托盘

小贴士:

如果信用证要求提供“中性装箱单”(Neutral Packing List),则装箱单名称仍可填写成“Packing List”,但装箱单内不能显示卖方的名称,也不能签署。

如果信用证规定包装单为“Plain paper”、“In plain”或“In white paper”等,则在包装单内即不显示卖方名称,也不显示买方名称,也不能签署。其他内容与普通包装单据的缮制要求一样。

三、判断题

1. 装箱单的出单日期可以早于发票日期,也可晚于发票日期1~2天。(　)
2. 重量单的签发日期可等于或迟于发票日期,也可早于发票签发日期。(　)

3. 装箱单据的英文名称通常有 PACKING LIST, WEIGHT LIST, SPECIFICATION LIST, ASSORTMENT LIST 等, 实际业务中,可根据商品特性买卖双方自行选择使用。( )

4. 装箱单上需要注明货物的单价和总价。( )

5. 装箱单的收货人是 CONSIGNEE。( )

6. 信用证没有明确规定,装箱单可以无须签字。( )

7. 出口危险品时,无须提供包装的性能证和使用证。( )

8. 在装箱单上必须写明货物原产地。( )

9. 装箱单上的总数量和总件数应与发票上的总数量和总件数一致。( )

10. 装箱单上的栏目填制可参考商业发票,并与商业发票保持一致。( )

岗前培训

一、装箱单缮制规范

表 5－1　装箱单缮制规范

项目顺序号	填写内容	要点提示
(1)单据名称 Name of doc	按照信用证规定的单据名称填写	与信用证规定的单据名称相一致
(2)出单人 Issuer	签发装箱单的人	①信用证项下为受益人 ②托收和电汇项下为合同卖方 ③有些公司可能已印就,无须填写
(3)受单人 To	抬头人	①信用证项下为开证申请人 ②托收和电汇项下为合同买方 ③信用证要求不显示抬头人时,可不填或填写"To whom it may concern"
(4)发票号 Invoice No.	此笔业务的发票号码	由卖方自行编制
(5)日期 Date	一般为发票日期	可略晚于发票日期,不能迟于信用证的有效期及提单日期
(6)运输标志 Marks and numbers	货物的唛头	①注意与信用证及合同规定的内容和形式完全一致 ②如合同和信用证无指定唛头,卖方可自行设计 ③如果没有唛头,填写"N/M"

续表

项目顺序号	填写内容	要点提示
(7)包装种类和件数、货物描述 Number and kind of packages, description of goods	包括货物的件数和货物描述	①可以用商品的统称 ②如果仅一种商品,可以无需填写商品的规格
(8)毛重 Gross weight 净重 Net weight 尺码 Measurement	填写货物的毛重、净重和尺码	若信用证要求列出单件毛重、净重和尺码时,应按照货物的实际情况填写,并且要符合信用证的规定
(9)自由处理区 Additional condition	用于表达格式中其他栏目不能或不便表达的内容	符合信用证要求
(10)签署 Signature	一般加盖出口商的英文名称加法人代表签字图章	①包装单据只能由 L/C 规定的受益人出具 ②无特殊规定,装箱单可以无需签署 ③若信用证要求手签,出单人要亲笔签署不能以盖章代替

二、装箱单缮制范例

<table>
<tr><td colspan="2">Issuer (2)
TIFERT TRADING CO., LTD.
NO. 86, ZHUJIANG ROAD, TIANJIN, CHINA</td><td colspan="3" rowspan="2">装 箱 单 (1)
PACKING LIST</td></tr>
<tr><td colspan="2" rowspan="2">To (3)
MARUBENI CORP
5-7, HOMMACHI, 2-CHOME, CHUO-KU, OSAKA, JAPAN</td></tr>
<tr><td colspan="2">Invoice No. (4)
INVOICE NO. 123456</td><td>Date (5)
APR 15, 2008</td></tr>
<tr><td>Marks and Numbers (6)</td><td>Number and kind of package
Description of goods (7)</td><td>G.W (8)</td><td>N.W (8)</td><td>Meas. (8)</td></tr>
<tr><td>MARUBENI
S/C 08TF0858
TOKYO
CTN 1-250</td><td>250 CARTONS GIRL JACKET
SYTLE NO.GJ234

PACKED IN CARTONS OF 20PCS EACH</td><td>25992.00KGS</td><td>24909.00KGS</td><td>24.548CBM</td></tr>
<tr><td colspan="5">(9) WE HEREBY CERTIFY THAT EACH ITEM HAS BEEN MARKED THE LABEL"MADE IN CHINA".

TIFERT TRADING CO., LTD
泰佛贸易有限公司
*

(10)</td></tr>
</table>

样例 5－1　女童夹克衫装箱单

三、缮制装箱单应注意问题

1. 如果信用证同时要求装箱单和重量单,受益人应分别出具两种单据,最好不要合二为一联合出具。如果受益人将两种单据名称印就在一起,来证仅要求其中一种时,最好将另一种单据的名称删除。

2. 如果没有特别要求,包装单据可以不显示收货人。

3. 装箱单上的唛头应与发票上的规定一致,唛头中如果有"C/NO 1 - UP",是指包装件号,应根据实际按序编写,这里的 UP 应理解为总箱数,缮制包装单据时要具体化,标明总件数。

4. 装箱单中的货物描述,可以与发票相同,也可在与信用证中货物描述不抵触的情况下只显示商品统称。

5. 包装单据中毛重应注明每个包装件的毛重和此包装件内不同规格、品种、花色货物各自的总毛重(sub total),最后在合计栏处标注所有货物的总毛重;净重应注明每个包装件的净重和此包装件内不同规格、品种、花色货物各自的总净重,最后在合计栏处标注所有货物总净重;尺码则要求注明每个包装件的尺寸和总尺码。

6. 包装单据一般不显示货物的单、总价。进口商转售时通常自制发票、使用出口商提供的原始包装单据,这样就可以避免泄露其购买成本。

7. 货物如装托盘,尺码单上应同时标明托盘本身尺码和连同托盘的总尺码。

8. 包装单据应如实反映货物的实际包装情况,并且要符合信用证关于装箱的规定。如信用证规定货物装 25 公斤或 50 公斤的编织袋内,货物实际装在 25 公斤的编织袋内,包装单据应该缮制成"Packed in pp woven bags of 25kgs net each."不应该照抄信用证原句。不管信用证是笼统规定(Sea worthy packing 或 standard export packing)还是具体要求(Packed in woven bags)等均应准确显示在单据之上。

9. 散装货物一般不需要提供包装单据。

10. 如来证规定包装单以"Plain Paper"、"in plain"或"in white paper"等形式出具,单据上不应显示进出口双方的名称,也不可签章。

上岗操作

任务栏

1. 通知:公司将有以下合同项下的货物装运出口,加工厂已将货物备妥,请根据有关资料缮制装箱单。

2. 目的:本项任务的目的是熟悉并掌握装箱单的缮制技巧。

3. 要求:下班前将缮制好的装箱单交给师傅审核。

一、动脑思考

1. 大都服装厂把合同项下衬衫备妥,码单显示总共1000箱,国外客户开来信用证中有指定唛头为:"ABC CORP/P. O. NO. 08F0018/HAMBURG/CTN NO. 1 - UP",作为单证员你在缮制包装单时,唛头应该如何缮制?

2. 如信用证规定货物装25公斤或50公斤的编织袋内(Packing in pp woven bags of 25kgs or 50kgs net each),货物实际装在25公斤的编织袋内,作为单证员你在缮制包装单时为了做到单证相符,你直接照抄原句Packing in pp woven bags of 25kgs or 50kgs net each,这样做是否可以?如果不可以,应该如何缮制?

3. 信用证对包装单据的规定为:"Packing/weight list issued by beneficiary in three photo copies, showing carton marks, style no, color, size, quantity, g. wt, n. wt, dimension per carton, packing method and break down of total quantity shipped in pieces, per style, per color, per size and must show invoice No. and description of goods."你作为单证员,请问如何缮制包装单才能符合信用证要求?

二、动手操作

1. 初级训练

泰佛贸易公司向日本伊藤忠株式会社出口棉毯一批,单证员已经完成商业发票(见样例5-2)的缮制,请根据商业发票及补充信息(每箱毛重18公斤、净重16公斤、尺码55×50×45公分)缮制一份装箱单(见样例5-3)。

2. 中级训练

泰佛贸易公司与美国NEW WORLD INTERNATIONAL INC客户就出口女士拖鞋达成一笔交易,美国客户已将信用证(见样例5-4)开抵泰佛贸易公司,作为单证员,请你根据信用证摘录信息及相关补充信息,利用空白装箱单(样例5-5)独立缮制一份装箱单。

其他补充信息如下:

(1) SIZE: EACH CARTON CONTAINING 37/10 38/10 39/10 40/10

(2) PACKING: IN CARTONS OF 40 PAIRS EACH

(3) MEASUREMENT: 0.356M3/CTN

(4). GW: 15KGS/CTN NW: 14KGS/CTN

(5) SHIPPING MARK: NW/ LOS ANGELES/NO. 1 - UP

(6) INVOICE NO. LS628 DATED AUG 20, 2008

Issuer TIFERT TRADING CO., LTD. NO. 86, ZHUJIANG ROAD, TIANJIN, CHINA	商 业 发 票
To MARUBENI CORP 5-7, HOMMACHI, 2-CHOME, CHUO-KU, OSAKA, JAPAN	**COMMERCIAL INVOICE** No.: INVOICE NO. 08TF0916 / Date: APR 15, 2008
Transport Details SHIPMENT FROM TIANJIN TO YOKOHAMA BY SEA	S/C No.: 08TF0858 / L/C No.: Terms of payment 30% T/T IN ADVANCE 70% T/T AFTER SHIPMENT

Marks and numbers	Number and kind of packages, Description of goods	Quantity	Unit price	Amount
			CIF YOKOHAMA	
MARUBENI	500 CARTONS 100% COTTON BLANKET	12500PCS	USD6.50/PC	USD52500.00
S/C 08TF0858	SIZE 150X210CM			
YOKOHAMA	BLUE COLOR			
CTN 1-250				

PACKED IN CARTONS OF 25PCS EACH

WE HEREBY CERTIFY THAT THE GOODS ARE OF CHINESE ORIGIN

TIFERT TRADING CO., LTD
泰佛贸易有限公司
*

王 宏

样例 5－2 商业发票

Issuer	装箱单 PACKING LIST
To	Invoice No. / Date

Marks and Numbers	Number and kind of package Description of goods	Quantity	Package	G.W	N.W	Meas.

TOTAL:

SAY TOTAL:

样例 5 – 3　空白装箱单

SEQUENCE OF TOTAL	27: 1/1
FORM OF DOCUMENTARY CREDIT	40A: IRREVOCABLE
APPLICABLE RULES	40E: UCP LATEST VERSION
DOCUMENTARY CREDIT NUMBER	20 : 00IM01413
DATE OF ISSUE	31C: 080731
DATE AND PLACE OF EXPIRY	31D: 080915 CHINA
APPLICANT	50: NEW WORLD INTERNATIONAL INC 129 HAYWARD WAY CA 91733, USA
BENEFICIARY	59: TIFERT TRADING CO., LTD NO. 86, ZHUJIANG ROAD, TIANJIN, CHINA
CURRENCY CODE, AMOUNT	32B: USD30940,00
AVAILABLE WITH ... BY	41D: ANY BANK BY NEGOTIATION
DRAFTS AT	42C: AT SIGHT FOR 100 PCT OF INVOICE VALUE
DRAWEE	42D: CATHAY BANK LOS ANGELES, CA.
PORT OF LOADING	44E: TIANJIN PORT, CHINA
PORT OF DISCHARGE	44F: LOS ANGELES PORT, CA, USA
LATEST DATE OF SHIPMENT	44C: 080831
DESCRPT OF GOODS/SERVICES	45A: 2000PAIRS LADIES SLIPPERS FOB TIANJIN, CHINA
DOCUMENTS REQUIRED	46A:

\+ SIGNED COMMERCIAL INVOICE IN 1 ORIGINAL AND 3 COPIES

\+ PACKING LIST IN 1 ORIGINAL AND 3 COPIES INDICATING THE CONTENTS OF EACH OF PACKAGE, TOTAL GROSS WEIGHT, NET WEIGHT AND MEASUREMENT.

……

样例 5-4　信用证

3. 高级训练

泰佛贸易公司与德国时尚服装公司（FASHION GARMENTS CO., LTD）经过友好洽商就出口男士衬衫达成一出口合同，数量5000件，金额12000美元，付款方式即期付款交单（D/P at sight）。随后泰佛贸易公司与天津新华衬衣厂签订购货合同，委托其代为加工。新华衬衣厂如期把合同项下5000件衬衫备妥，详见工厂传真过来的花色码单，作为单证员请你根据买卖双方签订的合同（见样例5-6）和加工厂提供的码单（见样例5-7）缮制装箱单（见样例5-8）以便办理出口报验工作。

<table>
<tr><td colspan="2" rowspan="1">Issuer</td><td colspan="6" rowspan="2">装 箱 单

PACKING LIST</td></tr>
<tr><td colspan="2">To</td></tr>
<tr><td colspan="2"></td><td colspan="3">Invoice No.</td><td colspan="3">Date</td></tr>
<tr><td>Marks and Numbers</td><td>Number and kind of package
Description of goods</td><td>Quantity</td><td>Package</td><td>G.W</td><td>N.W</td><td>Meas.</td><td></td></tr>
<tr><td></td><td></td><td></td><td></td><td></td><td></td><td></td><td></td></tr>
<tr><td colspan="8">TOTAL:
SAY TOTAL:</td></tr>
</table>

样例 5 – 5　空白装箱单

Sales Confirmation

No. 08TF0010

Dated: Jan 18, 2008

THE SELLER: TIFERT Trading Co., Ltd
No. 86, Zhujiang Road, Tianjin, China

THE BUYER: Fashion Garments Co., Ltd
Daichi Bldg 2 - 5 - 25, Hamburg, Germany

The undersigned Sellers and Buyers have agreed to close the following transaction according to the terms and conditions stipulated below:

Commodity & Specification	Quantity	Unit Price	Amount
100% Cotton Men's Shirt Style No. A - 118 B - 116 Size: S M L XL Color: Pink Blue Green	5000pcs	USD2.65/pc CIF Hamburg	USD13250.00

REMARKS: With 5% more or less both in amount and quantity at the seller's option

PACKING: In cartons and packing method as per P. O. No. FG0058 dated 2008 - 1 - 15

SHIPMENT: To be effected not later than Mar 15, 2008 from Tianjin to Hamburg allowing partial shipments and transshipment.

INSURANCHE: To be covered for 110 % of invoice value against All Risks and War Risk as per and subject to Ocean Marine Cargo Clauses of CIC dated 1/1/1981.

PAYMENT: The buyer shall pay against documentary draft drawn by the seller at sight upon first presentation. The shipping documents are to be delivered against payment only.

THE SELLER	THE BUYER
Tifert Trading Co., Ltd	Fashion Garments Co., Ltd
王宏	Johnson

样例5 - 6　销售确认书

天津新华衬衣厂

天津市海河东路 118 号

电话：24458896　传真：24458899

花色码单

商品名称：男士衬衣　　　　订单号：GY0058

款式号：A-118 和 B-116　　　　颜色：粉/蓝/绿

毛重：15 公斤/箱　　　　净重：14 公斤/箱

唛头：GOYOO　　　　尺码：45×35×30 公分/箱

08TF0010

HAMBURG

C/T NO.1-139

C/NO 箱号	CTNS 箱数	STYLE 款式	COLOR 颜色	SIZE 尺码 ASSORTMENT				QTY/CTN 数量/箱	TTL QTY 总数量
				S	M	L	XL		
1-112	112	A-118	粉	1	1	6	4	36 件	4032 件
			蓝	1	3	6	2		
			绿	2	1	6	3		
113-136	24	B-116	粉	1	1	6	4	36 件	864 件
			蓝	1	3	6	2		
			绿	2	1	6	3		
137	1	A-118	粉	2	1	8	3	36 件	36 件
			蓝		1	6	3		
			绿	1		6	5		
138	1	B-116	粉	2	2	4	4	34 件	34 件
			蓝	1	3	6	2		
			绿		1	6	3		
139	1	A-118	粉	2	2	4	4	34 件	34 件
			蓝	1	3	6	2		
		B-116	绿		1	6	3		
	139								5000 件

检验员：张丽丽　　日期：2008-3-10

样例 5－7　花色码单

TIFERT TRADING CO. , LTD

NO. 86, ZHUJIANG ROAD, TIANJIN, CHINA

TEL: 0086 -22 -8835 8888 FAX: 0086 -22 -8845 6666

Packing List

INV NO. TF080310

DATE:

样例 5 -8　空白装箱单

任务六 缮制检验证书

岗前测试

一、单选题

> 温馨提示：
>
> 在采用信用证付款方式下，由于银行仅凭单付款，不管交付货物的质量如何，也不受买卖双方签订合同的约束，所以为使卖方交付的货物质量符合合同约定品质，买方可在开证时要求卖方提交商检证书作为议付货款的单据之一。

1. 检验证书的签发流程为(　)。

A. 抽样—报检—检验—发证

B. 检验—报检—抽样—发证

C. 报检—抽样—检验—发证

D. 发证—报检—抽样—检验

2. 国家质量监督检验检疫总局的英文缩写是(　)。

A. QSIQ　　B. AQSIQ

C. AQSI　　D. AQSIB

3. 各地出入境检验检疫局的英文缩写是(　)。

A. CCIB　　B. CCIC　　C. CIB　　D. CIQ

4. 用于证明出口的冻畜肉、冻禽、禽畜罐头、冻兔、皮张、毛类、绒类、猪鬃等动物产品或食品经过检疫合格的证书是(　)。

A. 卫生证书　　B. 消毒检验证书　　C. 健康证书　　D. 兽医检验证书

5. 用于证明出口的粮谷、油籽、豆类等商品，以及包装用木材与植物性填充物等，已经过熏蒸灭虫的证书是(　)。

A. 熏蒸证书　　B. 消毒检验证书　　C. 健康证书　　D. 兽医检验证书

6. 法定检验检疫的出境货物，在报关时必须提供出入境检验检疫机构签发的(　)，海关据此放行货物。

A. 入境货物通关单　　B. 通关单

C. 出境货物通关单　　D. 报关单

7. 法定检验检疫的入境货物，在报关时必须提供出入境检验检疫机构签发的(　)，海关据此放行货物。

A. 入境货物通关单　　B. 通关单

C. 出境货物通关单　　D. 报关单

8. 对产地和报关地相一致的出境货物，经检验检疫合格的，出入境检验检疫机构签发(　)。

A. 入境货物通关单　　B. 出境货物换证凭单
C. 出境货物换证凭条　　D. 出境货物通关单

9. 熏蒸证必须由(　)签发。

A. 出口商　　B. 生产商
C. 出入境检验检疫局　　D. 进口商

10. 信用证中要求出具的下列检验证书,其中具有软条款性质的是(　)。

A. Inspection certificate of Quality and Quantity in duplicate issued by Entry – Exit Inspection and Quarantine Bureau

B. Clean inspection certificate issued, stamped and signed by the authorized signatures of DC applicant (Whose signatures must be in conformity with the record held in DC issuing bank's file and will only be verified by the office of the DC issuing bank at the time of presentation of documents) certifying that the goods have been inspected and accepted and showing the total number of inspection

C. Pre – shipment inspection for quantity, quality, description, classification and price should be carried out by SGS for issuance of a Clean Report Of Findings (CRF). The final invoice and packing list shall be endorsed by SGS with number and date of issuance of the CRF which must accompany shipping documents

D. Inspection certificate issued by manufacturer acceptable

小贴士:

换证凭单与换证凭条

相同点:换证凭单和换证凭条都是出境货物报检的凭证。两者都是报检地与出境地不同的情况下去出境地检验检疫机构换取正本《通关单》的凭证。

不同点:换证凭单可以一次报检,分批核销。也就是说可以一次将货物进行检验然后分批出口。但是必须带换证凭单正本到出境地核销并换通关单。
换证凭条是电子转单的凭证,也就是在报检地通过报检后有关数据就已通过系统自动传送到出境地检验检疫机构,企业只需凭换证凭条上的转单号或者换证凭条的传真件就可以到出境地检验检疫机构换取正本通关单。

两者比较:换证凭单速度慢、需要正本,但是可以一次报检分批核销;换证凭条速度快、无须正本、货物一证一批。

二、多选题

1. 检验检疫证书的签发机构可以是(　)。

A. 官方　　B. 非官方　　C. 生产商　　D. 进口商

2. 目前在国际上比较有名望、有权威的民间商品检验机构有(　)。

A. 瑞士通用公证行(SGS)

B. 英国英之杰检验集团(ITS)

C. 中国质量监督检验检疫总局(AQSIQ)

D. 日本海事检定协会(NKKK)

3. 用于证明可供人类食用的出口动物产品、食品等经过卫生检验或检疫合格的证件是(　)。

A. 卫生证书　B. 消毒检验证书　C. 健康证书　D. 兽医检验证书

4. 报检地与出境地不同的情况下,可凭(　)到出境地检验检疫机构换取正本《通关单》。

A. 报关单　B. 换证凭单　C. 检验证书　D. 换证凭条

5. 检验证书的签发日期(　)。

A. 可早于运输单据日期

B. 可等同于运输单据日期

C. 可晚于运输单据日期

D. 可晚于运输单据日期但在证书中要注明是在装船前施检

三、判断题

1. 检验证书是各种进出口商品检验证书、鉴定证书和其他证明书的统称。(　)

2. 某些商品必须由出口国或进口国政府指定的机构检验后才能出口或进口,这种检验是非法定检验。(　)

3. 财产价值鉴定证书,是作为国际贸易当事人和司法、仲裁、验资等有关部门索赔、理赔、评估或裁判的重要依据。(　)

4. 经人工合成或经加热、加压等深度加工的胶合板、刨花板、纤维板等属于木制包装。(　)

5. 出境货物的检验检疫工作程序是先检验检疫,后放行通关。(　)

6. 换证凭条可以一次报检,分批核销。(　)

7. 对于出口的法检商品,商检机构接受报验之后,可以派员赴货物存放地点进行现场抽样,也可以由报检单位送样至检验机构。(　)

8. 凡列入《检验检疫商品目录》内的出口商品,经检验检疫机构检验合格后都必须签发检验证书。(　)

9. Legalized(认证)指有关文件由进口国驻出口国使、领馆或相关协会进行确认。(　)

10. 检验证书的更改除了在更正处加盖“更正”章外,还应加上“变更内容已经出单人授权”字样。(　)

岗前培训

一、检验证书缮制规范

表 6－1　检验证书缮制规范

项目顺序号	填写内容	要点提示
(1)签证机构 Issuer	官方机构和非官方机构	如信用证未规定具体单位,则由出口商决定
(2)检验证书的名称 Name of certificate	填写证书名称	应与合同或信用证规定相符
(3)发货人 Consignor	出口商名称	一般只填写名称不填写地址
(4)收货人 Consignee	* * * * * *	不用填写具体的名称,中性单据可填写“To whom it may concern”
(5)货物描述 Description of goods	商品名称	可用统称,与其他单据保持一致
(6)报检的数量/重量 Quantity/weight declared	实际出运的数量或重量	应与装箱单和提单中的数量或重量一致
(7)包装的种类及数量 Number and kind of packages	货物的包装单位数量	应与包装单据和提单中的包装件数一致
(8)运输工具 Means of conveyance	海运 By sea freight 空运 By air freight 陆运 By rail/truck	应与实际运输方式相符
(9)标记及号码 Marks & No.	具体的唛头 没有唛头填 N/M	①此栏不能留空 ②应与其他单据的唛头保持一致
(10)检验结果 Result of inspection	所检验货物的实际的现状	是检验证书中最重要的一项,应该与信用证或合同要求的品质标准相符,否则会遭到银行或进口商的拒付
(11)签证地点 Place of issue	此笔业务证书的签发地点	一般与货物装运港一致
(12)签证日期 Date of issue	此笔业务证书的签发日期	一般不迟于提单日期
(13)授权人签字 Authorized signature	证书签署人姓名的汉语拼音	
(14)签名 Signature	证书签署人亲笔签名	可用中文
(15)签章 Official stamp	签证机构的公章	

二、检验证书缮制范例

中华人民共和国出入境检验检疫 (1) 正 本

ENTRY-EXIT INSPECTION AND QUARANTITE ORIGINAL
OF THE PEOPLE'S REPUBLIC OF CHINA

编号 No.:07CIQ1187

QUALITY CERTIFICATE (2)

发货人 (3)
Consignor TIFERT TRADING CO., LTD

收货人 (4)
Consignee ****

品名 (5)
Description of Goods GIRL JACKET

报检数量/重量 (6)
Quantity/Weight Declared 5000PCS

包装种类及数量 (7)
Number and Type of Packages 250CARTONS

运输工具 (8)
Means of Conveyance BY SEA FREIGHT

标记及号码 (9)
Mark & No.

MARUBENI
S/C 08TF0858
TOKYO
CTN 1-250

检验结果 (10)
Result of inspection

SAMPLES WERE DRAWN AT RANDOM FROM THE WHOLE LOT OF GOODS
AND INSPECTED STRICTLY ACCORDING TO THE S/C NO. 08TF0858
THE ABOVE RESULTS OF INSPECTION ARE IN CONFORMITY
WITH THE REQUIREMENTS IN THE SAID CONTRACT.

(15) (11) (12)

签证地点 Place of Issue TIANJIN 签证日期 Date of Issue APR 25, 2008

印章: (13) (14)
Official Stamp 授权签字人 Authorized Officer ZHANG CHI 签名 Signature 张驰

我们已尽所和最大能力实施上述检验，不能因我们签发本证书而免除卖方或其他方面根据合同和法律所承担的产品质量责任和其他责任。

All inspection are carried out conscientiously to the best of our knowledge and ability. This certificate dose not in any respect absolve the seller and other related parties from his contractual and legal obligations especially when product quality is concerned.

样例 6－1 女童夹克检验证书

三、缮制检验证书应注意问题

1. 如信用证对检验证书的签发机构有明确规定，则必须由该机构对商品实施检验检疫并出具相关检验证书。如没有具体规定，则可由任何机构包括出口商自己签发检验证书亦可。

2. 检验证书是官方机构或由商会、协会或同业公会设立的民间商品检验机构签发的文件，进出口商不能擅自涂改，如需修改有关内容，须要向签证机关申请办理证书变更手续。

3. 检验证书的签发日期应早于运输单据的日期，因为必须是在出运前办理有关检验检疫手续，以证明出口商所交货物是否与合同约定的品质规格相符。

4. 检验证书的种类和证书内容应符合信用证的要求，并且应做到货证、事（货物的事实状态）证和证证（同一批货物各种证书之间）的“三相符”。

5. 检验证书所列明的货物规格、品质、数量等与发票一致。

6. 检验证书的更改除了在更正处加盖“更正”章外，还应加上“变更内容已经出单人授权”字样。

7. 信用证要求装运前检验证书（Pre – shipment Inspection Certificate）作为议付的单据之一时，其签发日期绝对不能晚于装运日期。当信用证要求检验证书（Inspection Certificate）作为议付的单据之一，其的签发日期最好不要迟于运输单据的签发日期，说明是在装运前对货物实施的检验；如果一旦签发日期晚于运输单据的签发日期，最好通过标题或内容来表明检验发生在装运之前或装运当天，只是证书签发略晚些，以免遭信誉不好的、挑剔的银行拒付。

8. “商检软条款”是信用证中软条款最为集中的项目，对列有由申请人或其授权人签发检验证书且其签字与银行留存签字样本一致条款的信用证一般不宜接受，对不能或很难办到的商检条款应及时接洽进口商通过开证行改证，保证安全收汇。

上岗操作

任务栏

1. 通知：公司将有以下合同项下的货物装运出口，加工厂已将货物备妥，请根据有关资料缮制报检单和检验证书。

2. 目的：本项任务的目的是熟悉并掌握报检单和检验证书的缮制技巧。

3. 要求：下班前将缮制好的报检单和检验证书交给师傅审核。

一、动脑思考

1. 中国昌盛贸易公司向西班牙出口一批羊皮，请问出境报关时出口商需提供哪些检验证书？

2. 中国光大贸易公司向德国出口一批商品，需用木制托盘，请问这种情况下出口商需要做哪些必要工作？需提供哪些证书？如果托盘是用胶合板制成，是否仍需要此类证书？

3. 泰佛贸易公司委托南通服装厂生产一批工装，现工厂已将货物备妥，经查该商品属于法检商品，请问该批货应该在哪里报商检？谁来办理报检手续，是泰佛贸易公司还是南通服装加工厂？如果由南通服装加工厂办理报检手续，泰佛贸易公司需提供哪种单据给南通服装加工厂？信用证规定由上海港出运，检验机构施检后签发换证凭单还是换证凭条？两者有何区别？

二、动手操作

1. 初级训练

泰佛贸易公司向韩国 ORIENT CROWN ASIA LIMITED CORP 出口全棉精梳坯布一批，现在供货商泰佛贸易公司已将合同（见样例 6－2）项下的 4750 米面料备好，你作为报检员请根据合同和有关资料缮制报检单（见样例 6－3），争取如期将货物出运。

Sales Contract

No：08TY0986
Date ：AUG25，2008
Signed at：TIANJIN

Sellers：TIFERT TRADING CO. , LTD
Address：NO. 86, ZHUJIANG ROAD, TIANJIN, CHINA
Buyers：ORIENT CROWN ASIA LIMITED CORP
Address：NO. 16, DACHI STREET, BUSAN, KOREA

The undersigned buyers and sellers have agreed to close the following transactions according to the terms and conditions stipulated below：

Art No.	Description	Quantity	Unit Price	Amount
5689	100% COMBED COTTON	5000METERS 10% MORE OR LESS ALLOWED	USD1. 25/M CFR BUSAN	USD6250. 00

Total Amount: Say US DOLLARS SIX THOUSAND TWO HUNDRED AND FIFTY ONLY.

Packing: EXPORT STANDARD PACKING

METERS/CTN: 50M/CARTON PCAKING SIZE: 53 × 32 × 39cm

Time of shipment: Shipment should be made before or on OCT 15, 2008

Port of loading and destination: From any Chinese Port to BUSAN with Partial shipments and Transshipment allowed.

Insurance: To be covered by the buyer.

Payment mode: The buyers shall open with a bank acceptable to the Sellers and irrevocable, confirmed, without recourse, transferable L/C by draft at sight in the favor of the sellers. L/C to reach the sellers 30days before the month of shipment, valid for negotiation in China until 15th days after the month of shipment. In the Buyer's L/C, no terms and conditions should be added or altered without prior to the Sellers consent. The Buyers must amend the L/C, if it is inconsistent with the stipulations of this contract, and the amendment must reach the Sellers at least 15days before the month of shipment stipulated in this contract.

Shipping Marks: ORIENT/08TY0986/BUSAN/NO. 1 – UP

Commodity Inspection: It is mutually agreed that the Certificate of Quality and Quantity issued by the CIQ at the sellers' place shall be considered as the basis of delivery.

Claims: Claims concerning quality shall be made within 30days and claims concerning quantity shall be made within 10days after the arrival of the goods at the destination. Claims shall be supported by a report issued by a reputable surveyor approved by the Sellers, claims in respect of matters within the responsibility of the insurance company or of the shipping company will not be considered or entertained by the Sellers.

Arbitration: All disputes arising from the execution of this agreement shall be settled through friendly consultations. In case no settlement can be reached, the case in dispute shall then be submitted to the Foreign Trade Arbitration Commission of the China Council for the Promotion of International Trade for Arbitration in accordance with its Provisional Rules of Procedure. The decision made by this commission shall be regarded as final and binding upon both parties. Arbitration fees shall be borne by the losing party, unless otherwise awarded.

Remarks:

This contract total 3 pages and shall be valid from the date when it is signed by both parties; should any dispute happens, the two parties should take this contract as the basis.

Sellers:	Buyers:
田辉	朴承国

样例6－2 销售合同

中华人民共和国出入境检验检疫
出境货物报检单

报检单位（加盖公章）： * 编号________________

报检单位登记号： 联系人： 电话： 报检日期：

发货人	（中文）	
	（外文）	
收货人	（中文）	
	（外文）	

货物名称（中/外文）	H. S. 编码	产地	数/重量	货物总值	包装种类及数量

运输工具名称号码		贸易方式		货物存放地点	
合同号		信用证号		用途	
发货日期		输往国家（地区）		许可证/审批号	
启运地		到达口岸		生产单位注册号	
集装箱规格、数量及号码					

合同订立的检验检疫条款或特殊要求	标 记 及 号 码	随附单据（划“√”或补填）	
		□合同 □信用证 □发票 □换证凭单 □装箱单 □厂检单	□包装性能结果单 □许可/审批文件 □ □ □ □

需要证单名称（划“√”或补填）		* 检验检疫费	
□品质证书 _正_副 □重量证书 _正_副 □数量证书 _正_副 □兽医卫生证书 _正_副 □健康证书 _正_副 □卫生证书 _正_副 □动物卫生证书 _正_副	□植物检疫证书 _正_副 □熏蒸/消毒证书 _正_副 □出境货物换证凭单 □出境货物通关单 □ □	总金额（人民币元）	
		计费人	
		收费人	

报检人郑重声明： 签名：________________	领 取 证 单	
	日 期	
	签 名	

注：有“*”号栏由出入境检验检疫机关填写 ◆国家出入境检验检疫局制

样例 6 – 3 空白报检单

2. 中级训练

泰佛贸易公司向英国出口沙滩伞一批，货物经天津出入境检验检疫局检验已达到合同约定的品质要求，作为天津出入境检验检疫局的单证员，请你根据下面提供的信息，缮制一份品质检验证书（见样例6－4）。

（1）出口商： TIFERT TRADING CO. , LTD
NO. 86, ZHUJIANG ROAD, TIANJIN, CHINA

（2）运输标志： BB CORP
S/C NO. HT222
LONDONG
NO. 1 – UP

（3）货物描述：
BEACH UMBRELLA ART NO. B68 200PCS USD10. 00/PC
ART NO. B94 300PCS USD15. 00/PC
CIF LONDON
PACKING IN CARTONS OF 10PCS EACH

（4）检验结果：SAMPLES WERE DRAWN AT RANDOM FROM THE WHOLE LOT OF GOODS AND INSPECTED STRICTLY ACCORDING TO THE S/C NO. HT222

THE ABOVE RESULTS OF INSPECTION ARE IN CONFORMITY WITH THE REQUIREMENTS IN THE SAID CONTRACT

（5）签发地点：TIANJIN

（6）签证时间：MAY 10,2008

（7）签证机关有权签字人：李丽

（8）证书号：08TJCIQ0526

3. 高级训练

泰佛贸易公司向法国SMART公司出口芸豆200公吨，为防止病虫害的发生，法国客户要求出运前对芸豆进行熏蒸处理，经处理后没有发现任何虫害，你作为天津出入境检验检疫局检验的单证员，请根据下面提供的信用证（样例6－5）摘录信息和补充信息，利用空白熏蒸证书（样例6－6）独立填写一份熏蒸证书。

信用证有关资料摘录如下：

27/ SEQUENCE OF TOTAL： 1/1
40A/ FORM OF DOCUMENTARY CREDIT： IRREVOCABLE
40E/APPLICABLE RULES： UCP LATEST VERSION
20/ DOCUMENTARY CREDIT NUMBER： M19EBNU00018
31C/ DATE OF ISSUE： 080806
31D/ DATE AND PLACE OF EXPIRY： 081020

中华人民共和国出入境检验检疫　　　　正　本

ENTRY-EXIT INSPECTION AND QUARANTITE　ORIGINAL
OF THE PEOPLE'S REPUBLIC OF CHINA

编号 No.:

QUALITY CERTIFICATE

发货人
Consignor________________________________

收货人
Consignee________________________________

品名
Description of Goods________________________　标记及号码 Mark & No.

报检数量/重量
Quantity/Weight Declared________________________

包装种类及数量
Number and Type of Packages________________________

运输工具
Means of Conveyance________________________________

检验结果
Result of inspection

印章:　签证地点 Place of Issue ____________ 签证日期 Date of Issue______________

Official Stamp

授权签字人 Authorized Officer___________ 签名 Signature_________________

我们已尽所和最大能力实施上述检验，不能因我们签发本证书而免除卖方或其他方面根据合同和法律所承担的产品质量责任和其他责任。

All inspection are carried out conscientiously to the best of our knowledge and ability. This certificate dose not in any respect absolve the seller and other related parties from his contractual and legal obligations especially when product quality is concerned.

样例 6－4　空白品质检验证书

	IN BENEFICIARY'S COUNTRY
50/ APPLICANT：	SMART TRADING CO. , LTD.
	220 VTRA MARSEILLES FRANCE
59/ BENEFICIARY：	TIFERT TRADING CO. , LTD
	NO. 86, ZHUJIANG ROAD, TIANJIN, CHINA.
32B/ CURRENCY CODE AMOUNT：	USD 24000. 00
41D/ AVAILABLE WITH/BY：	ANY BANK BY NEGOTIATION
42C/ DRAFT AT：	30DAYS AFTER SIGHT
44A/ ON BOARD/DISP/TAKING CHARGE：	CHINA PORT
44B/ FOR TRANSPORTATION TO：	MARSEILLES
44C/ LATEST DATE OF SHIPMENT：	080930

45A/ DESCR GOODS AND/OR SERVICES：

200MT CHINESE SOYBEANS 2008 CROP AT USD120/MT FOB TIANJIN

PACKING IN GUNNY BAGS OF 50KGS NET EAHC DETAILS AS PER S/C NO. 08RF0056

46A/ DOCUMENTS REQUIRED

+ SIGNED COMMERCIAL INVOICE IN TRIPLICATE
+ CERTIFICATE OF FUMIGATION ISSUED BY CIQ STATING THAT THE GOODS ARE FREE FROM LIVE WEEVIL.

……

样例 6－5　信用证

其他补充信息如下：

(1) SHIPPING MARKS：

SMART/08RF0056/MARSEILLES/NO. 1 – UP

(2) RESULT：

THE SOYBEANS HAVE BEEN FUMIGATED FOR 48HOURS BEFORE

SHIPMENT AND THE GOODS ARE FREE FROM LIVE WEEVIL.

(3) DATE OF ISSUE：SEPT 28, 2008

(4) PLAE OF ISSUE：TIANJIN

(5) AUTHORIZED SIGNATURE：陈立

中华人民共和国出入境检验检疫　　　　正　本

ENTRY-EXIT INSPECTION AND QUARANTITE OF THE PEOPLE'S REPUBLIC OF CHINA　　　　ORIGINAL

编号 No.:

FUMIGATION CERTIFICATE

发货人
Consignor______________________________

收货人
Consignee______________________________

品名 Description of Goods______________ 报检数量/重量 Quantity/Weight Declared______________ 包装种类及数量 Number and Type of Packages______________ 运输工具	标记及号码 Mark & No.

Means of Conveyance______________________________

检验结果
Result of inspection

印章：　　签证地点 Place of Issue ____________ 签证日期 Date of Issue____________

Official Stamp

授权签字人 Authorized Officer____________ 签名 Signature____________

我们已尽所和最大能力实施上述检验，不能因我们签发本证书而免除卖方或其他方面根据合同和法律所承担的产品质量责任和其他责任。

All inspection are carried out conscientiously to the best of our knowledge and ability. This certificate dose not in any respect absolve the seller and other related parties from his contractual and legal obligations especially when product quality is concerned.

样例 6 – 6　空白熏蒸检验证书

任务七　缮制原产地证书

岗前测试

一、单选题

> 温馨提示：
>
> 原产地证书是货物的经济国籍，在国际贸易中扮演非常重要的角色，关系到货物在进口国通关所适用的进口关税税率，对提高我出口产品的竞争力具有非常重要的作用。

1.（　）是出口国的特定机构出具的证明所出口货物为该国家（或地区）原产的一种证明文件。

A. 商业发票　　B. 原产地证书

C. 海运提单　　D. 领事发票

2. 根据我国有关规定，出口企业最迟应于货物出运前（　）天，向签证机构申请办理原产地证书。

A. 1 天　　B. 2 天　　C. 3 天　　D. 4 天

3. 目前出口到世界上大部分国家、地区的商品只要符合中国原产地规则都可以申领（　）。

A. FORM A 原产地证书　　B. 一般原产地证书

C. 区域性原产地证书　　D. 纺织品原产地证书

4. 原产地证书签发后，如果发现有错误，（　）。

A. 可以申请在原证书上更改

B. 一旦签发不能更改

C. 出口商可自己更改

D. 可以提出更改申请，并退回原签发证书，换发新证

5. 原产地证书签发后，如果遗失，（　）。

A. 不能补发新证

B. 出口商可自行签发代替

C. 经签证当局同意可以重发证书

D. 无须经签证当局同意就可重新申领新证

6. "GSP 产地证"表示（　）。

A. 一般原产地证书　　B. 欧共体纺织品专用产地证

C. 普惠制原产地证书　　D. 对美国出口纺织品声明书

7. 普惠税是指（　）。

A. 发展中国家给予发达国家的优惠进口关税

B. 发达国家给予发展中国家的优惠进口关税

C. WTO 成员国之间相互给予的优惠进口关税

D. 自由贸易区成员国之间相互给予的优惠进口关税

8. 普惠制产地证主要有三种形式,其中(　)使用范围较广。

A. 普惠制产地证明书

B. 普惠制产地证明书格式 59A

C. 普惠制产地证书明格式 APR

D. 普惠制产地证明书格式 A

9. 出口业务中,国外客户往往要出口方提供"GSP"产地证。在我国这种证书的签发机构是(　)。

A. 中国出入境检验检疫局

B. 中国国际贸易促进委员会

C. 行业公会

D. 贸促会

10. H. S. code (H. S. 编码)是海关合作理事会(　)的英文缩写。

A.《进出口商品的目录对照表》

B.《商品名称及编码协调制度》

C.《跟单信用证统一惯例》

D.《2000 年国际贸易术语解释通则》

二、多选题

1. 出口企业申请办理一般原产地证书时应提供的文件有(　)。

A.《一般原产地证明书申请单》

B.《中华人民共和国原产地证明书》

C. 商业发票

D. 保险单

2. 原产地证书是由出口国政府有关机构签发的一种证明货物原产地或制造地的证明文件。通常多用于不需要提供(　)的国家或地区。

A. 海关发票　　B. 领事发票

C. 证实发票　　D. 联合发票

3. 一般原产地证书是证明出口商品的生产地,并符合《中华人民共和国出口货物原产地规则》的一种文件,如果信用证或合同对签证机构未作具体规定,一般由(　)签发。

A. 中国出入境检验检疫局　　B. 中国国际贸易促进委员会
C. 国际商会　　D. 出口商所在地银行

4. 出口企业在向签证机构申领普惠制原产地证书 Form A 时，应递交的文件有(　)。

A. 普惠制产地证明书申请书　　B. 普惠制产地证明书 Form A
C. 商业发票　　D. 签证机构要求的其他文件

5. 一般原产地证书是证明货物原产于某一特定国家或地区，享受进口国正常关税(最惠国)待遇的证明文件，其主要作用是(　)。

A. 征收关税　　B. 贸易统计
C. 歧视性数量限制　　D. 反倾销和反补贴

小贴士：

手签员与申领员

原产地证明书手签员必须是经申领单位法人代表授权，并在贸促会备案注册，可在《原产地证》第十一栏中签名的人员。

原产地证明书申领员是经申领单位委派，并在贸促会备案注册的具体申办人员。申领员申办原产地证时，须持签证机关颁发的《产地证申领员证》。

手签员和申领员可以是同一人，也可以是不同的人。

三、判断题

1. 如信用证未规定原产地证书上的收货人，则可在收货人栏填写中间商。(　)

2. 原产地证书必须在表面上与发票的货物相关联，其中的货物描述可以使用与信用证不相矛盾的货物统称，但不能太笼统。(　)

3. 一般原产地证明书的第 3 栏(MEANS OF TRANSPORT AND ROUTE)必须填写运输方式和运输路线，无须填写中转港的名称。(　)

4. 原产地证书不可以显示信用证受益人或运输单据上的托运人之外的第三方为发货人/出口商。(　)

5. 海关规定的实质性加工是指产品加工后，在海关进出口税则中的税号(四位数一级的税则号)已有改变。(　)

6. 货物经过加工后，增值部分占新产品总值的比例已经达到 20% 和 20% 以上的产品，海关认定是经过了实质性加工。(　)

7. 普惠制原产地证格式 A 上收货人栏目必须详细填写本批货物最终目的地给惠国收货人的名称、地址、国别。如果有中间商，还应详细填写中间商的名称、地址、国别。(　)

8. 普惠制原产地证书上的原产地标准应按货物原料进口成分的实际情况分别按

比例填制，“W”表示出口加拿大货物中的进口成分在40%以下。（ ）

9. 普惠制原产地证书中的第6栏（MARKS AND NUMBER OF PACKAGES）唛头，不可以笼统填写成“AS PER INVOICE NO...”。（ ）

10. 我国某贸易商把从日本进口的布料剪裁缝制为服装再出口至日本，因为布料是进口的所以不能申请办理《普惠制原产地证书 FORMA》。（ ）

岗前培训

一、原产地证书缮制规范

表7－1 一般原产地证书缮制规范

项目顺序号	填写内容	要点提示
证书号码 Certificate No.	证书号码	符合签证机构证书号码的编排规则
(1)出口方 Exporter	此栏填写出口商的详细地址，包括街道名、门牌号码等	中国地名的英文译音应采用汉语拼音
(2)收货人 Consignee	最终收货人名称、地址和国家（地区）名，通常是出口合同中的买方或信用证上规定的提单通知人	如信用证规定所有单证收货人一栏留空，在这种情况下，此栏应加注“To Whom It May Concern”或“To Order”，但此栏不得留空
(3)所知航运方式和航线 Means of transport and route	具体的装货港、卸货港名称及运输方式，若经转运，还应注明转运地	对输往内陆给惠国的商品，如瑞士、奥地利，由于这些国家没有港口，因此如系海运，都须经第三国，再转运至该国，在填写时应注明
(4)目的地国家（地区） Country/region of destination	目的地国家（地区）的名称	一般应与最终收货人的国别（或地区）相一致，不能填写中间商国家名称
(5)签证机构用栏 For certifying authority use only	正常情况下证书申领单位应将此栏留空	由签证机构在签发后发证、补发证书或加注其他声明时使用
(6)运输标志 Marks and numbers	与发票相同	不可简单填写“按照发票”（As Per Invoice No ×××）或者“按照提单”（As Per B/L No ×××）；货物如无唛头，应填写“NO MARK”字样，此栏不得留空

续表

项目顺序号	填写内容	要点提示
(7)包装数量及种类、商品描述 Number and kind of packages; description of goods	按发票填写，包括商品的件数和货物描述，并应加结束符	①包装件数必须用大小写同时表示 ②商品名称要填写具体，可以用统称，但不能过于笼统 ③如货物为散装，在商品名称后加注"In Bulk"字样 ④信用证有关产地证的特殊要求可以在此加列 ⑤不要遗落结束符(* * *)，以防加添内容
(8)商品编码 H. S. Code	此笔业务的商品海关编码，应与报关单一致	一般填写前4位，此栏不得留空
(9)数量 Quantity	出口商品的数量及计量单位	如果只有毛重时，则需填"G. W."
(10)发票号码及日期 Number and date of invoice	此笔业务的商业发票号码及日期	此栏不得留空，发票的日期和号码与申请签证时随附的发票的发票号一致，为避免对月份、日期的误解，月份一律用英文(可用缩写)表示
(11)出口方声明 Declaration by the exporter	出口商所在地点及申报日期，由已在签证机构注册的人员签名并加盖有中英文的印章	此栏日期不得早于发票日期(第10栏)(最早是同日)，盖章时应避免覆盖进口国名称和手签人姓名
(12)由签证机构签字、盖章 Certification	签证地点、日期，签证机构签证人经审核后在此栏(正本)签名，并盖签证印章	本栏日期不得早于发票日期(第10栏)和申报日期(第11栏)

表7-2　普惠制原产地证书缮制规范

项目顺序号	填写内容	要点提示
证书号码 Reference number	证书号码	符合签证机构证书号码的编排规则
(1)出口商 Goods consigned from	出口商的详细地址，包括街道名、门牌号码等	中国地名的英文译音应采用汉语拼音
(2)收货人 Goods consigned to	给惠国的最终收货人名称和详细地址	如果信用证未明确最终收货人，可以填写商业发票的抬头人，但不可填写中间商的名称

续表

项目顺序号	填写内容	要点提示
(3)所知航运方式和航线 Means of transport and route	具体的装货港、卸货港名称及运输方式，若经转运，还应注明转运地	对输往内陆给惠国的商品，如瑞士、奥地利，由于这些国家没有港口，因此如系海运，都须经第三国，再转运至该国，在填写时应注明
(4)供官方使用 For official use	正常情况下留空	特殊情况，签证当局在此栏加注
(5)商品项目号 Item number	按不同品种、发票号等分列	单项商品，此栏填"1"，如果有两项以上，按顺序填写1、2、3……
(6)唛头及包装号 Marks and numbers of packages	与发票相同	①填写具体唛头，不可笼统填写成"As per Invoice No. ×××" ②没有唛头，应填写"NO MARK"(N/M)，不能留空
(7)包装件数、包装种类及商品的名称 Number and kind of packages, description of goods	按发票填写，包括商品的件数和货物描述，并应加结束符	①包装件数必须用大小写同时表示 ②商品名称要填写具体，可以用统称，但不能过于笼统 ③如货物为散装，在商品名称后加注"In Bulk"字样 ④信用证有关产地证的特殊要求可以在此加列 ⑤不要遗落结束符(* * *)，以防加添内容
(8)原产地标准 Origin criterion	如不含任何进口成分，此栏填写"P"	本栏是国外海关审核的核心项目，对含有进口成分的商品，应按照正本原产地证书背面的标准分不同情况填写
(9)毛重和其他数量 Gross weight or other quantity	商品的正常计量单位	以重量计算的则填毛重，只有净重的，填净重亦可，但要标上N. W. (NET WEIGHT)，以公斤为单位
(10)发票的日期和号码 Number and date of invoice	此笔业务的商业发票号码及日期	此栏不得留空，发票的日期和号码与申请签证时随附的发票的发票号一致，为避免对月份、日期的误解，月份一律用英文(可用缩写)表示
(11)签证当局的证明 Certificate	填写CIQ签证地点、日期，CIQ签证人经审核后在此栏(正本)亲笔签名并盖签证印章	本栏日期不得早于发票日期(第10栏)和申报日期(第12栏)
(12)出口商声明 Declaration by the exporter	在生产国横线上填写"中国"(China)；进口国横线上填最终进口国，进口国必须与第3栏目的国别一致	申请单位应由授权的手签员在此栏手签，标明申报地点、日期，并加盖申报单位中英文印章，手签员手迹必须在CIQ注册备案；此栏日期不得早于发票日期(第10栏)(最早是同日)，盖章时应避免覆盖进口国名称和手签员姓名

二、原产地证书缮制范例

ORIGINAL

<table>
<tr><td>1.Exporter
TIFERT TRADING CO., LTD.
NO. 86, ZHUJIANG ROAD, TIANJIN, CHINA</td><td rowspan="2">Certificate No.　081210

CERTIFICATE OF ORIGIN
OF
THE PEOPLE'S REPUBLIC OF CHINA</td></tr>
<tr><td>2.Consignee
MARUBENI CORP
5-7, HOMMACHI, 2-CHOME, CHUO-KU, OSAKA, JAPAN</td></tr>
<tr><td>3.Means of transport and route
SHIPMENT FROM TIANJIN TO TOKYO BY SEA</td><td rowspan="2">5.For certifying authority use only</td></tr>
<tr><td>4.Country / region of destination
JAPAN</td></tr>
</table>

6.Marks and numbers	7.Number and kind of packages; description of goods	8.H.S.Code	9.Quantity	10.Number and date of invoices
MARUBENI S/C 08TF0858 TOKYO CTN 1-250	250（TWO HUNDRED AND FIFTY） CARTONS OF GIRL JACKET L/C NO. A-08-0058 NAME AND ADDRESS OF MANUFACTURER: NO. 1 GARMENT FACTORY 88, HONG XING ROAD, TIANJIN, CHINA * * * * *	6204	5000PCS	INVOICE NO.123456 APR. 15, 2008

<table>
<tr><td>11.Declaration by the exporter
The undersigned hereby declares that the above details and statements are correct, that all the goods were produced in China and that they comply with the Rules of Origin of the People's Republic of China.

TIFERT TRADING CO., LTD
泰佛贸易有限公司
*

TIANJIN　APR. 15, 2008　王宏

Place and date, signature and stamp of authorized signatory</td><td>12.Certification
It is hereby certified that the declaration by the exporter is correct.

中国国际贸易促进委员会
天津分会

TIANJIN　APR.15, 2008　陈凯

Place and date, signature and stamp of certifying authority</td></tr>
</table>

样例 7－1　女童夹克一般原产地证书

1. Goods consigned from (Exporter's business name, address, country)

TIFERT TRADING CO., LTD.
NO. 86, ZHUJIANG ROAD, TIANJIN, CHINA

Reference No. 08A3-0308

GENERALIZED SYSTEM OF PREFERENCES

CERTIFICATE OF ORIGIN

(Combined declaration and certificate) FORM A

2. Goods consigned to (Consignee's name, address, country)

MARUBENI CORP
5-7, HOMMACHI, 2-CHOME, CHUO-KU,
OSAKA, JAPAN

Issued in CHINA
(country)

See Notes overleaf

3. Means of transport and route (as far as known)

SHIPMENT FROM TIANJIN TO TOKYO BY SEA

4. For official use

5. Item number	6. Marks and numbers of packages	7. Number and kind of packages; description of goods	8. Origin criterion (see Notes overleaf)	9. Gross weight or other quantity	10. Number and date of invoices
1	MARUBENI S/C 08TF0858 TOKYO CTN 1-250	250(TWO HUNDRED AND FIFTY) CARTONS OF GIRL JACKET L/C NO. A-08-0058 NAME AND ADDRESS OF MANUFACTURER: NO. 1 GARMENT FACTORY 88, HONG XING ROAD, TIANJIN, CHINA * * * *	"P"	5000PCS	INV NO. 123456 APR 15, 2008

11. Certification

It is hereby certified, on the basis of control carried out, that the declaration by the exporter is correct.

中华人民共和国 天津 出入境检验检疫局

TIANJIN APR. 15, 2008

Place and date, signature and stamp of certifying authority

12. Declaration by the exporter

The undersigned hereby declares that the above details and statements are correct, that all the goods were produced in

CHINA
(country)

and that they comply with the origin requirements specified for those goods in the Generalized System of Preferences for goods exported to

JAPAN

TIFERT TRADING CO., LTD.

TIANJIN APR. 15, 2008

Place and date, signature and stamp of authorized signatory

样例 7－2 女童夹克普惠制原产地证书

三、缮制原产地证书应注意问题

1. 如果信用证要求原产地证书做成第三方单据，原产地证书的出口商不能填写成合同中卖方或信用证的受益人，而应该填写成指明的一方。

2. 如果合同是通过中间商达成的，货物直运最终用户所在国，原产地证书的收货人应填写最终收货人的名称和地址，出于商业秘密，中间商可能不会告知出口商真正的最终买主，在此种情况下可以填写成"To whom it may concern"或"To order"，不能填写成中间商。

3. 唛头一定要严格参照发票或提单填写，并且要与发票或提单中的唛头一致，不能简单地填写成"As per invoice No. × ×"、"As per B/L No. × ×"或留空。

4. 目的地国家、地区应该填写为最终用户所在国或所在地区名称，不能填写中间商所在国、所在地区名称。

5. 货物名称应该详细，详尽到在海关税则中能找到对应的 HS Code，不能太笼统，无须填写商品的牌号、等级等内容。

6. 包装单位件数的大小写应该相符，最后不要漏写"ONLY"字样。

7. 信用证要求在原产地证书中要加注一些内容，如信用证证号、许可证证号、制造商或生产商的名称和地址等，应严格按要求填写，一般加注在货物描述后面即可。

8. 货物描述最后不要漏打" * * * "以示结束。

9. 发票日期的月份应该用英文的缩写表示，不要用六位阿拉伯数字填写以免产生异议。

10. 发票号应与申请原产地证一起随附的发票相符，使签证机关能够看出两者之间的关联。

11. 出口货物的海关编码应能准确反映实际出运的货物。

12. 货物中如果含有进口成分(百分比)，在原产地标准中应填写正确的原产地标准代码，不能笼统填写成"P"，申领原产地证书同时要提交进口成分明细表。

13. 注意原产地证书上几个日期的逻辑关系，申领日期不能早于发票日期，可略晚，最早可以与发票日期同一天；签发日期不能早于申领日期，可略晚，最早可以与申领日期相同，同时注意签发日期也不能晚于装运日期，否则被视为后发证。

14. 证书内容过多有附页的情况下，附页要由签证机构签字盖章，同时也要盖骑缝章，以示其是证书的组成部分。

上岗操作

任务栏

1. 通知:公司将有以下合同项下的货物装运出口,加工厂已将货物备妥,请根据有关资料缮制原产地证明书申请单和原产地证书。

2. 目的:本项任务的目的是熟悉并掌握原产地证明书申请单和原产地证书的缮制技巧。

3. 要求:下班前将缮制好的原产地证明书申请单和原产地证书交给师傅审核。

一、动脑思考

1. 泰佛贸易公司在完成一笔出口业务时,须在香港进行转口,转口商是香港大明公司(Hong Kong Da Ming Co., Ltd)请问:单证员在缮制一般原产地证书的出口商和收货人两个栏目时,各应如何填写?

2. 泰佛贸易公司在一笔出口贸易中收到国外客户的信用证,证中规定:所有单证收货人一栏留空。请问:业务员在缮制一般原产地证书的收货人一栏时应如何填写?

3. 泰佛贸易公司向瑞士出口一批商品,从天津出运,由于瑞士属于内陆国家,因此须先运往法国马赛再转运至瑞士苏黎世。请问单证员在填制普惠制原产地证书的所知航运方式和航线一栏时应如何填写?

二、动手操作

1. 初级训练

泰佛贸易公司向荷兰联合海外进出口公司供应童帽1000打,盛祥制帽厂用全部国产原料已经把货备妥,经出入境检验检疫局检验童帽符合合同约定品质,并预计走2月15日从天津港直运至鹿特丹的船。进口商荷兰联合海外进出口公司为了在进口通关时享受最低的进口关税税率,要求泰佛贸易公司向银行议付货款时提交普惠制原产地证书,为此泰佛贸易公司向天津出入境检验检疫局申领普惠制原产地证书。作为泰佛贸易公司的原产地证书的申领人员,请你依据缮制好的商业发票(见样例7-3)填写普惠制原产地证书申请书(见样例7-4),尽快办理普惠制原产地书申领事宜。(泰佛贸易公司在出入境检验检疫局的注册号为G3503)

TIFERT TRADING CO., LTD
INVOICE

Inv. No.: TF080220

Date: 2008-02-08

Sold to Messrs: OVERSEAS INDUSTRY IMPORT& EXPORT CO., LTD
A-602F JULAN, SULAN ROAD #01-20 SULTAN PLAZA, HOLLAND

Shipped per TONGHE V.114 FROM TIANJN TO ROTTERDAM

Maks and Nunbers	Description of Goods	Amount
OVS	500CARTONS -1000DOZ	
--------------	CHILDREN'S CAPS	CIF ROTTERDAM
ROTTERDAM	STYLE NO. KH5067	
NO.1-500	@USD80.00/DOZ	USD80000.00
	PACKED:2DOZ/CTN	
	HS CODE: 6506999000	
	INSURANCE PREMIUM: USD120.00	
	FREIGHT CHARGES: USD850.00	
	TIFERT TRADING CO., LTD 泰佛贸易有限公司 *	

样例7－3 商业发票

普惠制产地证明书申请书

申请单位（盖章）：

注册号：　　　　　　　　　　　　　　　　　　　　证书号：No

申请人郑重声明：

本人是被正式授权代表出口单位办理和签署本申请书的。

本申请书及普惠制产地证格式 A 所列内容正确无误，如发现弄虚作假，冒充格式 A 所列货物，擅改证书，自愿接受签证机关的处罚及负法律责任。现将有关情况申报如下：

现提交中国出口商业发票副本一份，普惠制产地证证明书格式 A（FORMYA）一正二副，以及其他附件　　　份。请予审核签证。

<table>
<tr><td>生产单位</td><td colspan="3"></td><td colspan="2">生产单位联系人电话</td><td></td></tr>
<tr><td>商品名称
(中英文)</td><td colspan="3"></td><td colspan="2">H. S税目号
(以六位数码计)</td><td></td></tr>
<tr><td colspan="3">商品（FOB）总值（以美元计）</td><td colspan="2"></td><td>发 票 号</td><td></td></tr>
<tr><td>最终销售国</td><td colspan="2"></td><td colspan="2">证 书 种 类 划“√”</td><td>加 急 证 书</td><td>普 通 证 书</td></tr>
<tr><td colspan="3">货 物 拟 出 运 日 期</td><td colspan="4"></td></tr>
<tr><td colspan="7">贸 易 方 式 和 企 业 性 质（请在适用处划“√”）</td></tr>
<tr><td>正常贸易</td><td>灵活贸易</td><td>中外合资
H</td><td>中外合作
Z</td><td>外商独资
D</td><td>零　售
Y</td><td>展　卖
M</td></tr>
<tr><td></td><td></td><td></td><td></td><td></td><td></td><td></td></tr>
<tr><td colspan="3">包装数量或毛重或其他数量</td><td colspan="4"></td></tr>
<tr><td colspan="7">原产地标准：
本项商品系在中国生产，完全符合该给惠国给惠方案规定，其原产地情况符合以下第　　条：
(1)　“P”（完全国产，未使用任何进口原材料）；
(2)　“W”（含进口成分或来料加工）；
(3)　“F”（对加拿大出口产品，其进口成分不超过产品出厂价值的 40%）。
本批产品系：1.直接运输从 ________ 到 ________；
2.转口运输从 ________ 中转国（地区）________ 到 ________ 。</td></tr>
<tr><td colspan="4">申请人说明</td><td colspan="3">领证人（签名）
电　话：
日期：　　年　　月　　日</td></tr>
</table>

注：凡含有进口成分的商品，必须按要求提交《含进口成分受惠商品成本明细单》。

样例 7－4　空白普惠制原产地证书申请书

2. 中级训练

泰佛贸易公司与泰国 MOUN 公司经过友好洽商就出口男士休闲裤达成一份出口合同,数量 1800 条,CFR BANGKOK,付款方式提单日后 60 天远期信用证(L/C at 60 days after B/L date)。作为单证员请你根据下列信息,缮制一般原产地证书(见样例 7-5)。

信用证中与原产地证书相关的主要条款如下:

……

59: BENEFICIARY: TIFERT TRADING CO. , LTD
NO. 86, ZHUJIANG ROAD, TIANJIN, CHINA

50: APPLICANT: MOUN CO. , LTD.
NO. 443, 249, ROAD,
BANGKOK, THAILAND

32: CURRENCY CODE AMOUNT: USD19800,00

44E: PORT OF LOADING TIANJIN

44F: PORT OF DISCHARGE BANGKOK

44C: LATEST DATE OF SHIPMENT 080531

45A: DESCRIPTION OF GOODS/SERVICE

1800 PCS OF MEN'S LEISURE PANTS AT USD11.00/PC CFR BANGKOK, THAILAND, PACKING IN 150 CARTONS

SHIPPING MARK: MOUN / BANGKOK/C/NO. 1-150/MADE IN CHINA

46A: DOCUMENTS REQUIRED

+CERTIFICATE OF ORIGIN IN ONE ORIGINAL AND ONE COPY ISSUED BY CCPIT CERTIFYING THAT GOODS ARE OF CHINESE ORIGIN INDICATING L/C NO.

……

其他补充信息如下:

(1)发票号码: 45678

(2)发票日期: 2008 年 5 月 5 日

(3)毛重: 16200KGS

(4)H. S 编码: 6201.9310

(5)申请日期: 2008 年 5 月 15 日

(6)一般原产地证书编号: 08EA7894

ORIGINAL

1.Exporter	Certificate No. CERTIFICATE OF ORIGIN OF THE PEOPLE'S REPUBLIC OF CHINA
2.Consignee	
3.Means of transport and route	5.For certifying authority use only
4.Country / region of destination	

6.Marks and numbers	7.Number and kind of packages; description of goods	8.H.S.Code	9.Quantity	10.Number and date of invoices

11.Declaration by the exporter The undersigned hereby declares that the above details and statements are correct, that all the goods were produced in China and that they comply with the Rules of Origin of the People's Republic of China. ------------------------------ Place and date, signature and stamp of authorized signatory	12.Certification It is hereby certified that the declaration by the exporter is correct. ------------------------------ Place and date, signature and stamp of certifying authority

样例 7－5　空白一般原产地证书

3. 高级训练

泰佛贸易公司与日本 TOSHU 公司有着长期的友好业务关系，TOSHU 公司每年都向泰佛贸易公司订购男士衬衫。合同 08JA7031KL 项下男士衬衫 142800 件已经备妥，并经检验合格，现按照信用证要求需要申领普惠制原产地证书。作为泰佛贸易公司的单证员，请你根据以下信用证（见样例 7－6）摘录信息及补充相关信息，缮制普惠制原产地证书（见样例 7－7）。

信用证有关资料摘录如下：

SEQUENCE OF TOTAL	27：1/1
FORM OF DOCUMENTARY CREDIT	40A：IRREVOCABLE
APPLICABLE RULES	40E：UCP LATEST VERSION
DOCUMENTARY CREDIT NUMBE	20：G/FO－7752807
DATE OF ISSUE：	31C：080403
DATE AND PLACE OF EXPIRY	31D：080615 TIANJIN CHINA
APPLICANT	50：TOSHU CORPORATION OSALM 12－36，KYUTARO － MACHI 4 － CHOME CHUO － KU，OSAKA 561 － 8177 JAPAN
BENEFICIARY	59：TIFERT TRADING CO.，LTD NO. 86，ZHUJIANG ROAD，TIANJIN，CHINA
CURRENCY CODE，AMOUNT	32B：USD201780.00
AVAILABLE WITH ... BY ...	41D：ANY BANK BY NEGOTIATION
PORT OF LOADING	44E：TIANJIN
PORT OF DISCHARGE	44F：YOKOHAMA
LATEST DATE OF SHIPMENT	44C：080531
DESCRPT OF GOODS/SERVICES	45A：

MAN'S SHIRT（CONTRACT NO. 08JA7031KL）

ST/NO.　Q'TY UNIT PRICE CIF YOKOHAMA

71 － 800 67200PCS USD 1.43/PC　USD96096.00

71 － 801 48000PCS USD 1.46/PC　USD70080.00

71 － 802 27600PCS USD 1.29/PC　USD35604.00

DOCUMENTS REQUIRED　46A：

＋ COMMERCIAL INVOICE IN QUINTUPLICATE

＋ PACKING LIST IN 3 COPIES

＋ GSP CERTIFICATE OF ORIGIN FORM A IN 3 COPIES SHOWING THE NAME AND ADDRESS OF MANUFACTURER AND CERTIFYING THE GOODS ARE WHOLLY PRODUCED IN CHINA.

……

样例 7－6　信用证

其他补充信息如下：

(1)SHIPPING MARKS：

TOSHU/08JA7031KL/YOKOHAMA/MADE IN CHINA

(2)INVOICE NO 08FZ008 DATED MAY20，2008

(3)PACKED IN CARTONS OF 50 PIECES EACH

<table>
<tr><td>1. Goods consigned from (Exporter's business name, address, country)</td><td rowspan="2">Reference No.
GENERALIZED SYSTEM OF PREFERENCES
CERTIFICATE OF ORIGIN
(Combined declaration and certificate) FORM A
Issued in THE PEOPLE'S REPUBLIC OF CHINA
(country)
See Notes overleaf</td></tr>
<tr><td>2. Goods consigned to (Consignee's name, address, country)</td></tr>
<tr><td>3 Means of transport and route (as far as known)</td><td>4. For official use</td></tr>
<tr><td colspan="2">5. Item number | 6. Marks and numbers of packages | 7. Number and kind of packages; description of goods | 8. Origin criterion (see Notes overleaf) | 9. Gross weight or other quantity | 10. Number and date of invoices</td></tr>
<tr><td>11. Certification
It is hereby certified, on the basis of control carried out that the declaration by the exporter is correct.</td><td>12. Declaration by the exporter
The undersigned hereby declares that the above details and statements are correct, that all the goods were
produced in ____________
(country)
and that they comply with the origin requirements specified for those goods in the Generalized System of Preferences for goods exported to
____________</td></tr>
<tr><td>____________
Place and date, signature and stamp of certifying authority</td><td>____________
Place and date, signature and stamp of authorized signatory</td></tr>
</table>

样例 7－7　空白普惠制原产地证书

任务八　缮制海运提单

岗前测试

一、单选题

> 温馨提示：
>
> 海运提单是国际贸易中最重要的单据之一，它是物权凭证，收货人或提单的合法持有人有权凭提单在目的港向承运人索要提单项下的货物。谁拥有提单，谁就有权力要求承运人交付货物，因此海运提单是有价证券，可以买卖转让，具有质押权。

1. 提单收货人一栏显示“TO ORDER”的字样，这种提单(　)。

A. 不可转让

B. 可以由持有人提货

C. 不经过背书即可以转让

D. 经背书，可以转让

2. 信用证要求港至港海运提单，若受益人提交的提单为备运提单，且该提单上注明的收货地与起运港不同，应该(　)。

A. 批注“ON BOARD”及装船日期

B. 另外批注装货港及船名

C. A 和 B 缺一不可

D. 无需做任何批注

3. 下列提单上已装船日期批注符合《跟单信用证统一惯例 UCP600》规定的是(　)。

A. GOODS DELIVERED TO SHIPPING COMPANY FOR SHIPMENT ON MAY 28, 2008

B. GOODS SHALL BE SHIPPED ON BOARD ON JUNE 1, 2008

C. GOODS SHIPPED ON BOARD ON JUNE 3, 2008

D. GOODS SHALL BE SHIPPED ON JUNE 4, 2008

4. 根据《跟单信用证统一惯例 UCP600》的规定，一般银行不接受(　)。

A. 转运提单　　　　B. 第三方托运人提单

C. 多式联运提单　　D. 注明货装舱面的提单

5. 根据《跟单信用证统一惯例 UCP600》的规定，以下提单显示所注内容可以被接受的是(　)。

A. SHIPPED ON DECK

B. THE GOODS MAY BE CARRIED ON DECK

C. FOUR CARTONS ARE BROKEN

D. PACKAGE IS NOT SUFFICIENT FOR THE SEA JOURNEY

6. 在买卖合同和信用证中一般都规定卖方须提供(　)。

A. 备运提单　　B. 已装船清洁提单

C. 已装船提单　　D. 记名提单

7. 在货物装运后,承运人对货物的外表状况良好,未加有关货损或包装不良之类批注的提单是(　)。

A. 不清洁提单　　B. 清洁提单

C. 备运提单　　D. 已装船提单

8. 如果出口货物采用海运与其他运输方式联合运输,由第一程承运人签发包括全程运输,并能在目的港或目的地凭以提货的提单是(　)。

A. 直达提单　　B. 转船提单

C. 备运提单　　D. 联运提单

9. 在信用证付款方式下,提单中的收货人一栏应按信用证规定填写。如信用证规定"Full set of B/L made out to order",此栏则填(　)。

A. "To order"　　B. "To order of . . . Bank"

C. "To order of shipper"　　D. "To order of . . . "

10. FOB 合同规定的最迟装运日为 5 月 4 日,下列日期中,正确的是(　)。

A. 货于 5 月 4 日送交船公司　　B. 货于 5 月 4 日开始装船

C. 货于 5 月 4 日全部装船完毕　　D. 货于 5 月 4 日抵达日本

二、多选题

1. 关于已装船提单叙述正确的是(　)。

A. 提单上印就"已装船"字样或加盖"已装船"戳记

B. 注明船名和装船日期

C. 对收货人按时收货有保障

D. 由船公司收到货物时签发

2. 运输单据是托运人将货物交付承运人或其代理人办理装运时,由承运人或其代理人向托运人签发的,用以证明托运货物已装运的收据。依据运输方式不同,运输单据有(　)。

A. 海运提单　　B. 航空运单　　C. 联合运输提单　　D. 铁路运单

3. 提单的主要作用有(　)。

A. 货物收据　　B. 物权凭证

C. 装船依据　　D. 运输合同的证明

4. 构成不清洁提单的批注为(　)。

A. "铁条松散"(iron strap loose or missing)

B. “发货人装箱点数并铅封”(shipper’s load, count & seal)

C. “旧麻袋”(packed in used gunny bags)

D. “短装 2 桶”(short shipped 2 drums)

5. 国外来证装运期为“on or about March 15, 2008”,则我出口提单的日期可以是(　)。

A. 3 月 10 日　　B. 3 月 15 日　　C. 3 月 20 日　　D. 3 月 21 日

小贴士:

一份提单上可能会出现的图章有:

①签发提单的公司印章(最多出现两处);

②提单更正章(一般不应超过三处);

③已装船批注章(标明已装船);

④日期文字章(表明装船完毕);

⑤电放章(电放货物时使用)等。

三、判断题

1. 海运提单和海运单都是物权凭证,都可背书转让,而其他运输单据,则为非物权凭证,不得转让。(　)

2. 承运人在提单上加注任何批注均构成不清洁提单。(　)

3. 正本提单如出具一式几份,则每份具有相同的效力,只要其中一份凭以提货,其他各份立即失效。(　)

4. 根据《跟单信用证统一惯例 UCP600》的规定,承运人或船长的任何签字或证实,必须表明“承运人”或“船长”的身份。(　)

5. 根据《跟单信用证统一惯例 UCP600》的规定,全套提单可以只有一份正本或一份以上正本,如信用证要求提交全套正本提单时,只要提单上注明的正本份数全部提交即可。(　)

6. 根据《跟单信用证统一惯例 UCP600》的规定,与发票不同,除非信用证另有规定,提单上的货名可以使用统称。(　)

7. 无论是清洁提单还是不清洁提单,只要收货人的名称与信用证的规定相符,银行都予以接受。(　)

8. 全式提单是指提单除有正面条款之外,还在背面印有承运人和托运人权利、义务等详细条款的提单。略式提单仅有提单正面内容,如船名、货号、标志、件数、装运港、目的港,而略去了提单背面全部条款的提单。因此,两者效力不同。(　)

9. 除非信用证另有规定,银行可接受甲板提单。(　)

10. 提单签发日不得超过信用证规定的装运日期，也不得早于信用证的最早装运日期。(　)

岗前培训

一、海运提单缮制规范

表 8－1　海运提单缮制规范

项目顺序号	填写内容	要点提示
(1)提单号 B/L No.	按照装货单编号填写	与装货单中编号一致
(2)托运人 Shipper	一般为信用证受益人或合同卖方	①信用证项下为受益人 ②托收和电汇项下为合同卖方
(3)收货人 Consignee	抬头人，应完全按照信用证和合同要求填写	一般为指示式： ①To Order ②To Order of Shipper ③To Order of ××× Bank ④To Order of ＋ 开证人的具体名称
(4)被通知人 Notify party	应完全按照信用证要求填写	一般是进口商或其代理人，承运人凭此栏内容通知其办理提货，所以提单的被通知人的名称和地址一定要详细
(5)前程运输 Pre－carriage by	前程运输方式	如货物需转运，此栏填第一程船船名；如不需转运，此栏留空
(6)装运港 Port of loading	装运港名称	按信用证规定填写实际装运货物的港口
(7)船名 Vessel name	应填写货物所装船的船名及航次	如货物需转运，填写第二程船船名；如不需转运，填第一程船船名
(8)转运港 Port of transshipment	转运港名称	如不需转运，此栏留空
(9)卸货港 Port of discharge	货物实际卸下的港口名称	如有重名，在港口后面一定要加注国别
(10)最终目的地 Final destination	填最终目的地名称	如最终目的地就是目的港，此栏可留空

续表

项目顺序号	填写内容	要点提示
(11)集装箱号、铅封号及唛头 Container seal No. or Marks & Nos.	此笔业务的集装箱号、铅封号及唛头	唛头应与商业发票、装箱单上的一致
(12)包装的种类和数量 Number and kind of package	按实际包装具体情况填写	总件数除小写外,还要用文字大写叙述,且大小写应一致
(13)货物名称 Description of goods	按信用证规定填写,可用统称	要与其他单据如发票等保持一致
(14)毛重 Gross Weight	填写总毛重	除非信用证另有规定,一般重量以公斤表示,保留两位小数
(15)尺码 Measurement	填写总尺码	除非信用证另有规定,一般体积以立方米表示,保留三位小数
(16)运费条款	按信用证要求加注运费条款	应注意与使用的贸易术语一致,凡是F组术语填写“Freight to collect”,C组术语其写“Freight prepaid”
(17)装船批注的日期 On board notation	货物的装船完毕日期	此栏可与18栏日期相同,也可能略晚于提单的签发日期,但不能晚于信用证规定的最迟装运期
(18)提单签发地点及日期 Place and date of issue	提单的签发地点和签发日期	不能晚于信用证规定的最迟装运期
(19)正本提单签发份数 No. of original B/L	应按信用证的规定提供要求的份数	此栏必须用英文大写数字表示
(20)承运人签章 Signed for the carrier	承运人或其代理人的签字	常见签署方式: ①承运人或其代理人签署 ②船长或其代理人签署

二、海运提单缮制范例

Shipper (2)	B/L No. SINO081216 (1)
TIFERT TRADING CO., LTD NO.86, ZHUJIANG ROAD, TIANJIN,CHINA	中国外运天津公司 SINOTRANS TIANJIN COMPANY OCEAN BILL OF LADING
Consignee or order (3) TO ORDER	
Notify address (4) MARUBENI CORP 5-7, HOMMACHI, 2-CHOME, CHUO-KU, OSAKA, JAPAN TEL NO. 8745 9986	SHIPPED on board in apparent good order and condition (unless otherwise indicated) the goods or packages specified herein and to be discharged at the mentioned port of discharge or as near thereto as the vessel may safely get and be always afloat. The weight, measure, marks and numbers, quality, contents and value, being particulars furnished by the Shipper, are not checked by the Carrier on loading. The Shipper, Consignee and the Holder of this Bill of Lading hereby expressly accept and agree to all printed, written or stamped provisions, exceptions and conditions of this Bill of Lading, including those on the back hereof. IN WITNESS whereof the number of original Bills of Lading stated below have been signed, one of which being accomplished the other(s) to be void.

Pre-carriage by (5)	Port of loading (6) TIANJIN, CHINA
Vessel (7) SHUNFENG V.0827	Port of transshipment (8)
Port of discharge (9) TOKYO, JAPAN	Final destination (10)

Container. seal No. or marks and Nos. (11)	Number and kind of package (12)	Description of goods (13)	Gross weight (kgs.) (14)	Measurement (m^3) (15)
MARUBENI S/C 08TF0858 TOKYO CTN 1-250	250 CARTONS SAY TWO HUNDRED AND FIFTY CARTONS ONLY	GIRL JAKET PREPAID FREIGHT (16)	24909.00KGS	24.548CBM ON BOARD DATE: APR.30, 2008 (17)

Freight and charges			REGARDING TRANSHIPMENT INFORMATION PLEASE CONTACT
Ex. rate	Prepaid at	Freight payable at	Place and date of issue (18) TIANJIN, APR.30, 2008
	Total prepaid	Number of original Bs/L (19) THREE	Signed for or on behalf of the Carrier (20) SINOTRANS TIANJIN COMPANY 张涛

样例 8－1　女童夹克海运提单

三、缮制海运提单应注意问题

1. 提单中的货物描述可只填写商品名称，无需填写规格、牌号等详情。如果涉及的商品较多，则可只填写商品的统称，但不得与信用证中货物描述有抵触。

2. 提单上最好不要加注关于包装状况的描述，如“新袋”（New Bag）、旧箱（Old Carton）等词语。

3. 提单上的修正和变更必须经过证实。证实从表面看来必须是由承运人、船长或其代理人所为（该代理人可以与出具或签署提单的代理人不同），只要表明其作为承运人或船长的代理人身份即可。

4. 对于正本提单上可能已做的任何修正或变更，不可转让副本提单，无需任何签字或证实。

5. 如果信用证要求提单注明运费已付或到目的港支付，则提单必须有相应标注。即使信用证对此未做具体规定，也应根据所采用的贸易术语，在运费支付栏填写“Freight to Collect”或“Freight Prepaid”。

上岗操作

任务栏

1. 通知：公司将有以下合同项下的货物装运出口，加工厂已将货物备妥，并且完成报检和原产地证书申请工作，请根据有关资料缮制托运委托书和海运提单。

2. 目的：本项任务的目的是熟悉并掌握托运委托书和海运提单的缮制技巧。

3. 要求：下班前将缮制好的托运委托书和海运提单交给师傅审核。

一、动脑思考

1. 泰佛贸易公司在一笔出口贸易中收到国外进口商的信用证，证中规定：

Applicant:	ABC Corporation No. 123, New Street, New York, USA
Beneficiary:	Tifert Trading Co., Ltd No. 86, Zhujiang Road, Tianjin, China
Issuing Bank:	Bank of China, New York Branch

Full set of clean on board B/L issued to our order, notifying applicant and marked freight prepaid and showing full name and address of the relative shipping agent in USA.

请问:作为单证员你应如何填写提单中的托运人、收货人和通知人？提单上的运费支付方式应如何填写？是否还有其他制单要求？

2. 泰佛贸易公司在一笔出口贸易中收到国外进口商的信用证,证中规定：

Applicant:	ABC Corporation No. 123, New Street, New York, USA
Beneficiary:	Tifert Trading Co. , Ltd No. 86, Zhujiang Road, Tianjin, China
Issuing Bank:	Bank of China, New York Branch

Full set clean on board ocean bill of lading, made out to order and blank endorsed, evidencing shipment from Tianjin to New York port not later than April 05 2008, marked freight prepaid and notify the applicant.

请问:作为单证员你应如何填写提单中的托运人、收货人和通知人？提单上的运费支付方式应如何填写？是否还有其他制单要求？在交单结汇时提单应如何背书,由谁首次背书？提单的签发日期是否有限制？

3. 泰佛贸易公司在一笔出口贸易中收到国外进口商的信用证,证中规定：

Applicant:	ABC Corporation No. 123, New Street, New York, USA
Beneficiary:	Tifert Trading Co. , Ltd No. 86, Zhujiang Road, Tianjin, China
Issuing Bank :	Bank of China, New York Branch

Full set of clean shipped on board marine bill of lading, made out to our order, marked freight prepaid, notify opener, indicating LC No. and S/C No. , received for shipment B/L not acceptable.

请问:作为单证员你应如何填写提单中的发货人、收货人和通知人？提单上的运费支付方式应如何填写？是否还有其他制单要求？信用证对提单的种类是否有限制？

二、动手操作

1. 初级训练

泰佛贸易公司向加拿大 FASHION FORCE 公司出口全棉女士衬衣 2550 件,加工厂已经委托出入境检验检疫局对货物进行了施检,检验结果完全合格。付款方式 20% T/T 预付,80% 即期信用证,信用证规定不允许分批、不允许转运,最迟装运期为 2008 年 11 月 30 日。你作为公司的货代员,请依据已经缮制好的商业发票(见样例 8 - 2)填写一份出口货物订舱委托书(见样例 8 - 3),递交给友通国际货运代理公司办理租船订舱事宜,争取装上 11 月 25 日开航的“EASTWIND VOY. 78”的船期。

Issuer TIFERT TRADING CO., LTD NO.86, ZHUJIANG ROAD, TIANJIN, CHINA	商 业 发 票 **COMMERCIAL INVOICE**	
To FASHION FORCE CO., LTD NO. 56, NEW TERMINAL STREET, OTTAWA, CANADA	No.: NT01F F004	Date: NOV.9, 2008
Transport Details SHIPMENT FROM TIANJIN CHINA TO MONTREAL CANADA BY VESSEL	S/C No. F01LC B08127	L/C No.
	Terms of payment 20% BY T/T IN ADVANCE, 80% BY L/C AT SIGHT	

Marks and numbers	Number and kind of packages, Description of goods	Quantity	Unit price	Amount
			CIF MONTREAL	
FASHION FORCE F01LCB08127 CTN NO.1-85 MONTREAL MADE IN CHINA	85 CARTONS LADIES BLOUSE 100% COTTON 40SX20S/140X60	2550PCS	USD12.80/PC	USD32640.00

TOTAL PACKAGE: 85 CARTONS
GROSS WEIGHT : 1615KGS
NET WEIGHT : 1445KGS
MEAS: 21.583 CBM

NAME OF OPENING BANK: BNP PARIS (CANADA)

TIFERT TRADING CO., LTD

王宏

样例 8－2　商业发票

出 口 货 物 订 舱 委 托 书

日期　　月　　日

1）发货人	4)信用证号码	
	5)开证银行	
	6)合同号码	7）成交金额
	8)装运口岸	9）目的港
2）收货人	10）转船运输	11)分批装运
	12）信用证有效期	13)装船期限
	14）运费	15)成交条件
	16）公司联系人	16)电话/传真
3）通知人	18）公司开户行	19)银行账号
	20）特别要求	

21）标记唛码	22）货号规格	23）包装件数	24）毛重	25)净重	26)数量	27）单价	28）总价

29）总件数	30）总毛重	31）总净重	32）总尺码	33）总金额

34)备注

样例 8－3　空白出口货物订舱委托书

2. 中级训练

天津长城电子公司向西班牙 ABC 公司出口空调 10000 台,合同(见样例 8 - 4)要求分两批出运,3 月 31 日前出运 3000 台,4 月 15 日前出运 7000 台。3 月份的 3000 台已经出运,现余下的 7000 台空调也已经备好,请与中国外运天津公司联系订舱事宜并且缮制海运提单(见样例 8 - 5)。

售 货 确 认 书

SALES CONFIRMATION

Sellers: TIANJIN GREATWALL
ELECTRIC CO., LTD
35 YINGBING ROAD, ,CHINA

S/C No. TJIN04006

Date: FEB. 15, 2008

Signed at: TIANJIN, CHINA

Buyers: ABC CORPORATION LIMITED
CTRADE XABIA, KM5 53620 GATA DE GORGOS
ALICANTE, SPAIN

The undersigned Sellers and Buyers have agreed to close the following transaction according to the terms and conditions stipulated below

货 号 Article No.	品名及规格 Description of Goods	数 量 Quantity	单 价 Unit price	金 额 Amount
80230019	AIR CONDITIONER KFR - 35GW/NL MODEL R407C, 220V	10000 SETS	FOB TIANJIN USD160.00/SET	USD1600000.00

With 5% more or less both in amount and quantity allowed at the Sellers' option

Total Value: US DOLLARS ONE MILLION SIX HUNDRED THOUSAND ONLY.

Packing: ONE SET IN TWO CARTONS, TOTAL 20,000 CARTONS

Time of shipment: 3,000 SET BY MARCH 31, 2008 AND 7,000 SET BY APRIL 15, 2008 PARTIAL SHIPMENT AND TRANSSHIPMENT ARE ALLOWED.

Loading port & Destination: FROM TIANJIN TO VALENCIA SPAIN

Insurance: TO BE COVERED BY THE BUYERS.

Terms of payment: BY IRREVOCABLE LETTER OF CREDIT TO BE AVAILABLE BY 30 DAYS AFTER SIGHT DRAFT TO REACH THE SELLERS BEFORE MAR. 13, 2008 AND TO REMAIN VALID FOR NEGOTIATION IN CHINA UNTIL THE 15TH DAY AFTER THE AFORESAID TIME OF SHIPMENT.

Shipping Mark: ABC/TJIN04006/CHARLESTON/NO. 1 - UP

Documents required:

+ SIGNED COMMERCIAL INVOICE IN DUPLICATE INDICATING S/C NO.
+ PACKING LIST IN TRIPLCATE SHOWING G. W., N. W. AND MEASUREMENT
+ FULL SET OF ORIGINAL CLEAN SHIPPED ON BOARD B/L, MADE OUT TO ORDER OF SHIPPER, MARKED "FREIGHT TO COLLECT" AND NOTIFY APPLICANT WITH FULL ADDRESS AND INDICATING L/C.

SELLERS　　　　BUYERS

徐进　　　　陈述

样例 8 - 4 销售合同

其他补充信息如下：

(1)空调的详细包装情况为：

	尺码	毛重	净重
外箱一	85×55×45CM	55KGS	52KGS
外箱二	75×50×45CM	45KGS	42KGS

(2)船名：HANJIN EXPRESS V. 38

(3)提单号：SINO98563

(4)提单日：APR 15,2008

(5)承运人有权签字人：张强

Shipper

B/L No.

中国外运天津公司

SINOTRANS TIANJIN COMPANY

Consignee or order

OCEAN BILL OF LADING

Notify address

SHIPPED on board in apparent good order and condition (unless otherwise indicated) the goods or packages specified herein and to be discharged at the mentioned port of discharge or as near thereto as the vessel may safely get and be always afloat.

The weight, measure, marks and numbers, quality, contents and value, being particulars furnished by the Shipper, are not checked by the Carrier on loading.

The Shipper, Consignee and the Holder of this Bill of Lading hereby expressly accept and agree to all printed, written or stamped provisions, exceptions and conditions of this Bill of Lading, including those on the back hereof.

IN WITNESS whereof the number of original Bills of Lading stated below have been signed, one of which being accomplished the other(s) to be void.

Pre-carriage by	Port of loading
Vessel	Port of transshipment
Port of discharge	Final destination

Container. seal No. or marks and Nos.	Number and kind of package	Description of goods	Gross weight (kgs.)	Measurement (m^3)

Freight and charges			REGARDING TRANSHIPMENT INFORMATION PLEASE CONTACT
Ex. rate	Prepaid at	Freight payable at	Place and date of issue
	Total prepaid	Number of original Bs/L	Signed for or on behalf of the Carrier As Agent

样例 8－5　空白海运提单

3. 高级训练

天津国际进出口公司与美国 NICHIMEN 公司就面料出口达成一出口合同，信用证已开抵天津国际进出口公司，面料加工厂已经准备就绪，且舱位已订妥，请依据下列信用证（见样例 8 - 6）及补充信息缮制海运提单（见样例 8 - 7）。

DOCUMENTARY CREDIT

27　SEQUENCE OF TOTAL：1/1

40A　FORM OF DOC. CREDIT：IRREVOCABLE

40E　APPLICABLE RULES：UCP LATEST VERSION

20C　DOC. CREDIT NO. DCMTN55123

31C　DATE OF ISSUE：080212

31D　PLACE/DATE OF EXPIRY：080409 IN CHINA

51　ISSUING BANK：THE NORINCHUK BANK NEW YORK

50　APPLICANT：　NICHIMEN CORPORATION
　　2 - 2 NAKANOSHIMA，NEW YORK，
　　AMERICA

59　BENEFICIARY：TIANJIN INTERNATIONAL IMP. & EXP. CORP.
　　8TH FLOOR FOREIGN TRADE BUILDING
　　200 ZHANQIAN ROAD，TIANJIN，CHINA

41D　AVAILABLE WITH ANY BANK BY NEGOTIATION

32B　AMOUNT：USD64000. 00

42C　DRAFT AT SIGHT FOR 98PCT OF INVOICE VALUE

42D　DRAWEE：ISSUING BANK

43　PARTIAL SHIPMENT AND TRANSSHIPMENT ALLOWED

44E　LOADING PORT：TIANJIN

44F　FOR TRANSPORATION TO：CHARLESTON，USA

44C　LATEST SHIPMENT DATE：MARCH 20，2008

45A　DESCRIPTION OF GOODS：
　　100 PCT COTTON GREIGE PRINT CLOTH
　　ART. NO. 3042 FIRST QUALITY
　　SIZE：30X30 68X68 50" EXPORT PACKING IN SEAWORTHY BALES
　　TOTAL QUANTITY：ABOUT 200 000YDS
　　PRICE USD0. 32/YD CIF CHARLESTON
　　AS PER CONTRACT NO. J515

46A　DUCUMENT REQUIRED：

+ SIGNED COMMERCIAL INVOICE IN 5 COPIES

+ FULL SET OF CLEAN ON BOARD OCEAN BILL OF LADING MADE OUT TO ORDER AND BLANK ENDORSED AND MARKED FREIGHT PREPAID AND NOTIFY APPLICANT. BILL OF LADING MUST SHOW L/C NO. AND THE EXACT OCEAN FREIGHT AMOUNT PAID BY BENEFICIARY TO THE STEAMSHIP CO.

+ CERTIFICATE OF ORIGIN G. S. P. FORM A IN 2 COPIES

47A　ADDITIONAL CLAUSES：

+ ALL DOCUMENTS MUST BEAR THE L/C NO.

+ DOCUMENT MUST BE PRESENTED WITHIN 15 DAYS AFTER SHIPMENT.

……

样例 8 - 6　信用证

Shipper

B/L No.:

Consignee

Notify Party

中国远洋运输公司

BILL OF LADING ORIGINAL

CHINA OCEAN SHIPPING CO

Pre carriage by	*Place of Receipt
Ocean Vessel Voy. No.	Port of Loading

Port of discharge	*Final destination	Freight payable at	Number original Bs/L

Marks and Numbers	Number and kind of packages; Description	Gross weight	Measurement

TOTAL PACKAGES(IN WORDS)

Freight and charges

Place and date of issue

Signed for the Carrier

Applicable only when document used as a Through Bill of Loading

样例 8－7　空白海运提单

其他有关补充信息如下：

(1) 包装明细：布包（IN BALE)

件号	货号	包装率	每包毛重	每包净重	每包尺码
1－166	3042	1200YDS/BALE	141 KGS	139KGS	95X68X50CM

(2) 出运数量:199200YDS

(3) 船名:MSC SARAH V.6A

(4) 提单号:DMDF2390

(5)提单日期:2008.3.20

(6)承运人代理：CHINA NATIONAL FOREIGN TRADE TRANSPORT CORPORATION

(7)有权签字人：黎明

(8)SHIPPING MARK:J－515
NAGOYA
PKG. NO. 1－166

(9)支付的总运费：USD1200.00

任务九　缮制保险单

岗前测试

一、单选题

> 温馨提示：
>
> 国际贸易买卖双方相距甚远，一般货物需要经过长时间运输，为转移运输途中的风险，需要办理相应的投保手续。依据买卖双方所采用的贸易术语的不同，有时由卖方负责办理投保手续，有时则由买方负责办理投保手续。

1. 根据《伦敦保险协会海运保险条款》的规定，承保范围最小的基本险别是(　)。

A. ICC(A)　　B. ICC(B)

C. ICC(C)　　D. ICC War Clause

2. 合同或信用证没有规定投保加成率，根据《跟单信用证统一惯例 UCP600》的规定，卖方可在 CIF 总值的基础上(　)投保。

A. 加二成　　B. 加一成

C. 加三成　　D. 加四成

3. 保险单中“IOP”是指(　)。

A. 一种一般附加险　　B. 一种特殊附加险

C. 计免赔率　　D. 不计免赔率

4. 我方按 CIF 条件出口一批罐头食品，按下列(　)投保是正确的。

A. 平安险 + 水渍险　　B. 一切险 + 偷窃提货不着险

C. 水渍险 + 偷窃提货不着险　　D. 战争险 + 偷窃提货不着险

5. 在我国海洋运输货物保险业务中，下列(　)险别不适用“仓至仓”条款。

A. WAR RISK　　B. WA or WPA

C. FPA　　D. ALL RISKS

6. 在海运过程中，被保险货物茶叶经水浸已不能饮用，这种海上损失属于(　)。

A. 单独海损　　B. 共同海损

C. 推定全损　　D. 实际全损

7. 某公司出口货物一批，按 CIF 价值的 110% 投保了水渍险，在此基础上还可加保(　)。

A. 平安险和渗漏险　　B. 破碎险和战争险

C. 一切险和战争险　　D. 平安险和战争险

8. 出口商出运 100 公斤香料，单价为 USD100/KG CIFC5% LONDON，加成率为 10%，保险费率为 1%，出口商应付保险费(　)。

A. USD110　　B. USD500
C. USD1000　　D. USD100

9. 若信用证没有特殊规定,一般保险单的被保险人是(　)。

A. 开证行　　B. 受益人
C. 申请人　　D. 议付行

10. 根据我国"海洋货物运输保险条款"的规定,一切险包括(　)。

A. 平安险加11种一般附加险　　B. 一切险加11种一般附加险
C. 水渍险加11种一般附加险　　D. 11种一般附加险加特殊附加险

二、多选题

1. 根据我国海运货物保险条款(即CIC条款)的规定,海洋运输货物保险中的基本险包括(　)。

A. 平安险　　B. 水渍险　　C. 一切险　　D. 附加险

2. 以下关于保险凭证的正确叙述是(　)。

A. 俗称小保单,是一种简化的保险单　　B. 既有正面内容,又有背面条款
C. 与保险单具有同等效力　　D. 在实务中,保险单可以代替保险凭证

3. 以下关于保险单作用的正确选项是(　)。

A. 物权凭证　　B. 索赔证明　　C. 保险合同证明　　D. 货物收据

4. 在我国海洋运输货物保险业务中,下列险别均可适用"仓至仓"条款(　)。

A. ALL RISKS　　B. F. P. A　　C. T. P. N. D　　D. WAR RISK

5. 构成共同海损的条件是(　)。

A. 必须是有意的、合理的措施造成的损失
B. 必须是为船、货共同安全而采取的措施
C. 必须是属于非常性质的损失
D. 必须是确实遭遇的危难

小贴士:

1. 保险单是保险人对保险单所列货物,在其所负责期间和所负承保责任范围内,承担货物灭失和损害的赔偿责任的凭证;
2. 保险单是保险人与被保险人之间的一种契约,通过保险单上的保险条款,规定了保险人与被保险人的权利和义务;
3. 当保险单上所列的被保险货物在保险人的责任范围内遭受灭失和损害时,保险单是被保险人或合法持有人向保险公司要求赔偿的凭证;
4. 当保险单上所列的被保险货物在保险人的责任范围内遭受灭失和损害时,保险单是保险公司处理被保险人赔偿要求的主要理赔依据。

三、判断题

1. 根据《跟单信用证统一惯例 UCP600》的规定，信用证规定提供保险单时，出口商可以用保险凭证代替。（　）

2. 根据《跟单信用证统一惯例 UCP600》的规定，银行拒绝接受表明投保生效日期迟于装运日期的保险单。（　）

3. 一切险的责任范围涵盖所有险别，包括偷窃、提货不着险及战争险。（　）

4. 保险单是一种权利的凭证，经背书后可以随货物所有权的转移而进行转让。（　）

5. 保险单的赔付地一般为装运港（地），如有特殊要求，可事先说明。（　）

6. 保险凭证俗称“小保单”，是保险单的简化形式，省略了背面的保险条款，保险条款仍以保险单为准，与保险单具有同等的法律效力。（　）

7. 预约保险单亦称预约保险合同，是保险公司与投保人事先订立的在一定时期内承保多批货物的保险合同。凡在合同约定时期内，由出口商向保险公司发出“装运通知”或“保险声明”，保险公司就对货物自动承保。（　）

8. 保险单的包装及数量应填最大包装件数，如为散装货应填“N/M”。（　）

9. 保险单的货物名称一栏应按发票品名填写。如发票品种名称繁多，可填写商品的统称。（　）

10. 批单是保险公司对已经签发保单的更改或补充。（　）

岗前培训

一、保险单缮制规范

表 9－1　保险单缮制规范

项目顺序号	填写内容	要点提示
(1)保险公司名称 Name of Insurance Company	保险公司名称	一般在保险单顶端已印好
(2)发票号 Invoice No.	本批投保货物所对应的发票号码	必须与所随附发票的发票号码一致
(3)保险单号 Policy No.	保险公司编制的保单号码	由保险公司统一编号
(4)保险单据名称 Insurance Policy	由保险公司印好单据名称	应与信用证要求单据名称一致
(5)被保险人 Insured	投保人名称或称抬头人	①信用证项下为受益人 ②托收和电汇项下为合同卖方
(6)唛头 Marks & Nos.	具体唛头或填写 As per Invoice No…	按发票、提单上的唛头填写，如无唛头，可填写“N/M”

续表

项目顺序号	填写内容	要点提示
(7)保险货物项目 Description of Goods	参照发票、提单填写,可用商品统称	应与提单、产地证的货物描述相一致
(8)数量 Quantity	参照发票、提单,填写最大外包装的总件数	散装货要注明“In Bulk”,再填写重量
(9)保险金额 Amount Insured	发票毛值加上投保加成后的金额	此栏为小写金额,一般小数点后尾数一律进为整数,即保险金额不设辅币
(10)总保险金额 Total Amount Insured	保险金额的大写	计价货币也应填写全称, 大写、小写金额必须保持一致
(11)承保险别 Conditions	本批投保货物投保的险别、依据的保险条款及版本年份	险别内容必须与信用证(合同)规定的保险条款保持一致
(12)保费 Premium	as arranged	保险公司已在此栏印好
(13)装载运输工具 Per Conveyance S. S	运输工具名称及航次	应与提单上的运输工具的名称及航次相一致。若需转船,则应分别填写一程船名和二程船名,中间用“/”分开
(14)开航日期 Slg. on or about	As per B/L	不用填写实际开航日期
(15)运输起讫地 From … To…	提单的装运港和目的港	如需转运,则应加注转运港名称
(16)保险勘查代理人 Insurance Survey Agent	目的港保险代理人的名称、详细地址及联系方式	保险勘查代理人一般由保险公司自己选定,以便收货人在出险后通知其代理人联系有关查勘和索赔事宜
(17)赔付地点 Claim payable at…	应严格按信用证规定,若没有具体规定,目的港为赔付地点	一般信用证规定在赔款偿付地点后要注明偿付所使用的货币名称
(18)保险单签发日期和地点 Date and Place of Issue	此笔保险单签发日期和签发地点	保险单的签发日期应早于运输单据日期,以证明是在货物出运前办理的投保,签发地点一般为出口商所在地
(19)保险公司签章 Authorized Signature	保险公司名称及签章	保险单只有经保险公司或其代理签章后才生效

二、保险单缮制范例

中保财产保险有限公司(1)

The People's Insurance (Property) Company of China, Ltd

发票号码
Invoice No. INVOICE NO. 123456 (2)

保险单号次
Policy No. PICC08526 (3)

海洋货物运输保险单 (4)

MARINE CARGO TRANSPORTATION INSURANCE POLICY

被保险人：
Insured： TIFERT TRADING CO., LTD (5)

中保财产保险有限公司(以下简称本公司)根据被保险人的要求,及其所缴付约定的保险费,按照本保险单承担险别和背面所载条款与下列特别条款承保下列货物运输保险,特签发本保险单。

This policy of Insurance witnesses that the People's Insurance (Property) Company of China, Ltd. (hereinafter called "The Company"), at the request of the Insured and in consideration of the agreed premium paid by the Insured, undertakes to insure the under mentioned goods in transportation subject to conditions of the Policy as per the Clauses printed overleaf and other special clauses attached hereon.

唛头 (6) Shipping Marks	保险货物项目 (7) Descriptions of Goods	数量 (8) Quantity	保险金额 (9) Amount Insured
AS PER INV. NO. 123456	GIRL JACKET	250 CARTONS	USD57750.00

总保险金额： (10)
Total Amount Insured： U. S. DOLLARS FIFTY－SEVEN THOUSAND SEVEN HUNDRED AND FIFTY ONLY

承保险别 (11)
Conditions

COVERING ALL RISKS AND WAR RISK AS PER OCEAN MARINE CARGO TRANSPORTATION CLAUSES OF C. I. C. DATED 1/1/1981.

保费
Premium as arranged (12)

载运输工具
Per Conveyance S.S SHUNFENG V.0827 (13)

开航日期
Slg. on or abt AS PER B/L (14)

起运港
From TIANJIN (15)

目的港
To TOKYO

所保货物，如发生本保险单项下可能引起索赔的损失或损坏，应立即通知本公司下述代理人查勘。如有索赔，应向本公司提交保险单正本（本保险单共有 2 份正本）及有关文件。如一份正本已用于索赔，其余正本则自动失效。(16)

In the event of loss or damage which may result in acclaim under this Policy, immediate notice must be given to the Company's Agent as mentioned hereunder. Claims, if any, one of the Original Policy which has been issued in 2 original (s) together with the relevant documents shall be surrendered to the Company. If one of the Original Policy has been accomplished, the others to be void.

PICC TOKYO BRANCH

RM101, 10TH FLOOR SUPER BUILDING, TOKYO, JAPAN

TEL: 0081－61－2458 7531

赔款偿付地点
Claim payable at TOKYO IN USD (17)

日期
Date APR. 28 ,2008 (18) 在 At TIANJIN

THE PEOPLE'S INSURANCE (PROPERTY) COMPANY OF CHINA, LTD

蒋彩石

地址：
Address：

(19)

样例 9－1 女童夹克保险单

三、缮制保险单应注意的问题

1. 保险单据的转让无需取得保险人的同意,也无需通知保险人。

2. 保险单据的出单日期不得迟于运输单据所列货物装船或发运或承运人接受监管的日期。因此,办理投保手续的日期也不得迟于货物装运日期。

3. 保险单据必须在表面上看来是由保险公司或其代理人出具并签署,银行不接受由保险经纪人签发的暂保单。

4. 中国人民保险公司可以按照CIC条款签发保险单,也可以按照ICC条款签发保险单,但不允许在一份保单内部分险别依据CIC条款,而部分险别又依据ICC条款,两者不能混用。

上岗操作

任务栏

1. 通知:公司将有以下合同项下的货物装运出口,加工厂已将货物备妥,并且已经订妥舱位,请根据有关资料缮制投保单和保险单。
2. 目的:本项任务的目的是熟悉并掌握投保单和保险单的缮制技巧。
3. 要求:下班前将缮制好的投保单和保险单交给师傅审核。

一、动脑思考

1. 泰佛贸易公司在一笔出口贸易的发票中金额显示为:

	USD12356.00
LESS 3% COM	370.68
TOTAL AMOUNT	USD11985.32

请问:业务员在向保险公司投保时,保险金额应该以发票净值还是发票毛值为基础计算投保金额?为什么?具体金额应该如何填写?

2. 泰佛贸易公司在一笔CIF出口贸易中收到国外进口商的信用证,信用证对保险条款规定为:"INSURANCE POLICY OR CERTIFICATE IN DUPLICATE FOR 110% OF TOTAL INVOICE VALUE COVERING ALL RISKS AND WAR RISK AS PER CIC DATED 1/1/1981"未规定保险单是否需背书,请问:业务员在向银行交单时,是否有必要对保险单据进行背书?为什么?

3. 泰佛贸易公司在一笔出口贸易的结汇单据中保险单的签发日期比提单日期晚

一天,但保险单中加注有这样的词句:"THE COVER IS EFFECTIVE AT THE LATEST FROM THE DATE OF SHIPMENT OF THE GOODS AT THE PLACE STATED IN THE CREDIT",请问:在这种情况下向银行交单议付,银行会提出异议吗? 为什么?

二、动手操作

1. 初级训练

泰佛贸易公司与荷兰 FASHION TOY 公司就出口毛绒玩具达成一份出口合同,现货物已经备好,且已订妥 10 月 18 日舱位,请与中国人民财产保险股份有限公司办理投保手续,依据发票(见样例 9-2)及补充信息填写投保单(见样例 9-3)。

其他补充信息如下:

(1)买卖双方在合同中约定的保险条款为:

INSURANCE POLICY OR CERTIFICATE FOR FULL INVOICE VALUE PLUS 10% COVERING INSTITUTE CARGO CLAUSES (A) AND WAR CLAUSES OF INSTITUTE CARGO DATED 1/1/1982

(2)中国人保在阿姆斯特丹的代理为:

AGENT OF INSURANCE AT AMSTERDAM

THE PEOPLE'S INSURANCE COMPANY OF CHINA AMSTERDAM BRANCH

530#, ARIL ST. AMSTERDAM,

THE NETHERLANDS

电话:00315487665　传真:00315487666

(3)经查,毛绒玩具投保一切险的费率为 5‰

(4)保险单号次为:PICCSH088784

Issuer UNIVERSAL TRADING CO., LTD NO.6, ZHONGSHAN ROAD, SHANGHAI, CHINA	商 业 发 票 **COMMERCIAL INVOICE**		
To FASHION TOY CO., LTD NO. 56, TIMES STREET, AMSTERDAM NETHERLAND	No.: UNI08G0056	Date: OCT.12, 2008	
Transport Details SHIPPED PER S.S. PU HE VOY. 0011W FROM SHANGHAI CHINA TO AMSTERDAM NETHERLAND BY SEA	S/C No. 08UN128	L/C No.	
	Terms of payment 30% BY T/T IN ADVANCE, 70% BY D/P AT SIGHT		

Marks and numbers	Number and kind of packages, Description of goods	Quantity	Unit price	Amount
			CIF AMSTERDAM	
FASHION TOY 08UN128 AMSTERDAM CTN NO.1-930 MADE IN CHINA	930 CARTONS PLUSH TOYS ART NO.0042	18600PCS	USD1.85/PC	USD34 410.00

TIFERT TRADING CO., LTD

王宏

样例9－2 商业发票

海运出口货物投保单

1)保险人

2)被保险人

3)标记	4)包装及数量	5)保险货物项目	6)保险货物金额

7)总保险金额(大写)

8)运输工具 (船名) (航次)

9)装运港

10)目的港

11)投保险别

12)保险代理人

13)赔付地点

14)货物起运日期

15)投保日期

16)投保人签字

17)应缴保费

样例9-3 空白投保单

2. 中级训练

泰佛贸易公司与意大利 BIG TOWER 公司经过友好洽商，就出口台布达成一份出口合同，数量 5000 打，CIF GENOA，付款方式即期信用证（L/C at sight）。随后，泰佛贸易公司向中国人民保险公司进行投保，提交投保单。中国人民保险公司向泰佛贸易公司出具了保险单。作为保险公司的业务员，请你根据信用证（见样例 9－4）有关条款及补充信息缮制保险单（见样例 9－5）。

信用证中与提单相关的主要条款如下：

59：BENEFICIARY：　TIFERT TRADING CO.，LTD
NO.86，ZHUJIANG ROAD，TIANJIN，CHINA

50：APPLICANT：　BIG TOWER CORP
88，TOWER BUILDING，GENOA，ITALY

44E：LOADING ON BOARD/DISPATCH/TAKING IN CHARGE AT/FROM…TIANJIN

44F：FOR TRANSPORTATION TO　GENOA

44C：NOT LATER THAN 31ST MAY，2008

45A：DESCRIPTION OF GOODS/SERVICE

TABLE CLOTH　ART NO. T168 2000DOZ USD11.50/PC
ART NO. T294 3000DOZ USD12.80/PC
CIF LONDON
PACKING IN CARTONS OF 10PCS EACH

SHIPPING MARKS：　BIG TOWER
S/C NO. TF368
GENOA
NO. 1－UP

46A：DOCUMENTS REQUIRED

+MARINE INSURANCE POLICY OF CERTIFICATE IN DUPLICATE，ENDORSED IN BLANK，FOR 110% OF THE INVOICE COST INCLUDING OCEAN MARINE CARGO CLAUSES（ALL RISKS），OCEAN MARINE CARGO WAR RISK CLAUSES AND OCEAN MARINE CARGO STRIKES RISKS AND CIVIL COMMOTIONS CLAUSES OF THE PEOPLE'S INSURANCE COMPANY OF CHINA INCLUDING WAREHOUSE TO WAREHOUSE CLAUSE，CLAIMS PAYABLE IN GENOA IN CURRENCY OF DRAFTS.

样例 9－4　信用证

其他补充信息如下：

（1）INV. NO.　：　TJ8526
（2）POLICY NO.　：　PICC8526
（3）投保日期　：　MAY15，2008
（4）船名航次　：　SHUNFENG V55
（5）保险代理人　：　GENOA INSURANCE CO LTD
12，DONG JIN STREET，GENOA，ITALY.
TEL：0039 2 3789 4598
ATN：MR MARAY

PICC 中国人民财产保险股份有限公司

货物运输保险单 CARGO TRANSPORTATION INSURANCE POLICY

发票号码
Invoice No.

保险单号次
Policy No.

被保险人：
Insured：

中保财产保险有限公司(以下简称本公司)根据被保险人的要求及其所缴付约定的保险费,按照本保险单承担险别和背面所载条款与下列特别条款承保下列货物运输保险,特签发本保险单。

This policy of Insurance witnesses that the People's Insurance (Property) Company of China, Ltd. (hereinafter called "The Company"), at the request of the Insured and in consideration of the agreed premium paid by the Insured, undertakes to insure the under mentioned goods in transportation subject to conditions of the Policy as per the Clauses printed overleaf and other special clauses attached hereon.

唛头 Shipping Marks	保险货物项目 Descriptions of Goods	数量 Quantity	保险金额 Amount Insured

总保险金额：
Total Amount Insured：

承保险别
Conditions

保费
Premium ______________ 载运输工具
Per Conveyance S.S ______ 开航日期
Slg. on or abt ______________

起运港
Form ______________ 目的港
To ______________

所保货物，如发生本保险单项下可能引起索赔的损失或损坏，应立即通知本公司下述代理人查勘。如有索赔，应向本公司提交保险单正本（本保险单共有　　份正本）及有关文件。如一份正本已用于索赔，其余正本则自动失效。

In the event of loss or damage which may result in acclaim under this Policy, immediate notice must be given to the Company's Agent as mentioned hereunder. Claims, if any, one of the Original Policy which has been issued in original (s) together with the relevant documents shall be surrendered to the Company. If one of the Original Policy has been accomplished, the others to be void.

赔款偿付地点
Claim payable at

日期
Date ______________ 在
at ______________

地址：
Address：______________

样例 9-5　空白保险单

3. 高级训练

上海衣箱制造有限公司与丹麦 POWER CASSES/SAFE PRODUCTS 公司经过友好洽商，就出口衣箱达成一出口合同，数量 5600 件，CIF COPENHAGEN，付款方式为电汇加托收(T/T + D/P AT SIGHT)。随后，上海衣箱制造有限公司向中国平安保险公司投保，提交投保单。中国平安保险公司接受其投保后，向上海衣箱制造有限公司签发了保险单。你作为保险公司的业务员，请根据合同 TT6321(见样例 9－6)及补充信息缮制保险单(见样例 9－7)。

其他补充信息如下：

(1)发票号：ES2008502

(2)保险单号：PA200856

(3)提单日期：NOV 28，2008

(4)船名航次：SHUNFENG V728

(5)保险代理人：PING AN INSURANCE CO.，LTD. COPENHAGEN BRANCH
HOERKAER 34，2730 HERLEV，DENMARK

SALES CONTRACT

S/C No.: TT6321

Date: OCT 18, 2008

The Seller: SHANGHAI SUITCASE MANUFACTURE CO., LTD

Add: 3188 JINJIANG ROAD, SHANGHAI, CHINA

The Buyer: POWER CASSES/SAFE PRODUCTS APS

Add: PROEVENSVEJ 27, DK-2610 ROEDOVRE, COPENHAGEN, DEMARK

The seller agrees to sell and the buyer agrees to buy the under mentioned goods on the terms and conditions stated below:

(1)Marks & Nos.	(2) Commodity & Specifications	(3)Quantity (piece)	(4)Unit Price (USD)	(5)Total Amount (USD)
POWER TT6321 COPENHAGEN No.1-100	SUITCASE	5600PCS	USD2.43/PC CIF COPENHAGEN	USD13608.00
Total Value: THIRTEEN THOUSAND SIX HUNDRED AND EIGHT ONLY.				

(6) Time of Shipment: DURING NOV., 2008

(7) Port of Loading: SHANGHAI, CHINA

(8) Port of Destination: COPENHAGEN, DEMARK

(9) Insurance: TO BE COVERED BY THE SELLER FOR 110% OF CIF VALUE COVERING ALL RISKS AND WAR RISK AS PER OCEAN MARIN CARGO CLAUSES OF PICC DATED 1/1/1981.

(10) Terms of Payment: 30% BY T/T IN ADVANCE, 70% BY D/P AT SIGHT

(11) Packing: 56PCS TO A CARTON

Seller(signature):　　　　Buyer(signature):

王强　　　　Olsen

样例 9－6　销售合同

中国平安保险股份有限公司

PING AN INSURANCE COMPANY OF CHINA LTD.

货 物 运 输 保 险 单

CARGO TRANSPORTATION INSURANCE POLICY

被保险人
Insured:

中国平安保险股份有限公司根据被保险人的要求及其所交付约定的保险费，按照本保险单背面所载条款与下列特款，承保下述货物运输保险，特立本保险单。

This Policy of Insurance witnesses that **PING AN INSURANCE COMPANY OF CHINA, LTD.**, at the request of the Insured and in consideration of the agreed premium paid by the Insured, undertakes to insure the under mentioned goods in transportation subject to the conditions of Policy as per the clauses printed overleaf and other special clauses attached hereon.

保单号
Policy No.

赔款偿付地点
Claim Payable at

发票或提单号
Invoice No. or B/L No.

运输工具
Per Conveyance S.S.

查勘代理人
Survey By:

起运日期
Slg. on or abt.

自
From

至
To

保险金额
Amount Insured

保险货物项目、标记、数量及包装：
Description, Marks, Quantity & Packing of Goods:

承保条件
Condition:

签单日期
Date:

For and on behalf of
PING AN INSURANCE COMPANY OF CHINA, LTD.

Authorized Signature

复核：

制单

地址及电话

Address & Tel.

注：未加盖本公司保单专用章，保单无效。

样例9－7　空白保险单

任务十 缮制其他单据

岗前测试

一、单选题

> 温馨提示：
>
> 其他单据是国际贸易中常用的结汇单据之一，单据的种类繁多，缮制也比较灵活。依据证明内容的不同，可冠以不同的单据名称。

1. 在 FOB 或 CFR 条件下，一般要求出口商在货物离开启运港（地）后两个工作日内向进口商发出（ ），进口商需要据此为进口货物办理保险手续。

A. 受益人证明函 B. 寄样证明
C. 装船通知 D. 船龄证明

2. 主要说明航程中船舶停靠港口的证明是（ ）。

A. 船级证明 B. 货装具名船舶证明
C. 航程证明 D. 船长收据

3. 信用证中规定："The vessel carrying the goods is not Israeli and will not call on any Israeli ports while carrying the goods and that the vessel is not banned entry to the port of the Arab States for any reasons under whatever the laws and regulations of such Sates allowed"。该证明是（ ）。

A. 航程证明 B. 黑名单证明 C. 船籍证明 D. 船长收据

4. 信用证中规定："Shipping company's certificate stating that the carrying vessel has entered P&I Club and should be attached with the original documents"，该证明是（ ）。

A. 船籍证明 B. 货装具名船舶证明
C. 船级证明 D. 航运组织证明

5. 有些地区开来的信用证规定："Class certificate certifying that the shipment is made by a seaworthy vessel which are classified 100 A1 issued by Lloyds or equivalent classification society"，该证明是（ ）。

A. 黑名单证明 B. 船籍证明 C. 航程证明 D. 船级证明

6. 装船通知应该及时、充分，以便买方及时办理（ ）。

A. 订舱手续 B. 保险手续 C. 报关手续 D. 报检手续

7. 装运通知可细分为两种，一种是在装运前由买方发给卖方的，英文名称是（ ）。

A. SHIPPING INSTRUCTION B. SHIPPING DOCUMENTS
C. SHIPPING SAMPLE D. SHIPPING ADVICE

8. 装运通知可细分为两种,一种是在装运后由卖方发给买方的,英文名称是(　)。

A. SHIPPING INSTRUCTION　　B. SHIPPING DOCUMENTS

C. SHIPPING SAMPLE　　D. SHIPPING ADVICE

9. 如信用证规定装船后立即发装运通知("Immediately after shipment"),一般应掌握在提单后(　)内发送。

A. 一天　　B. 二天　　C. 三天　　D. 四天

10. 一般而言,装运通知除发送给进口商外,还可以发送给(　)。

A. 船公司　　B. 货代公司　　C. 保险公司　　D. 付款行

二、多选题

1. 发送装船通知的作用为(　)。

A. 办理货运保险　　B. 以便对方准备付款、赎单

C. 以便了解货物品质　　D. 便于船货衔接

2. 受益人向船公司或其代理人可索取的证明有(　)。

A. 船籍证明　　B. 航程证明　　C. 船龄证明　　D. 船级证明

3. 受益人证明主要包括(　)。

A. 装运证明　　B. 寄单证明　　C. 寄样证明　　D. 包装证明

4. 航运组织和公约证明通常包括(　)。

A. 寄单证明　　B. 黑名单证明

C. 安全符合证书　　D. 班轮公会证明

5. 受益人证明的主要作用包括(　)。

A. 向有关方面证实某件事实

B. 作为议付单据之一

C. 证明已经履行某种义务或完成某项工作

D. 向卖方进行索赔的依据

小贴士:

1. 船公司证明的种类很多,应依照合同或信用证的规定,要求船公司出具相关证明。如要求船龄证明,就必须签发船龄证明,而不能以船籍证明替代。
2. 缮制船公司证明不能完全照抄信用证条款内容,应具体化并在人称、时态等方面作相应变化。
3. 船公司证明签发日期一般与运输单据签发日期相同,或略晚些。
4. 船公司证明本身的性质决定其必须要签署。

三、判断题

1. 装运通知(Shipping Advice)是货物离开启运港(地)后,由出口商发送给进口商,通知后者一定数量的货物已经启运的通知文件。(　)

2. 有些国家或地区来证规定货物必须装载某国籍的船舶或禁止装载某国籍的船舶时,受益人在租船订舱时就必须考虑此要求,同时要求船公司或船代出具船级证明。(　)

3. 有的信用证规定,样品或单据副本交载货船舶的船长带交进口商,为满足信用证的这一规定,可要求船长出具运费收据,用于出口商向银行议付货款。(　)

4. 受益人证明通常是指信用证受益人根据信用证的要求出具的证明受益人已经履行了合同或信用证规定义务的证明。(　)

5. 其他单据是出口业务中常用的结汇单据之一,依据证明的内容不同,可冠以不同的单据名称。(　)

6. 有些国家或地区来证规定装载货物的船舶船龄不得超过15年,受益人必须要求船代或船公司出具载货船只的船龄证明书才能满足信用证要求,否则影响安全收汇。(　)

7. 如信用证要求:"A certificate from the shipping company or its agent stating that goods are shipped by APL",该证明是船籍证明。(　)

8. 信用证要求:"A certificate issued by the carrier, shipping Co or their agents certifying that shipment has been effected by conference line and/or regular line vessels only covered by institute classification clause to accompany the documents",该证明是班轮公会证明。(　)

9. 如果信用证没有特殊规定,证明函可以无须签署。(　)

10. 受益人证明函不能完全照抄信用证条款的内容,应具体化并在人称、时态等方面作相应变化。(　)

岗前培训

一、其他单据缮制规范

表10-1　装运通知缮制规范

项目顺序号	填写内容	要点提示
(1)单据名称 Name of Doc	Shipping Advice	应与信用证要求的单据名称一致
(2)日期 Date	发送装运通知的时间	一般与提单日期相同或略晚于提单日期
(3)通知对象 To	开证人或其他	按信用证要求填写

续 表

项目顺序号	填写内容	要点提示
(4)声明或证明文句 Statement	声明货物已出运	按信用证要求填写
(5)通知内容 Contents	合同号、信用证号、品名、数量、运输工具、开航日期、装运港、目的港、提单号等详细内容	按信用证要求填写
(6)激励性文句 Encourage sentence	希望对方满意的文句	不是必须的部分
(7)签署 Signature	受益人签章	一般可以不签署

表 10-2 船公司证明缮制规范

项目顺序号	填写内容	要点提示
(1)单据名称 Name of Doc	Certificate	单据名称应与信用证一致
(2)日期 Date	证明的日期	一般与提单日期相同
(3)抬头人 To	To whom it may concern	不填实际当事人
(4)证明文句 Contents	需证明的内容	按照信用证要求并结合实际情况作出证明
(5)签署 Signature	船公司或货代公司签章	应该与提单签单人一致

表 10-3 受益人证明函缮制规范

项目顺序号	填写内容	要点提示
(1)单据名称 Name of Doc	Certificate	单据名称应与信用证一致
(2)日期 Date	证明日期	应符合信用证规定
(3)发票号 Invoice No.	发票号码	
(4)抬头人 To	To whom it may concern	不填实际当事人
(5)证明文句 Contents	需证明的内容	应符合信用证规定，注意人称、时态、语态的变化
(6)签署 Signature	受益人签章	证明函无论信用证是否要求签署，必须要签署

二、其他单据缮制范例

TIANJIN TIFERT TRADING CO., LTD

NO. 86, ZHUJIANG ROAD, TIANJIN, CHINA

SHIPPING ADVICE (1)

TO: MARUBENI CORP. (3)　　　　DATE: APR 30, 2008 (2)

DEAR SIR,

WE ARE PLEASED TO INFORM YOU THAT THE FOLLOWING MENTIONED GOODS HAS BEEN SHIPPED OUT, FULL DETAILS AS FOLLOWS: (4)

1.COMMODITY: GIRL JACKET
2. QUANTITY: 250 CARTONS
3. BILL OF LADING NO.: SINO081216
4. OCEAN VESSEL: SHUNFENG V.0827 (5)
5. PORT OF LOADING: TIANJIN, CHINA
6. DATE OF SHIPPMENT: APR.30, 2008
7. PORT OF DESTINATION: TOKYO, JANPAN
8. TOTAL AMOUNT: USD52500.00
9. MARKS AND NUMBER ON B/L: MARUBENI
S/C 08TF0858
TOKYO
CTN 1-250

WE HOPE YOU ARE SATISFIED WITH THE QUALITY OF OUR GOODS AND LOOK FORWARD TO RECEIVING YOUR REPEAT ORDER SOON. (6)

TIFERT TRADING CO., LTD
泰佛贸易有限公司
*

(7)

王 宏

样例 10-1 女童夹克装运通知

CERTIFICATE OF VESSEL'S AGE (1)

TIANJIN，APR 30, 2008 (2)

TO: WHOM IT MAY CONCERN: (3)

THIS IS TO CERTIFY THAT THE M.S./S.S. SHUNFENG V.0827 WAS BUILT IN YEAR 1998 AND HAS THEREFORE NOT BEEN IN OPERATION FOR MORE THAN 15 YEARS AT TIME OF CARGO LOADING. (4)

SINOTRANS TIANJIN COMPANY

张涛 (5)

样例 10－2 女童夹克船公司证明

TIANJIN TIFERT TRADING CO., LTD

NO. 86, ZHUJIANG ROAD, TIANJIN, CHINA

CERTIFICATE (1)

DATE: APR 30, 2008 (2)

INVOICE NO: 123456 (3)

TO: WHOM IT MAY CONCERN (4)

WE CERTIFY THAT 1/3 ORIGINAL B/L AND ONE SET OF NON-NEGOTIABLE SHIPPING DOCUEMENTS HAVE BEEN SENT TO MARUBENI CORP WITHIN 48 HOURS AFTER SHIPMENT.

(5)

TIFERT TRADING CO., LTD

泰佛贸易有限公司

*

(6)

样例 10－3 女童夹克受益人证明函

三、缮制其他单据应注意的问题

1. 出口商应及时缮制装运通知,并严格按合同或信用证要求的时间发送装运通知。

2. 装运通知应该充分,以便买方或保险公司及时办理保险手续。信用证要求通知的内容必须一一列出,可以比信用证详尽,但不能与其他单据相同的信息相矛盾。

3. 证明函不能完全照抄信用证条款内容,应具体化并在人称、时态等方面作相应变化。

4. 证明函本身的性质决定该单据需要由受益人签署。

上岗操作

任务栏

1. 通知:公司有以下合同项下的货物装运出口,请根据有关资料缮制装运通知、船公司证明及受益人证明函。
2. 目的:本项任务的目的是熟悉并掌握装运通知、船公司证明或及益人证明函的缮制技巧。
3. 要求:下班前将缮制好的装运通知、船公司证明及受益人证明函交给师傅审核。

一、动脑思考

1. 泰佛贸易公司收到国外客户通过银行开立的信用证,来证规定:"Beneficiary is to fax Mr. . . . stating L/C No. , quantity shipped, name of vessel & ETD within 5 days after shipment, a copy of this fax must accompany the documents for negotiation."请问:该条款中提及"a copy of this fax"实际上指的是什么单据?受益人在缮制该单据时应该注意什么?如果向银行议付时遗漏提交"a copy of this fax",后果如何?

2. 泰佛贸易公司收到国外客户通过银行开立的信用证,来证规定:"One copy of invoice, packing list and original GSP Form A to be sent direct to applicant immediately after shipment and beneficiary's certificate to this effect and relative postal receipt should be required for negotiation",请问:一般情况下,受益人应该在装船后几日内将单据寄给开证申请人?除了按照要求邮寄单据外,在向银行议付货款时应提供哪些单据才能符合信用证要求?

3. 泰佛贸易公司在一笔信用证付款方式下的出口业务中,向银行议付货款时遭银行拒付并收到拒付电一纸。拒付理由是:漏提交"captain's receipt"。泰佛贸易公司于是仔细地核对留底单据与信用证,发现在信用证 47A 附加条件中有一条款规定为:"Full set of non – negotiable shipping documents to be sent to the captain of the carrying vessel and handed over to Messrs. × × × and captain's receipt accompanied by the original documents for negotiation."泰佛贸易公司认为银行拒付没有道理,于是与银行据理力

争,理由之一是该单据并没有出现在需要单据(46A:DOCUMENTS REQUIRED)条款中,而是出现在其他附加条件(47A:ADDITIONAL CONDITION),故没有必要提交该单据。你认为泰佛贸易公司的理由成立吗?为什么?在什么情况下泰佛贸易公司的理由才成立?请举例说明。

二、动手操作

1. 初级训练

泰佛贸易公司与澳大利亚一服装进口商(TIMES FASHION GARMENT CO. ,LTD)达成一批时装出口业务,信用证要求在大货出运前将船前样快递给客户确认,并出具寄样证明作为结汇单据之一。信用证具体条款是:Pre - shipment samples including different styles, different colors and different sizes to be sent direct by courier service to buyer before shipment and beneficiary's certificate to this effect is required. 作为单证员,请你按照信用证要求缮制寄样证明(见样例 10 - 4)。

TIFERT TRADING CO., LTD

NO. 86, ZHUJIANG ROAD, TIANJIN, CHINA

CERTIFICATE

DATE:

....

Authorized Signature

样例 10 - 4　空白寄样证明

2. 中级训练

泰佛贸易公司与挪威 Kuffert Kompagniet 公司经过友好洽商，就出口野餐篮子达成一份出口合同，数量 5000 套，CFR OSLO，付款方式即期信用证（L/C at sight），要求出运后发送装运通知给 Kuffert Kompagniet 公司以便办理投保手续。现在泰佛贸易公司已经完成交货义务，将 5000 套野餐篮子装上 2008 年 8 月 28 日开航的“EASTWIND VOY18”提单号为 COSO9969，作为单证员，请你根据信用证要求和补充信息缮制装运通知（见样例 10－5）。

信用证中与提单相关的主要条款如下：

27：SEQUENCE OF TOTAL　　1/1
40A：FORM OF DOC CREDIT　　IRREVOCABLE
40E：APPLICABLE RULES　　UCP LATEST VERSION
20：DOC CREDIT NUMBER　　QC08－0014578
59：BENEFICIARY　　TIFERT TRADING CO.，LTD
NO. 86，ZHUJIANG ROAD，TIANJIN，CHINA
50：APPLICANT　　KUFFERT KOMPAGNIET
BANEMARKSVEJ 50，NW－2605 BROENDBY，
NORWAY
32B：CURRENCY CODE，AMOUNT　　EUR8980.00
44E：LOADING ON BOARD/DISPATCH/TAKING IN CHARGE AT/FROM…TIANJIN
44F：FOR TRANSPORTATION TO　　OSLO
44C：NOT LATER THAN AUG 30，2008
45A：DESCRIPTION OF GOODS/SERVICE
PICNIC BASKETS　STYLE PB1158 5000SETS USD15.80/SET
CFR OSLO
PACKING IN CARTONS OF 1SET EACH
DETAILS AS PER S/C NO.08MM0965 DATED 5/7/2008
SHIPPING MARKS：KUFFERT
S/C NO.08MM0965
OSLO
NO.1－UP
MADE IN CHINA
46A：DOCUMENTS REQUIRED
＋SHIPMENT ADVICE WITH FULL DETAILS INCLUDING CTN NUMBERS，VESSEL'S NAME，B/L NUMBER，VALUE AND QUANTITY OF GOODS，SHIPPING MARKS MUST BE SENT ON THE DATE OF SHIPMENT TO APPLICANT.

SHIPPING ADVICE

DATE:

TO:

DEAR SIR，

RE: L/NO.

WE ARE PLEASED TO INFORM YOU THAT THE FOLLOWING MENTIONED GOODS HAS BEEN SIPPED OUT，FULL DETAILS FOLLOWS:

1.COMMODITY:

2. QUANTITY:

3. NUMBER OF KIND OF PACKAGES:

4. BILL OF LADING NO.:

5. OCEAN VESSEL:

6. PORT OF LOADING:

7. DATE OF SHIPPMENT:

8. PORT OF DESTINATION:

9. TOTAL AMOUNT:

10. SHIPPING MARKS:

WE HOPE YOU ARE SATISFIED WITH THE QUALITY OF OUR GOODS AND LOOK FORWARD TO RECEIVING YOUR REPEAT ORDER SOON.

....

Authorized Signature

样例 10 –5　空白装船通知

3. 高级训练

泰佛贸易公司与科威特一贸易商就出口毛毯达成一份出口合同，信用证规定货物需装中国籍船舶，并列举经停的港口且这些港口非属阿拉伯黑名单，其具体条款如下：

46A：DOCUMENTS REQUIRED

+SHIPPING COMPANY'S CERTIFICATE EVDENCING THAT THE CARRYING VESSEL FLYING THE FLAG OF P. R OF CHINA, FROM TIANJIN TO KUWAIT CALLING AT FOLLOWING PORTS DURING THIS PRESENT VOYAGE ACCORDING TO THE SCHEDULE, AND THAT THE VESSEL IS NOT BLACK LISTED BY THE ARABIAN COUNTRIES.

(1) HONGKONG

(2) DAMMAM

(3) BANGKOK

(4) SINGAPORE

(5) KARACHI

(6) DUBAI

货物已由中国籍的"TIANHE RIVER"装运出口，作为公司单证员，请你按照信用证要求缮制船公司证明（见样例10－6）。

CERTIFICATE

Date:

To whom it may concern:

....

Authorized Signature

样例10－6　空白船公司证明函

任务十一　缮制汇票

岗前测试

一、单选题

> 温馨提示：
>
> 汇票是无条件的支付命令，是国际贸易中使用最多的支付工具，它具有流通性、无因性等特点，是一种金融单据，为了不影响其流通转让，在实际业务中，汇票的缮制质量要求高，一般不允许有涂改的痕迹。

一、单选题

1. 如果一张汇票的出票日期为9月28日，见票后60天付款，则到期日为(　)。

A. 11月28日　　B. 11月30日

C. 11月27日　　D. 11月29日

2. 在假远期信用证支付方式下，受益人开具远期汇票，其利息由(　)负担。

A. 开证行　　B. 受益人

C. 开证人　　D. 付款行

3. 在其他条件相同的前提下，(　)的远期汇票对收款人最为有利。

A. 出票后30天后付款　　B. 货到目的港后30天付款

C. 见票后30天付款　　D. 提单签发日后30天付款

4. 信用证上若未注明汇票的付款人，根据《跟单信用证统一惯例UCP600》的规定，汇票的付款人应该是(　)。

A. 开证人　　B. 开证行　　C. 议付行　　D. 出口人

5. 由出口商签发的要求银行在一定时间内付款的汇票不可能是(　)。

A. 商业汇票　　B. 银行汇票　　C. 远期汇票　　D. 即期汇票

6. 国际贸易中经常使用的汇票多为(　)。

A. 光票　　B. 商业跟单汇票　　C. 银行汇票　　D. 银行承兑汇票

7. 托收和信用证两种支付方式使用的汇票都是商业汇票，都是通过银行收款，(　)。

A. 托收属于商业信用，信用证属于银行信用

B. 托收属于银行信用，信用证属于商业信用

C. 两者都属于商业信用

D. 两者都不属于银行信用

8. 汇票的抬头人有不同的形式，其中使用最多的是(　)。

A. 限制性抬头　　B. 指示性抬头　　C. 来人抬头　　D. 以上均不对

9. 商业汇票的出票人应该是(　)。

A. 进口商　　B. 进口地银行　　C. 出口地银行　　D. 出口商

10. 在国际货款结算业务中,需要办理承兑手续的汇票必然是(　)。

A. 远期汇票　　B. 即期汇票　　C. 商业汇票　　D. 银行汇票

二、多选题

1. 汇票与本票的区别在于(　)。

A. 前者是无条件支付命令,后者是无条件的支付承诺

B. 前者的当事人有三个,后者的当事人为两个

C. 前者在使用过程中可能有承兑,后者无须承兑

D. 前者的主债务人会因承兑而变化,后者的主债务人不会变化

2. 下列说法中,正确的是(　)。

A. 汇票有即期和远期之分　　B. 汇票的当事人有三个

C. 远期汇票承兑后可以贴现　　D. 汇票的付款人是出票人

3. 常见的规定远期汇票起算日期的方法有(　)。

A. 自开证日起算　　B. 自出票日起算

C. 自提单日起算　　D. 自见票日起算

4. 汇票背书的方式主要有(　)。

A. 限制性背书　　B. 空白背书

C. 指示性背书　　D. 记名背书

5. 汇票的收款人也叫抬头人,一般有以下几种表示方式(　)。

A. 记名抬头　　B. 限制性抬头

C. 指示性抬头　　D. 来人抬头

小贴士:

远期汇票的到期日一般掌握如下原则:

1. 无论起始日期之前用"after"或"from",均应从单据日期、装运日期或其他事件的次日起起算,不包括提及的日期在内,除非信用证特别规定包括该日。

2. 如期限按月计算,到期日应为付款当月的相同日期。如果没有相同日期,则到期日按当月的最后一天掌握。如见票为JAN31,见票后1个月、3个月付款的到期日分别为FEB28/29、APR30。

3. 信用证要求远期汇票,而提单上有多个装船批注,且所有装船批注均显示货物是从一个信用证允许的地理区域或地区装运,则将使用最早的装船批注日期计算汇票到期日。而一张汇票项下提交了不止一套提单,则最晚的提单日期将被用来计算汇票的到期日。

4. 到期日适逢节假日,则顺延至节假日后第一个营业日。

三、判断题

1. 信用证支付方式属于银行信用，所使用的汇票必然是银行汇票。(　)

2. 如果信用证未规定汇票的付款人，则应该理解为开证行是付款人。(　)

3. 追索(Recourse)是指汇票等票据遭到拒付时，持票人要求其前手背书人、出票人、承兑人等清偿汇票金额及有关费用的行为。(　)

4. 一张商业汇票上的收款人是"仅付给 ABC 有限公司"(Pay to ABC Co., Ltd Only)，这种汇票不能转让。(　)

5. 汇票经背书后，汇票的收款权利转让给被背书人，被背书人若日后遭拒付，可向前手行使追索权。(　)

6. 汇票、本票、支票均有即期和远期之分。(　)

7. 信用证支付方式下，汇票的付款人可以是开证申请人。(　)

8. 由于银行信用高于商业信用，所以银行承兑过的汇票比较容易被接受而给予贴现，或用以质押。(　)

9. 汇票按付款期限可分为即期和远期汇票，前者为见票即付；后者在未到期之前，持票人可以办理贴现，以便获取融资。(　)

10. 银行汇票的出票人是银行，付款人可以是银行，也可以是企业或个人。(　)

岗前培训

一、汇票缮制规范

表 11－1　汇票缮制规范

项目顺序号	填写内容	要点提示
(1)单据名称 Name of Doc	Bill of Exchange, Exchange 或 Draft	一般已印妥
(2)汇票编号 No.	此笔业务的发票号	与商业发票上的发票号保持一致
(3)日期和地点 Place and date	汇票的出票地点和日期	①出票地点一般为议付行和出票人所在地点 ②出票日期应在提单日后，信用证有效期和交单期前
(4)小写金额 Amount in figure	支付货币名称缩写和阿拉伯数字构成	不得超过信用证最高限额

续　表

项目顺序号	填写内容	要点提示
(5)付款期限 Tenor	①即期付款,在At和Sight之间填写＊＊＊或－－－ ②远期付款,在At和Sight之间填写具体的期限	远期付款的几种表示方法: ①见票后×××天付款 ②出票后×××天付款 ③提单日后×××天付款 ④指定日期付款
(6)收款人 Payee	①限制性抬头 ②指示性抬头,指示性抬头便于流通转让 ③来人抬头	①Pay to ×××only ②Pay to the order of… ③Pay to the bearer
(7)大写金额 Amount in words	用文字叙述支付货币名称和支付的金额	①习惯上,在货币名称前加"say",在大写金额后加"only"字样 ②大小写金额保持一致
(8)出票依据 Drawn under	①信用证项下,填写开证行名称、信用证号和开证日期 ②托收项下,填写For Collection	信用证有规定的文句照抄即可
(9)付款人 Drawee	①信用证方式下,一般为开证行或信用证指定的付款人 ②托收项下,填写进口商	信用证项下不能以开证人为付款人
(10)出票人 Drawer	受益人或合同中出口商	①加盖受益人签章 ②如果要求手签,则必须亲笔签名

二、汇票缮制范例

BILL OF EXCHANGE　(1)

No. INV NO. 123456　(2)　　　　Tianjin, China. MAY 5, 2008 (3)

Exchange for　USD52500.00　(4)

At　＊　＊　＊　(5) sight of this FIRST of Exchange(SECOND of exchange being unpaid), pay to the order of　TIFERT TRADING CO., LTD ONLY (6)　the sum of

U.S. DOLLARS FIFTY-TWO THOUSAND FIVE HUNDRED ONLY　(7)

Drawn under　BANK OF TOKYO　(8)

L/C No.　A-08-0058

Date　MAR 20, 2008

To: BANK OF TOKYO　(9)

TIFERT TRADING CO., LTD
泰佛贸易有限公司
＊
(10)

样例11－1　女童夹克汇票

三、缮制汇票应注意的问题

1. 票面必须整洁、干净、清楚,金额不得涂改,不得加注与汇票无关的内容。

2. 为防备单据在邮寄途中遗失,一般远洋单据都按两次邮寄,所以,汇票都应制成一式两联,“付一不付二”或“付二不付一”,两联具有同等效力。港澳地区一次寄单,可只出一联。

3. 一般情况下,汇票的金额与发票的金额一致,除非信用证另有规定。

4. 汇票必须由受益人或卖方出具。

5. 在信用证方式下,汇票的收款人从票据法的角度看应该为受益人,受益人向银行交单时,通过背书把收款权利转让给议付行,但在实际业务中也有直接做成议付行为收款人的情况。在托收方式下汇票的收款人一般为托收行。

上岗操作

任务栏

1. 通知:公司有以下合同项下的货物已装运出口,请根据有关资料缮制汇票。
2. 目的:本项任务的目的是熟悉和掌握汇票的缮制技巧。
3. 要求:下班前将缮制好的汇票交给师傅审核。

一、动脑思考

1. 泰佛贸易公司在一笔出口贸易中收到国外进口商的信用证,该证显示:

This L/C is available with us by payment at 30 days after receipt of full set of documents at our counters.

请问:这是什么性质的信用证?你作为单证员,在缮制汇票时付款期限应如何处理?汇票的付款人是谁?

2. 泰佛贸易公司在一笔出口贸易中收到国外进口商的信用证,信用证金额为6000澳元,货描为:30M/T of Chinese Wheat at AUD200.00/MT FOB Shanghai。出口商实际发货30.5 M/T如双方同意将货款超过信用证金额的部分采用托收方式付款。

请问:你作为单证员应如何缮制汇票?需要做几套汇票?信用证项下的汇票金额如何填写?

3. 泰佛贸易公司在一笔出口贸易中收到国外进口商的信用证,证中规定:Drafts to be drawn as follows: AUD30000.00—Drafts to be drawn at sight on National Australia Bank

Ltd., Brisbane, Australia. AUD20000.00—Drafts to be drawn at 45 days' sight on National Australia Bank Ltd., Brisbane, Australia. 请问：你作为制单员应出具几套汇票？汇票的内容有哪些区别？

二、动手操作

1. 初级训练

泰佛贸易公司与中间商香港家用电器公司达成一笔洗衣机出口合同，付款方式为 D/P 即期，货物由天津直接运往科威特，现在 1000 台洗衣机已经装运出口，请根据已缮制好的商业发票（见样例 11－2）缮制汇票（见样例 11－3），并通过中国银行天津分行托收货款。

TIFERT TRADING CO.,LTD

NO. 86, ZHUJIANG ROAD, TIANJIN, CHINA

COMMERCIAL INVOICE

Invoice No.: 2008TF018　　**Date:** MAY 15, 2008

Buyer: HONGKONG HOME ELECTRIC APPLIANCES CO., LTD.
312 SOUTH BRIDGE STREET, HONGKONG

L/C No.: 08-M-34985　　**Contract No.:** BD48001

From TIANJIN　　**to** KUWAIT

Marks and No.	Description of goods	Quantity	Unit Price	Amount
A.B.C. DUBAI NO.I-1000 MADE IN CHINA	WASHING MACHINES BRAND: MEIDI ART NO. P97811　KF-23GW ART NO. P97801　KF-25GW	500PCS 500PCS 1000PCS	@HKD 1000.00 @HKD1000.00 LESS 2% COM	**FOBTIANJIN** HKD500000.00 HKD500000.00 HKD1000000.00 20000.00 HKD980000.00

TIFERT TRADING CO., LTD
泰佛贸易有限公司
*

样例 11－2　商业发票

BILL OF EXCHANGE

No. ______________________

For ______________________ ______________________________

(amount in figure) (place and date of issue)

At ______________________________ sight of this FIRST Bill of exchange (SECOND being unpaid)

pay to ____ or order the sum of

____

(amount in words)

Value received for ______________________ of ______________________

(quantity) (name of commodity)

Drawn under ____

To: ______________________ For and on behalf of

____

____

(Signature)

样例 11－3 空白汇票

2. 中级训练

泰佛贸易公司与日本 ITOCHU 公司经过友好洽商，就出口女式针织衫达成一份出口合同，数量 1500 件，CIF KOBE，付款方式即期信用证（L/C at 30 days after bill of lading date）。作为单证员，请你根据信用证（见样例 11－4）有关条款和其他补充信息缮制汇票（见样例 11－5）。

信用证中与汇票相关的主要条款如下：

27：SEQUENCE OF TATOL	1/1
40A：FORM OF DOC. CREDIT	IRREVOCABLEABLE
44E：APPLICABLE RULES	UCP LATEST VERSION
20：DOC CREDIT NUMBER	ABL－AN107
31C：DATE OF ISSUE	081015
31D DATE AND PALCE OF EXPIRY	081130 AT NEGOTIATING BANK'S COUNTER
32B AMOUNT	CURRENCY GBP AMOUNT 16500,00
59：BENEFICIARY：	TIFERT TRADING CO., LTD NO.86, ZHUJIANG ROAD, TIANJIN, CHINA
50：APPLICANT：	ITOCHU CORP

	88, RED SUN BUILDING, TOKYO, JAPAN.
41D: AVAILABLE WITH/BY:	BANK OF CHINA, TIANJIN BRANCH BY NEGOTIATION
42C: DRAFT(S) AT:	DRAFT(S) AT 30 DAYS AFTER BILL OF LADING DATE FOR 97% OF TOTAL INVOICE VALUE
42D: DRAWEE:	MIZUHO CORPORATE BANK, LTD, TOKYO
44C: LATEST DATE OF SHIP.:	081115

样例 11-4 信用证

其他补充信息如下：

(1)发票号码为:INV. 1234

(2)发票金额为:GBP16500 00

(3)提单日期为:2008 年 11 月 10 日

(4)汇票日期为:2008 年 11 月 15 日

BILL OF EXCHANGE

No.____________________ Tianjin, China.____________

Exchange for

At____________sight of this FIRST of Exchange(SECOND of exchange being npaid) ,pay to order of ______________________________

the sum of

1

Drawn under______________________

L/C No.______________________

Date______________________

To:______________________

____

样例 11-5 空白汇票

3. 高级训练

天津福胜贸易公司与丹麦 MARMORHUSET 公司经过友好洽商,就出口家具达成一份出口合同,数量 1000 件,CIF COPENHAGEN,付款方式为电汇加托收(T/T + D/P AT SIGHT)。作为单证员,请你根据贸易合同有关条款(见样例 11-6)及其他补充信息缮制托收项下汇票(见样例 11-7),通过天津银行托收货款。

SALES CONTRACT

编号 No.: SC080216　　日期 Date : FEB16,2008

The sellers: TIANJIN FUSHENG TRADING CO., LTD

Add: NO.18 ZHUJIANG ROAD, TIANJIN,CHINA　　POST CODE: 300221

The buyers: MARMORHUSET A/S

Add: SMEDEGAARDSVEJ 6 A, TVIS, DK-7500 HOLSTEBRO, DEMARK

TEL: 0045-96135111

兹确认售予你方下列货品，其成交条款如下：

We hereby confirm having sold to you the following goods on the terms and conditions as specified below:

(1) 货物名称及规格 Name of Commodity and Specifications	(2)数量 Quantity	(3)单价 Unit price	(4)总值 Total Amount
FURNITURE			CIF COPENHAGEN
FNT110	600PCS	USD58.00	USD34800.00
FNT120	400PCS	USD46.00	USD18400.00
TOTAL:	1000PCS		USD53200.00

(5)包装：

Packing: PACKED IN ONE CARTON OF 1PC EACH

(6)装运唛头：

Shipping Mark: N/M

(7)装运期限：

Time of Shipment: NOT LATER THAN APRIL 10, 2008

(8)装运口岸：　　目的地：

Port of Shipment: TIANJIN　　Destination: COPENHAGEN

(9)付款条件：

Payment Terms: 20% T/T IN ADVANCE, THE OTHERS 80% D/P AT SIGHT.

(10)保险:卖方负责投保海运险按照 CIF 金额的 110% 投保一切险和战争险,如果发生索赔,在埃塞俄比亚用美元赔偿。

Insurance: THE SELLER SHALL ARRANGE MARINE INSURANCE COVERING ALL RISKS AND WAR RISK FOR 110% OF CIF VALUE. CLAIM, IF ANY, PAYABLE IN ETHIOPIA, IN CURRENCY OF USD.

(11)凡以 CIF 条件成交的业务,保额为发票价的 110%,投保险别以本销售合同中所开列的为限,买方如要求增加保额或保险范围应以装船前经售方同意,因此而增加的保险费由买方负责。

FOR TRANSACTIONS CONCLUDED ON CIF BASIS IT IS UNDERSTOOD THAT THE INSURANCE AMOUNT WILL BE FOR 110% OF THE INVOICE VALUE AGAINST THE RISKS SPECIFIED IN THE SALES CONTRACT, IF ADDITIONAL INSURANCE AMOUNT OR COVERAGE IS REQUIRED, THE BUYER MUST HAVE THE CONSENT OF THE SELLER BEFORE SHIPMENT, AND THE ADDITIONAL PREMIUM IS TO BE BORNE BY THE BUYER.

(12)品质/数量异议:如买方提出索赔,凡属品质异议,须于货到目的口岸之日起2个月内提出。凡属数量异议,须于货到目的口岸之日起15天内提出,对所装货物所提任何异议属于保险公司、轮船公司及期货有关运输机构所负责者,售方不负任何责任。

QUALITY/QUANTITY DISCREPANCY: IN CASE OF QUALITY DISCREPANCY, CLAIM SHOULD BE FILED BY THE BUYER WITHIN 2 MONTHS AFTER THE ARRIVAL OF THE GOODS AT THE PORT OF DESTINATION WHILE FOR QUANTITY DISCREPANCY CLAIM SHOULD BE FILED BY THE BUYER WITHIN 15 DAYS AFTER THE ARRIVAL OF THE GOODS AT THE PORT OF DESTINATION IT IS UNDERSTOOD THAT SELLER SHALL NOT BE LIABLE FOR ANY DISCREPANCY OF THE GOODS SHIPPED DUE TO CAUSES FOR WHICH THE INSURANCE COMPANY, SHIPPING COMPANY OTHER TRANSPORTATION ORGANIZATION ARE LIABLE.

(13)本合同内所述全部或部分商品,如因人力不可抗拒的原因,以致不能履约或延迟交货,售方概不负责。

THE SELLER SHALL NOT BE HELD LIABLE FOR FAILURE OR DELAY IN DELIVERY OF THE ENTIRE LOT OR PORTION OF THE GOOD S UNDER THIS SALES CONTRACT IN CONSEQUENCE OF ANY FORCE MAJEURE INCIDENTS.

确认签署 Confirmed by

MARMORHUSET A/S	TIANJIN FUSHENG TRADING CO., LTD
TOM	王强
买方(the buyers)	卖方(the sellers)

样例11-6 销售合同

其他补充信息如下:

(1)发票号码为:INV. DP0803

(2)发票日期为:2008年3月4日

(3)托收项下汇票日期为:2008年4月11日

BILL OF EXCHANGE

凭 不可撤销信用证
Drawn Under Irrevocable L/C No.
日期
Date 支取 Payable with interest @ % 按 息 付款
号码 汇票金额 天津
No. Exchange for Tianjin
见票 日后（本汇票之副本未付）付交
at sight of this FIRST of Exchange (Second of Exchange
Being unpaid) Pay to the order of
金额
the sum of

For and on behalf of
此致
To

样例 11－7 空白汇票

学习情境四　综合训练

任务十二　缮制全套单据

岗前测试

一、单选题

> 温馨提示：
>
> 国际贸易中买卖双方往往以交单代替交货，由于采用的贸易术语不同、付款方式不同、加之各个国家的通关手续不同每笔业务所需要的单据的种类、份数及缮制要求各不相同，买卖双方应该在合同中加以约定。特别是采用信用证付款方式，更应该严格按照信用证要求缮制全套单据，做到单证相符、单单相符、单内相符。

1. 除非特殊情况，通常开证行开立的信用证一般不是(　)。

A. 不可撤销信用证　　B. 议付信用证

C. 跟单信用证　　D. 预支信用证

2. 汇票的抬头人是(　)。

A. 受款人　　B. 发票的抬头人

C. 付款人　　D. 提单的收货人

3. 商业发票的抬头人一般是(　)。

A. 受益人　　B. 买方

C. 开证银行　　D. 卖方

4. 以下是出口合同中的保险条款，唯一正确的是(　)。

A. 一切险和水渍险　　B. 战争险

C. 易碎易破险　　D. 平安险

5. 航空运单(　)。

A. 代表物权，经背书可转让

B. 代表物权，但不能转让

C. 不代表物权，也不能凭以向承运人提货

D. 不代表物权，但可以作为提货凭证

6. H公司以CIF贸易术语进口一批货物，国外卖方提交的海运提单上有关“运费支付”一项应写成(　)。

A. Freight Prepaid　　B. Freight as Arranged

C. Freight Collect　　D. Freight Payable at Destination

7. 在集装箱运输中，能够实现“门到门”运输的集装箱货物交接方式是(　)。

A. LCL/LCL　　B. FCL/FCL　　C. LCL/FCL　　D. FCL/LCL

8. 下面四份海运提单,收货人填写不同,其中( )需托运人背书。

A. To Order

B. Pay to ABC Co., Ltd

C. To Order of Applicant

D. To Order of issuing bank

9. 根据《跟单信用证统一惯例 UCP600》的规定,如买卖合同规定立即装运,开来信用证的装运期规定为"尽速装运",该装运期应理解为(　)。

A. 开证行开出信用证之日起 30 天内装运

B. 通知行通知信用证之日起 30 天内装运

C. 受益人收到信用证之日起 30 天内装运

D. 银行将不予受理

10. 信用证的汇票条款注明"drawn on us",则汇票的付款人是(　)。

A. 开证申请人　　B. 开证行　　C. 议付行　　D. 受益人

二、多选题

1. 信用证的特点包括(　)。

A. 银行信用　　B. 商业信用　　C. 单据买卖　　D. 自足文件

2. 我国对外贸易货运保险包括(　)。

A. 海上运输保险　　B. 陆上运输保险　　C. 航空运输保险　　D. 邮包运输保险

3. 在我国海洋运输货物保险业务中,下列(　)险均可适用"仓至仓"条款。

A. ALL RISKS　　B. WA or WPA　　C. FPA　　D. WAR RISKS

4. 假远期信用证与远期信用证的区别是(　)。

A. 开证基础不同　　B. 付款人不同

C. 利息的负担者不同　　D. 收汇的时间不同

5. 属于逆汇法的支付方式有(　)

A. 汇款　　B. 托收　　C. 信用证　　D. 银行保函

小贴士:

必须签字、必须注明日期的单据有:

1.《UCP600》第 19、20、21、22、23 及 24 条规定的各种运输单据;

2.《UCP600》第 28 条规定的保险单据;

3. 证明、声明及能起到证明作用的单据;

4. 汇票。

三、判断题

1. 按国际保险市场惯例，大保单与小保单具有同等法律效力。(　)

2. 根据《跟单信用证统一惯例 UCP600》的规定，信用证经修改后，开证行即不可撤销地受该修改的约束，受益人收到修改通知后，原信用证的条款失效。(　)

3. 凡装在同一航次，同一条船上的货物，经同一航线同时运抵目的港，即使装运时间和装运地点不同，也不作分批装运。(　)

4. 本票可以是远期的，远期本票像远期汇票一样也存在承兑行为。(　)

5. 无论是 CIC 的战争险，还是 ICC 的战争险，都可以单独投保。(　)

6. 背对背信用证与未经保兑的可转让信用证一样对供货方有利。(　)

7. 信用证受益人收到信用证后，经审核如发现来证内容与成交合同不符，可经过通知行转告开证行，要求开证行修改不符之处。(　)

8. 偷窃提货不着险和交货不到险均在一切险范围内，所以只要投保一切险，收货人若提不到货，保险公司均应负责赔偿。(　)

9. 可转让信用证办理转让后，买卖合同也随之由第一受益人转让第二受益人。(　)

10. 在 CFR 条件下，如合同与信用证中均未规定卖方发送“装运通知”，卖方将货物在规定时间内装上海轮后，可以不必向买方发送装运通知。(　)

岗前培训

一、单证知识网络资源

在信息化高速发展的今天，我们的工作、生活和学习都和网络密切相关了。充分利用网络资源，发挥互联网的优势，使之更好地服务于学习、工作和生活，这是我们必须面对的事情，特别在终身教育的大潮下，在构建学习型社会的步伐里，面对社会的发展，我们应该学会充分利用网络资源进行学习、工作和生活。在此推荐一些比较好的单证知识网站，这里既有单证知识学习网站，也有各种职业资格证书考试网站和与单证业务操作相关的网站，更有一些单证制单软件网站，希望对大家学好单证有所帮助。

表 12－1　单证知识网络资源一览表

知识学习			
出口精英网	外贸英才论坛	精英外贸论坛	Export911(英文网站)
中华涉外网	世贸人才网	跨国外贸论坛	福步外贸论坛
东港物流网	外贸之家	起点外贸	外贸知识网

续 表

知识学习			
外贸知识网	外贸英才网	智美外贸网	国际贸易网
资格考试			
商务单证员考试	外贸跟单员考试	外贸业务员考试	中国对外经济贸易考试网
报关员考试	报检员考试	货代员考试	中华外贸网校
业务操作			
中国人民保险公司	中国银行	中华人民共和国商务部	中国对外贸易运输总公司
太平洋保险公司	国家外汇管理局	中国海关	马士基航运有限公司
中国平安保险公司	国家税务总局	产地证网上申领	中国远洋运输公司
在线广交会	国家质量监督检验检疫总局	中国电子口岸	中国国际货运网
外贸服装网	中国电子检验检疫业务网	中国进出口贸易网	中海发展股份有限公司
软件下载			
轻松制单	极限外贸制单	外贸制单系统	出口专家
外贸制单通	杰华外贸软件		

二、典型单证知识网络资源页面示例

图例 12－1　外贸精英网 http://www.cnexp.net/

图例 12－2 外贸知识网 http://www.trade－website.cn/

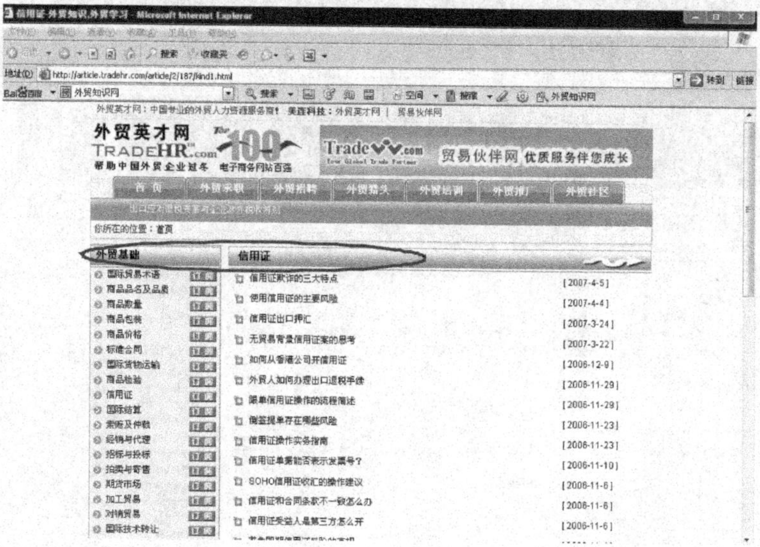

图例 12－3 外贸英才网 http://www.tradehr.com/

图例 12－4　外贸之家 http://www.waimao.org/

图例 12－5　智美外贸网 http://zmay.cn/trade/trade03/list9_1.html

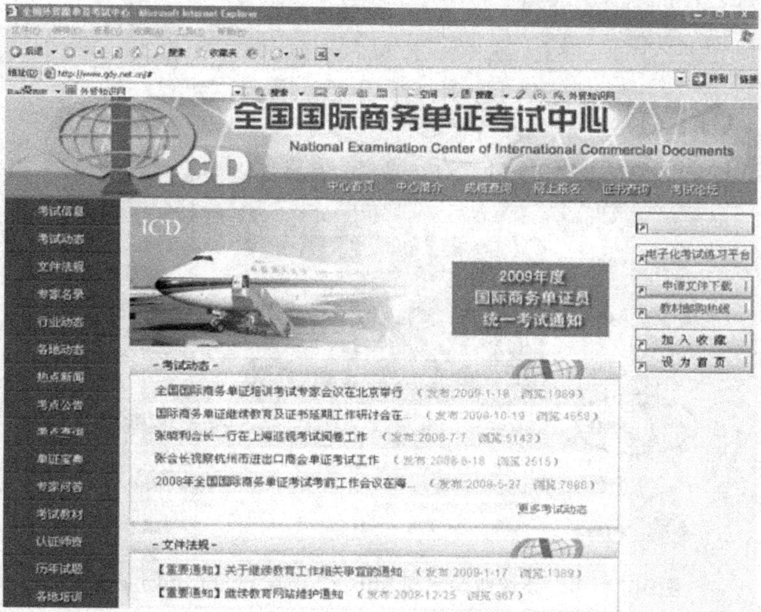

图例 12－6　国际商务单证员网 http://www.icd.net.cn/main.asp

图例 12－7　外贸跟单员网 http://www.gdy.net.cn/

图例 12 –8　外贸业务员网 http://www.chinawmks.com/

图例 12 –9　外贸服装网 http://www.wear.cn/weEnglish/DZSL

图例 12－10　商务部培训网 http://training. mofcom. gov. cn/jsp/sites

图例 12－11　轻松制单网 http://www. abin. com. cn/rjxz. htm

图例 12－12　出口专家网 http://www.51exp.com/

上岗操作

任务栏

1. 通知：公司有以下合同项下的货物已装运出口，请根据有关资料缮制全套结汇单据。

2. 目的：本项任务的目的是熟悉并掌握全套结汇单据的缮制技巧。

3. 要求：下班前将缮制好的全套结汇单据交给师傅审核。

一、动脑思考

1. 天虹食品公司向马来西亚出口 50 箱冻肉用鸡，规定航空运输。信用证要求提供已装运的航空运单（Shipped Airway Bill），天虹食品公司即按规定办理了空运，装运后交单议付。但单据到国外，开证行提出单证不符，拒绝接受。理由是信用证规定提供已装运的航空运单,而实际提供的航空运单未标明已装运字样(如类似“Shipped”等),所以不能接受。

天虹食品公司与议付行共同研究,反驳开证行并提出:我所提供的航空运单系国际上通用标准格式,运单上有两个日期,即“Executed on 28th May,2008.”和“Flight date:29th May 2008。”上述“Flight date”(起飞日期) 即可证实该批货物已装运,而且在本栏中又有民航局签章,完全符合信用证要求,请即付款。同时,天虹食品公司亦直接向买方进行说理解释工作,最后承付了货款。

请问:在此案例中,之所以开证行最后能同意付款,主要原因是什么?从中我们得出什么样的经验?请说明。

2. 2008 年 8 月天顺工业品进出口公司与英国 A 商人成交一笔交易,采用信用证付款,来证规定装运港为 CHINA PORT,货物在青岛港装船出运后,业务员在缮制提单时,在装运港栏目填写为 QINGDAO PORT,随后将全套单据交议付行议付,但单据到国外开证行后遭拒付,理由是从单据表面上看不出青岛是属于中国港口。出口商通过议付行多次与开证行进行交涉,青岛是中国主要的港口,这是任何人都知道的事实,开证行完全是无理挑剔。最后经过多方交涉,拖延了 4 个多月后开证行才同意付款,出口商损失利息达 10000 多元。请问:通过此案例,我们应该吸取什么教训?在缮制提单时如何填写装运港开证行就无懈可击了?请举例说明。

3. 南通正大集团出口一笔豆粕,合同规定以旧、修补麻袋包装。信用证对于包装条件规定:“Packed in gunny bags”(麻袋包装)。南通正大集团公司按合同规定,货物以旧、修补麻袋包装,提单按信用证规定“麻袋包装”缮制。承运人在签发提单时发现货物包装是旧袋且有修补,要求在提单上加注。南通正大集团公司考虑提单加添批注造成不清洁提单则无法议付,以为合同即规定允许货物以旧、修补麻袋包装,买方不会有异议,所以修改提单为货物以旧、修补麻袋包装。单据交议付行议付时,议付行也疏忽未发现问题,单到开证行却被拒付,其理由:信用证规定为“Packed in gunny bags.”(麻袋包装),而发票与提单却表示为“Packed in used and repaired gunny bags.”(旧、修补麻袋包装),故单证不符。南通正大集团几经交涉无果,结果以削价处理才结案。请问:通过案例,我们如何看待合同与信用证之间的关系?从中我们应吸取什么教训?

二、动手操作

1. 初级训练

大连纺织品进出口公司与韩国大宇家纺有限公司于 2008 年 5 月 8 日就台布达成一出口合同 08DRA207(见样例 12 - 1),随后,大连纺织品进出口公司抓紧按合同要求备货,并于2008年4月15日把4800条台布全部备妥,在清河轮185航次订妥舱位,货代公司要求4月18日下午5:00前把货送至大连指定仓库,下货纸号为BTB0810090,作为单证员,请你用空白单据(见样例12-2、12-3、12-4),按照合同要求缮制发票、提单和保险单等结汇单据。

SALES CONFIRMATION

卖方 DAWOO HOMETEXTILE CO. LTD.
Seller: C.P.O. BOX7155 SEOUL, KOREA

NO.: 08DRA207
DATE: MAY 20, 2008

买方 DALIAN TEXTILES IMPORT & EXPORT CORP.
Buyer: 4 YING CHUN STREET, DALIAN, CHINA

经买卖双方同意成交下列商品，订立条款如下：
This contract is made by and agreed between the BUYER and SELLER, in accordance with the terms and conditions stipulated below.

唛头 **Marks and Numbers**	名称及规格 **Description of goods**	数量 **Quantity**	单价 **Unit Price**	金额 **Amount**
DAEHO 08DRA207 KOREA CTN 1-240	TABLE CLOTH 100% COTTON 120×120CM	4800PCS	CIF DALIAN USD12.00/PC	USD57600.00

总值 **TOTAL:** U. S. DOLLARS FIFTY-SEVEN THOUSAND SIX HUNDRED ONLY.

Transshipment (转运):
□ Allowed (允许) ☒ not allowed (不允许)
Partial shipments (分批装运):
□ Allowed (允许) ☒ not allowed (不允许)
Shipment date (装运期):
NOT LATER THAN 30TH JUNE, 2008
Packing(包装):
1PC TO A PLASTIC BAG, 20BAGS TO A CARTON.
Insurance (保险):
To be covered by the SELLER FOR 110% of the invoice value covering ALL RISKS AND WAR RISK from DALIAN to BUSAN
Terms of payment (付款条件):
The buyers shall pay 30% of the sales proceeds by T/T remittance to the seller not later than MAY 5, 2008 AND 70% will be remitted to the sellers after the goods loaded on board.

THE SELLER 张天一

THE BUYER 朴金焕

样例12-1 合同

<table>
<tr><td rowspan="2">Issuer</td><td colspan="2" rowspan="2">商 业 发 票
COMMERCIAL INVOICE</td></tr>
<tr></tr>
<tr><td rowspan="2">To</td><td>No.:</td><td>Date:</td></tr>
<tr></tr>
<tr><td rowspan="2">Transport Details</td><td>S/C No.</td><td>L/C No.</td></tr>
<tr><td colspan="2">Terms of payment</td></tr>
</table>

Marks and numbers	Number and kind of packages, Description of goods	Quantity	Unit price	Amount

样例 12－2　空白发票

Shipper	B/L No.: **BILL OF LADING ORIGINAL** 中国远洋运输公司 **CHINA OCEAN SHIPPING CO**
Consignee	
Notify Party	

Pre carriage by	*Place of Receipt		
Ocean Vessel Voy. No.	Port of Loading		
Port of discharge	*Final destination	Freight payable at	Number original Bs/L
Marks and Numbers	Number and kind of packages; Description	Gross weight	Measurement

TOTAL PACKAGES(IN WORDS)

Freight and charges

Place and date of issue
Signed for the Carrier

Applicable only when document used as a Through Bill of Loading

样例 12－3　空白提单

中保财产保险有限公司

The People's Insurance (Property) Company of China, Ltd

发票号码
Invoice No.

保险单号次
Policy No.

海洋货物运输保险单

MARINE CARGO TRANSPORTATION INSURANCE POLICY

被保险人：
Insured：

中保财产保险有限公司（以下简称本公司）根据被保险人的要求，及其所缴付约定的保险费，按照本保险单承担险别和背面所载条款与下列特别条款承保下列货物运输保险，特签发本保险单。

This policy of Insurance witnesses that the People's Insurance (Property) Company of China, Ltd. (hereinafter called "The Company"), at the request of the Insured and in consideration of the agreed premium paid by the Insured, undertakes to insure the undermentioned goods in transportation subject to conditions of the Policy as per the Clauses printed overleaf and other special clauses attached hereon.

唛头 Shipping Marks	保险货物项目 Descriptions of Goods	数量 Quantity	保险金额 Amount Insured

总保险金额：
Total Amount Insured:

承保险别
Conditions

保费
Premium ____________ 载运输工具
Per conveyance S.S ____________ 开航日期
Slg. on or abt ____________

起运港
From ____________ 目的港
To ____________

所保货物，如发生本保险单项下可能引起索赔的损失或损坏，应立即通知本公司下述代理人查勘。如有索赔，应向本公司提交保险单正本（本保险单共有　　份正本）及有关文件。如一份正本已用于索赔，其余正本则自动失效。

In the event of loss or damage which may result in acclaim under this Policy, immediate notice must be given to the Company's Agent as mentioned hereunder. Claims, if any, one of the Original Policy which has been issued in____ original (s) together with the relevant documents shall be surrendered to the Company. If one of the Original Policy has been accomplished, the others to be void.

赔款偿付地点
Claim payable at

日期
Date ____________ 在
at ____________

地址：
Address： ____________

样例 12－4　空白保险单

2. 中级训练

上海现代贸易有限公司与荷兰通尼产业公司就出口运动套装达成合同一纸(见样例12－5),合同规定付款方式为50%见票后30天付款交单,50%提单日后30天信用证付款(见样例12－6),货物装"天河"轮38航次,提单号08TH2345,保险单号08TT123456,普惠制原产地证号CIQ080622,运费USD1.00/套,保险费率1‰,作为公司单证员,请你利用空白单据(见样例12－7、12－8、12－9、12－10、12－11、12－12、12－13)缮制全套结汇单据,争取早日收回货款。

售 货 合 同

SALES CONTRACT

THE SELLERS: XIANDAI TRADING CO., LTD　　S/C NO. XD08008

ADDRESS: RM 2-8, 55 ZHEJIANG ROAD　　DATE: MAR. 27 2008

SHANGHAI, CHINA

TEL: 021—3478526　FAX: 021—3478525 E-MAIL: christina@163.com

THE BUYERS: TONNY PRODUCTS PLC

ADDRESS: BERSTOFSGADE 48, AMSTERDAM, THE NETHERLANDS

TEL: +(31)74 12 37 08　FAX: +(31)74 12 37 09 E-MIAL: chila@tvl.com

AFTER FRIENDLY NEGOTIATION, THE SELLERS AGREE TO SELL AND THE BUYERS AGREE TO BUY THE UNDERMENTIONED GOODS ACCORDING TO THE TERMS AND CONDITIONS STIPULATED BELOW.

商品名称及规格 NAME OF COMMODITY &SPECIFICATI0N	数量 QUANTITY	单价 UNIT PRICE	总 值 TOTAL VALUE
JOGGING SUIT		CIFC3% ROTTERDAM	
Art. No. KB7900	840SETS	EUR15.20	EUR 12768.00
Art. No. KP6300	600SETS	EUR12.50	EUR 7500.00
Art. No. KY5200	600SETS	EUR10.60	EUR 6360.00
TOTAL:	2040SETS		EUR 26,628.00

PACKING: PACKED IN CARTONS OF 12 SETS EACH

SHIPPING MARKS: TONNY/XD06008/AMSTERDAM/NO.1-UP

PORT OF SHIPMENT: SHANGHAI CHINA

PORT OF DESTIMATI0N: AMSTERDAM THE NETHERLANDS

TIME OF SHIPMENT: NOT LATER THAN MAY 31,2008.

TERMS OF PAYMENT: 50% BY D/P AT 30 DAYS SIGHT;

50% BY L/C AT 30 DAYS AFTER B/L DATE

THE SELLERS:　　THE BUYERS:

李炜　　*STIVEN*

样例 12－5　售货合同

MT:700　ISSUE OF A DOCUMENTARY CREDIT

FROM: CITI - BANK AMSTERDAM, NETHERLANDS

SEQUENCE OF TOTAL:	*27:	1/1
FORM OF L/C	40A:	IRREVOCABLE
APPLICABLE RULES	*40E:	UCP LATEST VERSION
L/C NO.	*20:	68IM6895
DATE OF ISSUE	*31C:	080531
EXPIRY DATE AND PLACE	*31D:	080615 CHINA
APPLICANT	*50:	TONNY PRODUCTS PLC. BERSTOFSGADE 48, AMSTERDAM, THE NETHERLANDS
BENEFICIARY	*59:	XIANDAI TRADING CO., LTD RM 2 - 8, 55 ZHEJIANG ROAD SHANGHAI, CHINA
AMOUNT	*32B	EUR 13314, 00
AVAILABLE WITH BY	*41D:	WITH ANY BANK BY NEGOTIATION
DRAFTS AT	*42C:	AT 30 DAYS AFTER B/L DATE
DRAWEE	*42D:	CITI - BANK LOS ANGELES, CA.
PARTIAL SHIPMENT	*43P:	NOT ALLOWED
TRANSHIPMENT	*43T:	NOT ALLOWED
LOADING FROM	*44A:	CHINA PORTS
FOR TRANSPORTATION TO	*44B:	AMSTTERDAM, THE NETHERLANDS
LATEST DATE OF SHIPMENT	*44C:	080531

DESCRIPTION OF GOODS/SERVICES　*45A:

2040 SETS JOGGING SUIT DELIVERY CONDITION: CIF AMSTERDAM AS PER S/C XD08008

DOCUMENTS REQUIRED　*46A:

+SIGNED COMMERCIAL INVOICE IN 3 ORIGINAL AND 2 COPIES SHOWING FREIGHT CHARGES, PREMIUM AND FOB VALUE AND INDICATING THE ORIGIN OF GOODS IS CHINA.

+PACKING LIST IN 3 FOLDS.

+FULL SET OF CLEAN ON BOARD OCEAN BILLS OF LADING MADE OUT TO ORDER AND BLANK ENDORSED, MARKED "FREIGHT PREPAID" AND NOTIFYING APPLICANT.

+INSURANCE POLICY IN DUPLICATE FOR 110% OF INVOICE VALUE COVERING ALL RISKS AND WAR RISK SUBJECT TO CIC DATED JAN. 1ST, 1981.

+GSP CERTIFICATE OF ORIGIN FORM A ISSUED BY CIQ

+BENEFICIARY'S CERTIFICATE STATING THAT ONE SET OF NON - NEGOTIABLE SHIPPING DOCUMENTS HAVE BEEN SENT TO APPLICANT AFTER SHIPMENT.

ADDITIONAL CONDITIONS: *47A:

+ALL DOCUMENTS MUST SHOW THIS L/C NO

+A DISCREPANCY FEE OF USD 40.00 OR EQUIVALENT WILL BE DEDUCTED FROM THE PROCEEDS PAID UNDER ANY DRAWING WHERE DOCUMENTS PRESENTED ARE FOUND NOT TO BE IN STRICT CONFORMITY WITH THE TERMS OF THIS CREDIT.

CHARGES *71B: ALL BANKING CHARGES OUTSIDE OF OUR COUNTER ARE FOR ACCOUNT OF THE BENEFICIARY

PERIOD FOR PRESENTATION *48: WITHIN 15 DAYS FROM THE DATE OF B/L BUT NOT LATER THAN L/C EXPIRY DATE.

CONFIRMATION: *49: WITHOUT

MAC: A75A8689 CHK: 39D0ADB5BC9A

样例 12-6 信用证

<table>
<tr><td>Issuer</td><td colspan="2" rowspan="2">商 业 发 票
COMMERCIAL INVOICE</td></tr>
<tr><td rowspan="2">To</td></tr>
<tr><td>No.:</td><td>Date:</td></tr>
<tr><td rowspan="2">Transport Details</td><td>S/C No.</td><td>L/C No.</td></tr>
<tr><td colspan="2">Terms of payment</td></tr>
</table>

Marks and numbers	Number and kind of packages, Description of goods	Quantity	Unit price	Amount

样例 12-7 空白发票

Issuer	装 箱 单 PACKING LIST	
To	Invoice No.	Date

Marks and Numbers	Number and kind of package Description of goods	Quantity	Package	G.W	N.W	Meas.

TOTAL:

SAY TOTAL:

样例 12－8　空白装箱单

Shipper

B/L No.:

BILL OF LADING ORIGINAL

中国远洋运输公司

CHINA OCEAN SHIPPING CO

Consignee

Notify Party

Pre carriage by	*Place of Receipt
Ocean Vessel Voy. No.	Port of Loading

Port of discharge	*Final destination	Freight payable at	Number original Bs/L

Marks and Numbers	Number and kind of packages; Description	Gross weight	Measurement

TOTAL PACKAGES(IN WORDS)

Freight and charges

Place and date of issue

Signed for the Carrier

Applicable only when document used as a Through Bill of Loading

样例 12－9　空白提单

中保财产保险有限公司

The People's Insurance (Property) Company of China, Ltd

发票号码
Invoice No.

保险单号次
Policy No.

海洋货物运输保险单

MARINE CARGO TRANSPORTATION INSURANCE POLICY

被保险人：
Insured：

中保财产保险有限公司（以下简称本公司）根据被保险人的要求，及其所缴付约定的保险费，按照本保险单承担险别和背面所载条款与下列特别条款承保下列货物运输保险，特签发本保险单。

This policy of Insurance witnesses that the People's Insurance (Property) Company of China, Ltd. (hereinafter called "The Company"), at the request of the Insured and,in consideration of the agreed premium paid by the Insured, undertakes to insure the undermentioned goods in transportation subject to conditions of the Policy as per the Clauses printed overleaf and other special clauses attached hereon.

唛头 Shipping Marks	保险货物项目 Descriptions of Goods	数量 Quantity	保险金额 Amount Insured

总保险金额：
Total Amount Insured:

承保险别
Conditions

保费
Premium ____________ 载运输工具
Per conveyance S.S ____________ 开航日期
Slg. on or abt ____________

起运港
From ____________ 目的港
To ____________

所保货物，如发生本保险单项下可能引起索赔的损失或损坏，应立即通知本公司下述代理人查勘。如有索赔，应向本公司提交保险单正本（本保险单共有　　份正本）及有关文件。如一份正本已用于索赔，其余正本则自动失效。

In the event of loss or damage which may result in acclaim under this Policy, immediate notice must be given to the Company's Agent as mentioned hereunder. Claims, if any, one of the Original Policy which has been issued in original (s) together with the relevant documents shall be surrendered to the Company. If one of the Original Policy has been accomplished, the others to be void.

赔款偿付地点
Claim payable at

日期
Date ____________ 在
at ____________

地址：
Address： ____________

样例 12 – 10　空白保险单

<table>
<tr><td>1. Goods consigned from (Exporter's business name, address, country)</td><td rowspan="2">Reference No.
GENERALIZED SYSTEM OF PREFERENCES
CERTIFICATE OF ORIGIN
(Combined declaration and certificate) FORM A
Issued in THE PEOPLE'S REPUBLIC OF CHINA
(country)
See Notes overleaf</td></tr>
<tr><td>2. Goods consigned to (Consignee's name, address, country)</td></tr>
<tr><td>3 Means of transport and route (as far as known)</td><td>4. For official use</td></tr>
</table>

5. Item number	6. Marks and numbers of packages	7. Number and kind of packages; description of goods	8. Origin criterion (see Notes overleaf)	9. Gross weight or other quantity	10. Number and date of invoices

<table>
<tr><td>11. Certification
It is hereby certified, on the basis of control carried out, that the declaration by the exporter is correct.

____
Place and date, signature and stamp of certifying authority</td><td>12. Declaration by the exporter
The undersigned hereby declares that the above details and statements are correct, that all the goods were
produced in ______________________
(country)
and that they comply with the origin requirements specified for those goods in the Generalized System of Preferences for goods exported to
____

____
Place and date, signature and stamp of authorized signatory</td></tr>
</table>

样例 12－11　空白普惠制原产地证

BENEFICIARY'S CERTIFICATE

样例 12－12　空白受益人证明函

No.________________ Tianjin, China.____

Exchange for

At______________sight of this FIRST of Exchange(second of exchange being unpaid) , pay to the order of____

the sum of

1

Drawn under____

____

To:________________________

____

No.______________ Tianjin, China.____________

Exchange for

At____________sight of this SECOND of Exchange(first of exchange being unpaid) , pay to the order of____

the sum of

2

Drawn under____

____

To:______________________

____

样例 12－13　空白汇票

3. 高级训练

泰佛贸易公司 2008 年 7 月 15 日收到中国银行天津分行国际业务部的信用证通知函，告知美国联合纺织公司通过麦加利银行开来一份信用证。信用证通知书（见样例 12－14）和信用证（见样例 12－15）。作为单证员，请你马上找出该笔信用证所对应的合同（见样例 12－16），首先对信用证各条款进行审核，如发现信用证有关条款与合同不符且难接受，请填写审证记录（见样例 12－17）并交与主管该笔业务的业务员陈力，请其速与国外客户联系改证事宜。

中国银行
BANK OF CHINA

信用证通知书

Notification of Documentary Credit

ADDRESS: 80, JIEFANG BEI LU, TIANJIN, CHINA
CABLE: CHUNGKOU
TELEX: 23233 TJBOC CN
FAX: 0086 22 23128900　　　　DATE: JULY 15,2008

<table>
<tr><td colspan="2">To: 致
TIFERT TRADING CO., LTD
86, ZHUJIANG ROAD, TIANJIN, CHINA</td><td>When corresponding please quote our Ref No.</td></tr>
<tr><td colspan="2">Issuing Bank 开证行
STANDARD CHATERED BANK NEW YORK.
55 WATER STREET, ROOM 1702, NEW YORK U.S.A</td><td>Transmitted to us through 转递行</td></tr>
<tr><td>L/C No. 证号
DRG-LDLC01</td><td>Dated 开证日期
JUL 14, 2008</td><td>Amount 金额
USD895632.00</td></tr>
<tr><td>Expiry 效期
AUG 25, 2008</td><td>Tenor 远期</td><td>Charge 费用</td></tr>
<tr><td colspan="3">Dear Sirs,
迳启者：
We have pleasure in advising you that we have received from the a/m bank a(n)
兹通知贵司，我行收自上述银行
(　)telex issuing　电传开立　　　(　)ineffective　未生效
(　)pre-advising of　预先通知　　　(　)mail confirmation of　证实书
(X)original　正本　　　(　)duplicate　副本
letter of credit, contents of which are as per attached sheet(s).</td></tr>
</table>

This advice and the attached sheet(s) must accompany the relative documents when presented for negotiation.
信用证一份，现随附通知，贵司交单时，请将本通知书及信用证一并提示。
(X)Please note that this advice does not constitute our confirmation of the above L/C nor does it convey any engagement or obligation on our part.
本通知书不构成我行对此信用证之保兑及其他任何责任。
(　)Please note that we have added our confirmation to the above L/C, negotiation is restricted to ourselves only.
上述信用证已由我行加具保兑，并限向我行交单。

Remark

This L/C consists of 2 sheet(s), including the covering letter and attachment(s).
本信用证连同面函及附件共 2 纸。
If you find any terms and conditions in the L/C which you are unable to comply with and or any error(s), it is suggested that you contact applicant directly for necessary amendment(s) of as to avoid any difficulties which may arise when documents are presented
如本信用证中有无法办到的条款及/或错误，请迳与开证申请人联系进行必要的修改，以排除交单时可能发生的问题。

Yours faithfully
for BANK OF CHINA

样例 12 – 14　信用证通知函

FROM：STANDARD CHATERED BANK NEW YORK
TO：BANK OF CHINA TIANJIN BRANCH
80 JIEFANG BEI LU，TIANJIN
PEOPLE's REP. OF CHINA
TEST：FOR USD895632.00 ON DATE14/07/2008

PLEASE ADVISE BENEFICIARY OF THE FOLLOWING IRREVOCABLE LETTER OF CREDIT ISSUED BY US IN THEIR FAVOR SUBJECT TO UCP 600：
DOCUMENTARY CREDIT NUMBER：DRG – LDLC01
DATE AND PLACE OF EXPIRY：AUG 25，2008 IN U. S. A
APPLICANT：UNITED TEXTILES LTD.，1180 CHURCH ROAD NEW YORK，PA 19446 U. S. A.
BENEFICIARY：TIFERT TRADING CORP. No. 68 ZHUJIANG ROAD，TIANJIN，CHINA.
AMOUNT：USD895632.00

AVALIABLE WITH : ANY BANK BY NEGOTIATION OF BENEFICIARY'S DRAFT(S) AT 30 DAYS SIGHT DRAWN ON CHEMICAL BANK, NEW YORK, ACCOMPANIED BY THE DOCUMENTS

INDICATED HEREIN.

COVERING SHIPMENT OF :

COMMODITY	ART. NO.	QUANTITY
BED SHEETS	ART. NO. BS – 12	2400 DOZENS
	ART. NO. BS – 14	2000 DOZENS
PILLOW CASES	ART. NO. PC – 12	4800 DOZENS
	ART. NO. PC – 13	4800 DOZENS

PRICE TERMS : CIF NEW YORK

SHIPPING MARK: UNITED TEXTILES / LD – DRGSC01/NEWYORK/NO. 1 – UP

DETAILS AS PER S/C NO. LD – DRGSC01 DATED APR 1, 2008

DOCUMENTS REQUIRED:

+3 COPIES OF COMMERCIAL INVOICE SHOWING VALUE IN U. S. DOLLARS

AND INDICATING L/C NO. AND CONTRACT NO.

+2 COPIES OF PACKING LIST SHOWING GROSS/NET WEIGHT AND MEASUREMENT OF EACH CARTON.

+CERTIFICATE OF ORIGIN IN TRIPLICATE ISSUED BY CCPIT OR CHINA CHAMBER OF INTERNATIONAL COMMERCE.

+2 COPIES OF INSURANCE POLICY OR CERTIFICATE ENDORSED IN BLANK FOR THE INVOICE VALUE OF THE GOODS PLUS 130% COVERING ALL RISKS AND WAR RISK AS PER AND SUBJECT TO OCEAN MARINE CARGO CLAUSES OF THE PEOPLES INSURANCE COMPANY OF CHINA DATED 1/1/1981.

+3/3 SET AND ONE COPY OF CLEAN ON BOARD OCEAN BILLS OF LADING MADE OUT TO ORDER OF APPLICANT AND BLANK ENDORSED MARKED FREIGHT TO COLLECT AND NOTIFY APPLICANT.

+BENEFICIARY'S CERTIFICATE EVIDENCING THAT ONE FULL SET OF COPY OF SHIPPING DOCUMENTS TO BE SENT TO APPLICANT DIRECTLY AFTER SHIPMENT BY REGISTERED AIRMAIL.

PARTIAL SHIPMENTS:	PROHIBITED
TRANSSHIPMENTS:	PROHIBITED
SHIPMENT FROM	CHINA PORT
TO:	NEW YORK
NOT LATER THAN :	AUG 20, 2008

DOCUMENTS MUST BE PRESENTED WITHIN 7 DAYS AFTER SHIPMENT, BUT

WITHIN VALIDITY OF THE LETTER OF CREDIT.

INSTRUCTIONS TO THE PAYING/ACCEPTING /NEGOTIATING BANK

NEGOTIATING BANK IS TO FORWARD ALL DOCUMENTS IN ONE AIRMAIL TO STANDARD CHATERED BANK NEW YORK, 55 WATER STREET, ROOM 1702 , NEW YORK, NEW YORK 10041 U. S. A ATTN: LETTER OF CREDIT DEPARTMENT

样例 12 – 15　信用证

销售确认书
SALES CONFIRMATION

编号 No. LD-DRGSC01

日期 Date APRIL 1 2008

THE SELLERS:

TIFERT TRADING CO.，LTD

NO.86，ZHUJIANG ROAD，TIANJIN，CHINA

THE BUYERS:

UNITED TEXTILES LTD.

1180 CHURCH ROAD NEW YORK, PA 19446 U.S.A.

兹确认售予你方下列货品，其成交条款如下：

We hereby confirm having sold to you the following goods on the terms and conditions as specified below:

(1)货物名称及规格 Name of Commodity and Specifications	(2)数量 Quantity	(3)单价 Unit Price	(4)总值 Total Amount
BED SHEETS		CIFC3 NEWYORK	
ARTICLE NO. BS-12	2400DOZENS	USD127.52	USD306048.00
ARTICLE NO. BS-14	2400DOZENS	USD139.52	USD334848.00
PILLOWCASES			
ARTICLE NO. PC-12	4800DOZENS	USD23.53	USD112944.00
ARTICLE NO. PC-14	4800DOZENS	USD29.54	USD141792.00
TOTAL	14400DOZEN		USD895632.00

(4)包装：

PACKING：ART. NO. BS－12 & BS－14 TO PACKED IN CARTONS OF 12 DOZENS EACH

ART. NO. PC－12 & PC－14 TO PACKED IN CARTONS OF 24 DOZENS EACH

(5) 装运唛头：

SHIPPING MARK：AT THE SELLER'S OPTION

(6) 装运期限：收到可以转船及分批装运之信用证后 30 天内装出。

TIME OF SHIPMENT：WITHIN 30 DAYS AFTER RECEIPT OF L/C ALLOWING TRANSSHIPMENT AND PARTIAL SHIPMENTS

(7)装运口岸： 目的地：

PORT OF SHIPMENT：TIANJIN DESTINATION：NEWYORK

(8)付款条件:开给卖方100%不可撤销即期付款及可转让并无追索权之信用证,并须注明可在上述装运日期后十五天内在中国议付有效。

TERMS OF PAYMENT: BY 100% IRREVOCABLE, TRANSFERABLE AND WITHOUT RECOURSE LETTER OF CREDIT TO BE AVAILABLE BY SIGHT DRAFT AND TO REMAIN VALID FOR NEGOTIATION IN CHINA UNTIL THE 15TH DAY AFTER THE AFORESAID TIME OF SHIPMENT

(9)保险由卖方按发票金额的110% ,按照中国人民保险公司海洋运输货物保险条款(1981年1月1日)投保一切险和战争险。

INSURANCE: TO BE COVERED BY THE SELLER FOR 110% OF TOTAL INVOICE VALUE AGAINST ALL RISKS AND WAR RISK AS PER THE OCEAN MARINE CARGO CLAUSES OF THE PEOPLE'S INSURANCE COMPANY OF CHINA, DATED JAN1,1981.

(10)买方须于2008年7月15日前开出本批交易的信用证(或通知售方进口许可证号码)。否则,售方有权:不经通知取消本确认书,或接受买方对本售货确认未执行的全部或部分,或对遭受的损失提出索赔。

THE BUYER SHALL ESTABLISH THE COVERING LETTER OF CREDIT (OR NOTIFY THE IMPORT LICENSE NUMBER) BEFORE JULY 15TH 2008 FAILING WHICH THE SELLER RESERVES THE RIGHT TO RESCIND WITHOUT FURTHER NOTICE, OR TO ACCEPT WHOLE OR ANY PART OF THIS SALES CONFIRMATION UNFULFILLED BY THE BUYER, OR TO LODGE A CLAIM FOR DIRECT LOSSES SUSTAINED IF ANY.

(11)凡以CIF条件成交的业务,保额为发票价的110%,投保险别以本售货确认书中所开列的为限,买方如要求增加保额或保险范围应以装船前经售方同意,因此而增加的保险费由买方负责。

FOR TRANSACTIONS CONCLUDED ON C. I. F BASIS IT IS UNDERSTOOD THAT THE INSURANCE AMOUNT WILL BE FOR 110% OF THE INVOICE VALUE AGAINST THE RISKS SPECIFIED IN THE SALES CONFIRMATION, IF ADDITIONAL INSURANCE AMOUNT OR COVERAGE IS REQUIRED, THE BUYER MUST HAVE THE CONSENT OF THE SELLER BEFORE SHIPMENT, AND THE ADDITIONAL PREMIUM IS TO BE BORNE BY THE BUYER.

(12)品质/数量异议:如买方提出索赔,凡属品质异议,须于货到目的口岸之日起2个月内提出。凡属数量异议,须于货到目的口岸之日起15天内提出,对所装货物所提任何异议属于保险公司、轮船公司及其他有关运输机构负责者,售方不负任何责任。

QUALITY/QUANTITY DISCREPANCY: IN CASE OF QUALITY DISCREPANCY, CLAIM SHOULD BE FILED BY THE BUYER WITHIN 2 MONTHS AFTER THE ARRIVAL OF THE GOODS AT THE PORT OF DESTINATION WHILE FOR QUANTITY DISCREPANCY CLAIM SHOULD BE FILED BY THE BUYER WITHIN 15 DAYS AFTER THE ARRIVAL OF THE GOODS AT THE PORT OF DESTINATION IT IS

UNDERSTOOD THAT SELLER SHALL NOT BE LIABLE FOR ANY DISCREPANCY OF THE GOODS SHIPPED DUE TO CAUSES FOR WHICH THE INSURANCE COMPANY SHIPPING COMPANY OTHER TRANSPORTATION ORGANIZATION ARE LIABLE

(13)本确认书内所述全部或部分商品,如因人力不可抗拒的原因,以致不能履约或延迟交货,售方概不负责。

THE SELLER SHALL NOT BE HELD LIABLE FOR FAILURE OR DELAY IN DELIVERY OF THE ENTIRE LOT OR PORTION OF THE GOODS UNDER THIS SALES CONFIRMATION IN CONSEQUENCE OF ANY FORCE MAJEURE INCIDENTS.

UNITED TEXTILES LTD

RICHARD

买方 (the buyers)

TIFERT TRADING CO. , LTD

王宏

卖方(the sellers)

样例 12 - 16 合同

信用证审核记录

收证日期

信用证证号		合同号		订单号	
开证行				开证日期	
开证人					
受益人					
货物名称		数量		金额	
装运期		有效期		交单期	
装运港		目的港		可否分批	
贸易术语		汇票期限		可否转运	
特殊条款					

单据种类及份数	汇票	发票	装箱单	重量单	尺码单	保险单	提单正本	提单副本	原产地证	GSP产地证	品质证	重量证	植检证	船行证明	寄单证明	寄样证明	受益人证明	邮包收据	

需要修改内容	来证条款内容	应修改后条款内容

业务员签字		部门经理签字	

样例 12 – 17　审证记录

2008 年 7 月 18 日通过中国银行天津分行收到信用证 DRG－LDLC01 修改通知书（样例 12－18）和信用证的正式修改（见样例 12－19），经再次审核，客户已完全按要求改妥信用证。你作为单证员，请通知业务员可以办理出运手续，并在 8 月 15 日前与中远订妥舱位，请速办理报检、报关等具体事宜，同时，依据信用证及信用证修改备妥信用证项下的发票、装箱单、提单、保险单、原产地证、受益人证明函、汇票等所有结汇单据（见样例 12－20、12－21、12－22、12－23、12－24、12－25 及 12－26），最迟在交单期 9 月 5 日前将全套单据交到中国银行天津分行议付货款。

天津静海被服厂提供的码单资料及货代配妥的舱位资料如下：

毛重：15 公斤/箱

净重：14 公斤/箱

尺码：45×35×30 公分/箱

船名航次：HANJIN EXPRESS V. 138

下货纸号：COSCO20070818

海关编码：63023195

发票号：08TFFZ0068

中国银行 BANK OF CHINA

修改通知书

Notification of Amendment

ADDRESS：80, JIEFANG BEI LU, TIANJIN, CHINA

CABLE: CHUNGKOU

TELEX: 23233 TJBOC CN

FAX: 0086 22 23128900

DATE: JULY18, 2007

To: 致 TIFERT TRADING CO., LTD No. 86, ZHUJIANG ROAD, TIANJIN, CHINA	When corresponding please quote our Ref No.
Issuing Bank 开证行 STANDARD CHATERED BANK NEW YORK. 55 WATER STREET, ROOM 1702, NEW YORK U.S.A	Transmitted to us through 转递行
L/C No. 信用证号 DRG-LDLC01	Amendment No 修改次数 1
L/C advised 信用证通知日期 JULY 15, 2008	Amendment dated 修改日期 JULY 18, 2007

Dear Sirs,
迳启者：
We have pleasure in advising you that we have received from the a/m bank a(n)
兹通知贵司，我行收自上述银行

(X)telex of	电传开立	( )ineffective	未生效
( )original	正本	( )duplicate	副本

amendment to the captioned L/C, contents of which are as per attached sheet(s).
内容见附件。
This amendment should be attached to the captioned L/C advised by us, otherwise, the beneficiary will be responsible for any consequences arising there from.
本修改须附于有关信用证，否则，贵公司须对因此产生的后果承担责任。

Remark 备注

This L/C consists of 2 sheet(s), including the covering letter and attachment(s).
本信用证连同面函及附件共 2 纸。

Yours faithfully
for BANK OF CHINA

样例 12－18 信用证修改通知书

FROM：STANDARD CHATERED BANK NEW YORK
TO：BANK OF CHINA TIANJIN BRANCH
80 JIEFANG BEI LU，TIANJIN
PEOPLES REP. OF CHINA
TEST：FOR USD/895632.00 ON DATE14/07/2008

PLEASE ADVISE BENEFICIARY OF THE FOLLOWING AMENDMENT TO L/C NO. DRG－LDLC01 ISSUED BY US DATED 14/07/2008
DATE & NUMBER OF AMENDMENT：FIRST AMENDMENT ON JUL 18，2007 IN U.S.A

THE LETTER OF CREDIT BE AMENDED AS FOLLOWS：
1. THE CORRECT ADDRESS OF BENEFICIARY IS NO.86，ZHUJIANG ROAD，TIANJIN，CHINA.
2. BENEFICIARY'S DRAFT SHOULD BE AT SIGHT INSTEAD OF AT 30DAYS SIGHT
3. PILLOW CASE ART NO. PC－14 INSTEAD OF ART NO. PC－13
4. INSURANCE VALUE SHOULD BE INVOICE VALUE OF GOODS PLUS 10% NOT 130%
5. B/L SHOULD BE MADE OUT TO OREDR OF SHIPPER INSTEAD OF TO ORDER OF APPLICANT AND MARKED

FREIGHT PREPAID NOT FREIGHT TO COLLECT.
6. PARTIAL SHIPMENT AND TRANSHIPMENT SHOULD BE ALLOWED INSTEAD OF PROHIBITED.
7. DOCUMENTS SHOULD BE PRESENTED FOR NEGOTIATION WITHIN 15DAYS AFTER SHIPMENT INSTEAD OF 7DAYS.
8. VALIDITY SHOULD EXTEND TO SEPT 5, 2008
OTHER TERMS AND CONDITIONS REMAIN UNCHANGED.

样例 12－19　信用证修改

<table>
<tr><td colspan="2">Issuer</td><td colspan="3" rowspan="2">商业发票
COMMERCIAL INVOICE</td></tr>
<tr><td colspan="2" rowspan="2">To</td></tr>
<tr><td colspan="2">No.</td><td>Date</td></tr>
<tr><td colspan="2" rowspan="2">Transport details</td><td colspan="2">S/C No.</td><td>L/C No.</td></tr>
<tr><td colspan="3">Terms of payment</td></tr>
<tr><td>Marks and Numbers</td><td>Number and kind of package
Description of goods</td><td>Quantity</td><td>Unit Price</td><td>Amount</td></tr>
<tr><td></td><td></td><td></td><td></td><td></td></tr>
<tr><td colspan="5">Total:
Say total:</td></tr>
</table>

样例 12－20　空白商业发票

<table>
<tr><td colspan="3">Issuer</td><td colspan="5" rowspan="2">装箱单

PACKING LIST</td></tr>
<tr><td colspan="3" rowspan="2">To</td></tr>
<tr><td colspan="3">Invoice No.</td><td colspan="2">Date</td></tr>
<tr><td>Marks and Numbers</td><td>Number and kind of package
Description of goods</td><td>Quantity</td><td>Package</td><td>G.W</td><td>N.W</td><td>Meas.</td></tr>
<tr><td></td><td></td><td></td><td></td><td></td><td></td><td></td></tr>
<tr><td colspan="7">TOTAL:</td></tr>
<tr><td colspan="7">SAY TOTAL:</td></tr>
</table>

样例 12－21　空白装箱单

1. Shipper Insert Name, Address and Phone

B/L No.

中远集装箱运输有限公司
COSCO CONTAINER LINES

TLX: 33057 COSCO CN
FAX: +86(021) 6545 8984

ORIGINAL

Port-to-Port or Combined Transport

BILL OF LADING

2. Consignee Insert Name, Address and Phone

3. Notify Party Insert Name, Address and Phone
(It is agreed that no responsibility shall attach to the Carrier or his agents for failure to notify)

RECEIVED in external apparent good order and condition except as other-wise noted. The total number of packages or unites stuffed in the container, the description of the goods and the weights shown in this Bill of Lading are furnished by the Merchants, and which the carrier has no reasonable means of checking and is not a part of this Bill of Lading contract. The carrier has Issued the number of Bills of Lading stated below, all of this tenor and date, One of the original Bills of Lading must be surrendered and endorsed or signed against the delivery of the shipment and whereupon any other original Bills of Lading shall be void. The Merchants agree to be bound by the terms and conditions of this Bill of Lading as if each had personally signed this Bill of Lading.
SEE clause 4 on the back of this Bill of Lading (Terms continued on the back hereof, please read carefully).
*Applicable Only When Document Used as a Combined Transport Bill of Lading.

4. Combined Transport * Pre - carriage by	5. Combined Transport* Place of Receipt
6. Ocean Vessel Voy. No.	7. Port of Loading
8. Port of Discharge	9. Combined Transport * Place of Delivery

Marks & Nos. Container / Seal No.	No. of Containers or Packages	Description of Goods (If Dangerous Goods, See Clause 20)	Gross Weight Kgs	Measurement
		Description of Contents for Shipper's Use Only (Not part of This B/L Contract)		

10. Total Number of containers and/or packages (in words)
Subject to Clause 7 Limitation

11. Freight & Charges	Revenue Tons	Rate	Per	Prepaid	Collect

Ex. Rate:	Prepaid at	Payable at	Place and date of issue
	Total Prepaid	No. of Original B(s)/L	Signed for the Carrier, COSCO CONTAINER LINES

LADEN ON BOARD THE VESSEL
DATE BY

样例 12－22 空白海运提单

PICC 中国人民财产保险股份有限公司

货物运输保险单 CARGO TRANSPORTATION INSURANCE POLICY

发票号(INVOICE NO.)　　　　　　　　　　　　保单号次

合同号(CONTRACT NO.)　　　　　　　　　　　POLICY NO.

信用证号(L/C NO.)

被保险人(INSURED): ______________________

中国人民保险公司（以下简称本公司）根据被保险人的要求，由被保险人向本公司缴付约定的保险费，按照本保险单承保险别和背面所载条款与下列条款承保下述货物运输保险，特立本保险单。

THIS POLICY OF INSURANCE WITNESSES THAT THE PEOPLE'S INSURANCE COMPANY OF CHINA(HEREINAFTER CALLED "THE COMPANY") AT THE REQUEST OF THE INSURED AND IN CONSIDERATION OF THE AGREED PREMIUM PAID TO THE COMPANY BY THE INSURED,UNDERTAKES TO INSURE THE UNDERMENTIONED GOODS IN TRANSPORTATION SUBJECT TO THE CONDITIONS OF THIS OF THIS POLICY ASPER THE CLAUSES PRINTED OVERLEAF AND OTHER SPECIL CLAUSES ATTACHED HEREON.

标　记 MARKS&NOS	包装及数量 QUANTITY	保险货物项目 DESCRIPTION OF GOODS	保险金额 AMOUNT INSURED

总保险金额(TOTAL AMOUNT INSURED): ______________________

保费(PREMIUM):AS ARRANGED 启运日期(DATE OF COMMENCEMENT):______________

装载运输工具(PER CONVEYANCE): ______________ 自(FROM): ______ 至(TO): ______________

承保险别(CONDITIONS):

所保货物，如发生保险单项下可能引起索赔的损失或损坏，应立即通知本公司下述代理人查勘。如有索赔，应向本公司提交保单正本（本保险单共有____ 份正本）及有关文件。如一份正本已用于索赔，其余正本自动失效。

IN THE EVENT OF LOSS OR DAMAGE WITCH MAY RESULT IN A CLAIM UNDER THIS POLICY, IMMEDIATE NOTICE MUST BE GIVEN TO THE COMPANY'S AGENT AS MENTIONED HEREUNDER. CLAIMS, IF ANY,ONE OF THE ORIGINAL POLICY WHICH HAS BEEN ISSUED IN ____ ORIGINAL(S) TOGETHER WITH THE RELEVENT DOCUMENTS SHALL BE SURRENDERED TO THE COMPANY. IF ONE OF THE ORIGINAL POLICY HAS BEEN ACCOMPLISHED. THE OTHERS TO BE VOID.

PICC Property Casualty Company Limited Tianjin Branch

赔款偿付地点

CLAIM PAYABLE AT: ______________________

出单日期:

ISSUING DATE AND PLACE: ______________　　______________________

核保人:　　　　制单人:　　　　经办人:　　　　Authorized Signature

样例 12－23　空白保险单

ORIGINAL

<table>
<tr><td>1.Exporter</td><td rowspan="2">Certificate No.

CERTIFICATE OF ORIGIN
OF
THE PEOPLE'S REPUBLIC OF CHINA</td></tr>
<tr><td>2.Consignee</td></tr>
<tr><td>3.Means of transport and route</td><td rowspan="2">5.For certifying authority use only</td></tr>
<tr><td>4.Country / region of destination</td></tr>
</table>

6.Marks and numbers	7.Number and kind of packages; description of goods	8.H.S.Code	9.Quantity	10.Number and date of invoices

11.Declaration by the exporter	12.Certification
The undersigned hereby declares that the above details and statements are correct, that all the goods were produced in China and that they comply with the Rules of Origin of the People's Republic of China. ----------------------------------- Place and date, signature and stamp of authorized signatory	It is hereby certified that the declaration by the exporter is correct. ----------------------------------- Place and date, signature and stamp of certifying authority

样例 12－24　空白一般原产地证书

TIFERT TRADING CO. , LTD
86, ZHUJIANG ROAD, TIANJIN, CHINA

CERTIFICATE

Date

样例 12 – 25　空白证明函

BILL OF EXCHANGE

Drawn under ______________________ L/C NO. ______________

Dated ______________ Payable with interest@ ________ %

NO. ________ Exchange for Tianjin ________ (Date)

At ______________ Of this FIRST of Exchange (Second of Exchange being

Unpaid) Pay to the order of

the sum of

Value received

To: ______________________

(Authorized Signature)

样例 12 – 26　空白汇票

学习情境五　综合训练

任务十三　审核单据

岗前测试

一、单选题

> 温馨提示：
>
> 卖方向银行交单议付货款前，首先要对全套单据进行审核，并且要做到：
>
> ①交单须与信用证条款保持一致；
>
> ②交单须与《UCP600》的相关适用条款保持一致；
>
> ③交单须与国际标准银行实务《ISBP》保持一致；
>
> ④交单须与相关法规保持一致；
>
> ⑤交单须与贸易常规保持一致。

1. 发票的日期在全套结汇单据中应(　)。

A. 早于汇票的签发日期

B. 早于提单的签发日期

C. 早于保险单的签发日期

D. 是最早签发的单据

2. 如果信用证未规定交单期限，根据《UCP600》的规定，受益人必须在货物装船后(　)内交单议付，但不能超过信用证的有效期。

A. 3 天　　B. 7 天

C. 15 天　　D. 21 天

3. 海运提单日期应理解为(　)。

A. 货物开始装船的日期

B. 货物装船过程中任何一天

C. 货物装船完毕的日期

D. 签订运输合同的日期

4. 如信用证规定"shipment on or about 15th Oct. 2000"，那么装运期应为(　)。

A. 9 天　　B. 10 天　　C. 11 天　　D. 12 天

5. 在托收项下，单据的缮制通常以(　)为依据。如有特殊要求，应参照相应的文件或资料。

A. 信用证　　B. 发票　　C. 合同　　D. 提单

6. 保兑信用证的保兑行，其责任是(　)。

A. 在开证行不履行付款义务时履行付款义务

B. 在开证申请人不履行付款义务时履行付款义务

C. 承担第一性的付款义务

D. 开证行承担第一性的付款责任，保兑行承担第二性的付款责任

7. 使用 D/P，D/A 和 L/C 三种方式结算货款，就卖方的收汇风险而言，从大到小依次为（　）。

A. D/A、D/P 和 L/C　　B. D/P、D/A 和 L/C

C. L/C、D/P 和 D/A　　D. L/C、D/A 和 D/P

8. 一般附加险中不包括（　）。

A. 破损破碎险　B. 淡水雨淋险　C. 黄曲霉素险　D. 短量险

9. 对港铁路货物运输，发货人凭以向银行结汇的运输单据为（　）。

A. 铁路运单正本　B. 铁路运单副本　C. 承运货物收据　D. 到货通知

10. 轻工进出口公司出口电冰箱共 1 000 台，合同和信用证都规定不准分批装运。运输时有 30 台被撞，包装破裂，冰箱外观变形，不能出口。根据《UCP600》规定，只要货款不超过信用证总金额，交货数量允许有 5% 的增减。据此，轻工公司发货时，可以装运（　）。

A. 1000 台　B. 970 台　C. 950 台　D. 1050 台

二、多选题

1. 审核单据的依据是（　）。

A. 开证申请书　B. 合同　C.《UCP600》　D. 信用证

2. 下列单据，银行可以拒付的有（　）。

A. 迟于信用证规定的到期日提交的单据

B. 迟于装运期后 15 天提交的单据

C. 单据内容与信用证规定不相符的单据

D. 单据与单据互相之间不符的单据

3. 下列关于信用证与合同关系的表述正确的是（　）。

A. 信用证的开立以买卖合同为依据

B. 信用证业务受买卖合同的约束

C. 合同是审核信用证的依据之一

D. 银行按信用证规定处理信用证业务

4. 假远期信用证又称买方远期信用证，其主要特点是（　）。

A. 由开证行开出延期付款信用证

B. 由受益人开出远期汇票

C. 由指定的付款行负责贴现汇票

D. 由进口人负担贴现息和费用

5. 承兑交单开立的汇票是（　）。

A. 即期汇票　B. 远期汇票　C. 银行汇票　D. 商业汇票

小贴士：

各种单据的签发日期应符合逻辑性和国际惯例，通常提单日期是确定各单据日期的关键，汇票日期应晚于提单、发票等其他单据，但不能晚于 L/C 的效期。各单据日期关系如下：

1. 发票日期应在各单据日期之首；
2. 提单日不能超过 L/C 规定的装运期，也不得早于 L/C 的最早装运期；
3. 保单的签发日应早于或等于提单日期（一般早于提单 2 天），不能早于发票；
4. 装箱单应等于或迟于发票日期，但必须在提单日之前；
5. 产地证不早于发票日期，不迟于提单日；
6. 商检证日期不晚于提单日期，但也不能过分早于提单日，尤其是鲜货、容易变质的商品；
7. 受益人证明等于或晚于提单日；
8. 装船通知等于或晚于提单日后 3 天内；
9. 船公司证明等于或早于提单日。

三、判断题

1. 如信用证未规定交单期，则交单期不得迟于运输单据日期后的 15 天，且不得迟于信用证有效期。（　）

2. 海运提单、铁路运单、航空运单均为物权凭证，可以转让。（　）

3. 空白抬头、空白背书的提单是指提单收货人一栏内空白而不需要背书的提单。（　）

4. 发票的开立日期，不能早于信用证的开证日期，也不能迟于信用证的最迟交单日期。（　）

5. 非物权凭证的单据，如果来证要求提交若干份，受益人可以只提交一份正本，其余以副本来满足，开证行不得拒绝。（　）

6. 票汇业务和托收业务都是商业信用，使用的都是商业汇票。（　）

7. 根据《跟单信用证统一惯例 UCP600》，除非信用证另有规定，商业发票应由开证申请人签发，必须作成受益人的抬头。（　）

8. 汇票、提单和保险单的抬头人通常各是付款人、收货人、被保险人。（　）

9. 一张商业汇票上的收款人是："仅付给 ABC 有限公司"（Pay to ABC Co., Ltd. Only），这种汇票不能转让。（　）

10. 保险单出具后，如需要补充或变更保险内容，保险公司可根据投保人的请求出具修改保险内容的凭证，该项凭证称为批单。（　）

岗前培训

一、单据审核规范

表 13－1　单据常见差错

单据种类	常见差错
商业发票 Commercial Invoice	①发票名称与信用证规定不符 ②发票的抬头人与信用证要求不符 ③发票上启运港或目的港与提单不一致 ④发票的货描与信用证的货描不符或拼写错误 ⑤发票中的数量、单价和金额没有如实反映所装运的货物 ⑥发票上的金额超过信用证规定的金额或不在允许增减的机动幅度内 ⑦对佣金和折扣的处理不符合信用证的规定 ⑧发票上遗漏信用证要求表明和证明的内容，或缮制发票时机械照搬信用证中的证明词，没有作相应的变更
包装单据 Packing List	①装箱单据的名称不符合信用证规定 ②装箱单据的各项内容与发票、提单内容不符 ③装箱单据中误现单价和总金额，泄露了进口商的底价 ④装箱单的日期填写不合理 ⑤装箱单的内容与货物实际包装内容不完全相符 ⑥装箱单据的具体缮制要求不符合信用证规定
商检证书 Inspection Certificate	①检验证书的种类不符合信用证要求 ②检验证书的出证机构不符合信用证要求 ③检验证书的商品名称、数量与发票、提单等其他单据不符 ④唛头与信用证或其他单据不符 ⑤检验结果有瑕疵不符合信用证或合同规定的要求 ⑥检验日期晚于提单日期，鲜活、易腐易烂商品检验过早 ⑦漏授权人签署或漏检验部门签章 ⑧附页漏盖骑缝章 ⑨证书更改处漏“更改章”及授权人签字
原产地证书 Certificate of Origin	①原产地证书的出证机构不符合信用证要求 ②原产地证书出口商不符合信用证要求 ③原产地证书收货人不符合信用证要求 ④原产地书标准引用不正确 ⑤原产地证书上的日期顺序不合理 ⑥原产地证书中货物件数的大小写不符 ⑦原产地证书中货物描述太笼统，导致在海关编码中找不到对应的编码 ⑧遗漏信用证书中对原产地证书的其他要求

续表

单据种类	常见差错
海运提单 Ocean Bill of Lading	①提单单据提交的种类与信用证要求不符 ②提单正本的份数与信用证要求不符或漏填提单正本的份数 ③提单的运费支付批注不规范或漏注 ④收妥待运海运提单漏装船批注或批注内容不完整 ⑤提单上记载的包装件数与信用证或其他单据不符 ⑥提单上包装件数大小写不一致或漏填大写 ⑦提单没有按照信用证要求正确背书或遗漏背书 ⑧提单日或装船日超过信用证规定的装运期 ⑨提单托运人与信用证规定不符 ⑩提单收货人与信用证规定不符 ⑪提单被通知人与信用证规定不符或填写不完整 ⑫正本提单漏注签发日期和签发地点
保险单 Insurance Policy	①保险单的种类与信用证要求不符 ②保险单抬头人填写有误 ③保险金额不符合信用证规定 ④保险金额大小写不一致或大写金额不正确 ⑤保险金额所使用货币与信用证金额所使用货币不一致 ⑥保险单的投保险别与信用证规定险别不符或有遗漏 ⑦保险单上的船名与发票或提单上的船名不相符 ⑧保险单的出单日期晚于提单日期 ⑨漏注赔付地点或赔付货币 ⑩遗漏背书或背书错误
其他单据 Other Documents	①单据的名称与信用证要求不符 ②单据的内容不详尽 ③单据的出单日期不符合信用证或惯例规定 ④证明文句的内容照抄信用证原句 ⑤遗漏签署
汇票 Bill of Exchange	①汇票的金额与发票或信用证规定不符 ②汇票上金额大小写不一致或大写金额填写不正确、不规范 ③汇票上货币币别与信用证上货币币别不相符 ④汇票上付款期限不符合信用证或合同规定或即期、远期填写不规范 ⑤汇票漏出票人签署 ⑥汇票的出票条款内容与信用证不符 ⑦汇票的付款人与信用证规定不符 ⑧汇票提交的份数不正确

二、单据审核范例

IRREVOCABLE DOCUMENTARY CREDIT

TO：BANK OF CHINA

DEAR SIR,

IN ACCRDANCE WITH THE TERMS OF UCP 600 WE ADVISE HAVING RECEIVED THE FOLLOWING TELE-TRANSMISSION FROM CENTRAL BANK OF SPAIN.

（SWIFT ADDRESS：SPBSCATTMON）

27 SEQ OF TOTAL：

1/1

40A FORM OF DC：

IRREVOCABLE

40E APPLICABLE RULES

UCP LATEST VERSION

20 DC NO：

LCN038

31C DATE OF ISSUE：

NOV. 23, 2008

31D EXPIRY DATE AND PLACE ：

DEC. 31, 2008 IN BENEFICIARYS COUNTRY

50 APPLICANT：

SKY INTERNATIONAL I/E LTD.

1000 ALGECIRAS ST. , SPAIN

59 BENEFICIARY：

TIFERT TRADING CORP LTD.

NO. 86, ZHUJIANG RD. , TIANJIN, CHINA

32B DC AMT：

USD131512,30

41D AVAILABLE WITH /BY：

ANY BANK BY NEGOTIATION

42C DRAFTS AT：

SIGHT FOR FULL INVOICE VALUE

43P PARTIAL SHIPMENTS：

ALLOWED

43T TRANSHIPMENT：

ALLOWED

44C LATEST DATE OF SHIPMENT

DEC. 16, 2008

44A LOADING/DISPATCH AT/FROM:

TIANJIN, CHINA

44B FOR TANSPORTION TO:

BARCELONA, SPAIN

45A DESCRIPTION OF GOODS AND/OR SERVICES:

NAPKIN

MATERIAL: 50% COTTON, 50% POLYESTER

SIZE: 18 * 18CM

PACKING: 100PCS/CARTON

46A DOCUMENTS REQUIRED

+ SIGNED COMMERCIAL INVOICE IN 6 COPIES INDICATING INVOICE NO., CONTRACT NO. SCN036

+ FULL SET OF CLEAN ON BOARD OCEAN BILLS OF LADING MADE OUT TO ORDER AND BLANK ENDORSED, MARKED PREPAID FREIGHT AND NOTIFYING THE APPLICANT

+ INSURANCE POLICY/CERTIFICATE IN 3 COPIES FOR 110 % OF THE INVOICE VALUE SHOWING CLAIMS PAYABLE IN SPAIN IN CURRENCY OF THE DRAFT, BLANK ENDORSED, COVERING ALL RISKS AND WAR RISKS

+ PACKING LIST/WEIGHT MEMO IN 3 COPIES CERTIFYING THAT EACH ITEM HAS BEEN MARKED THE LABEL "MADE IN CHINA"

+ CERTIFICATE OF QUALITY IN 3 COPIES ISSUED BY CIQ INDICATING DETAILED AND DEFINITE INSPECTION RESULTS.

+ CERTIFICATE OF ORIGIN IN DUPLICATE ISSUED BY CCPIT SHOWING THE GOODS ARE WHOLLY PRODUCED IN CHINA

+ BENEFICIARYS CERTIFICATE CERTIFYING THAT ONE FULL SET OF NON NEGOTIABLE DOCUMENTS HAVE BEEN SENT TO APPLICANT DIRECTLY WITHIN 48 HOURS AFTER SHIPMENT

47A ADDITIONAL CONDITIONS:

+ ALL BANKING CHARGES OUTSIDE THE OPENING BANK ARE FOR BENEFICIARYS ACCOUNT.

+ DOCUMENTS MUST BE PRESENTED WITH 21 DAYS AFTER THE DATE OF ISSUANCE OF THE TRANSPORT DOCUMENTS BUT WITHIN THE VALIDITY OF THIS CREDIT.

THIS ADVICE CONSTITUTES A DOCUMENTARY CREDIT ISSUED BY THE ABOVE BANK AND SHOULD BE PRESENTED WITH THE DOCUMENTS/DRAFTS FOR NEGOTIATION /PATMENT /ACCEPTANCE , AS APPLICABLE.

ACCOUNT NO:88586 - 89778

BANK OF SPAIN

1000 MAIN STREET, ALGECIR SPAIN

TEL: 34 - 4 - 2125001

样例 13 - 1 信用证

Issuer TIFERT TRADING CO., LTD. NO.86, ZHUJIANG ROAD, TIANJIN, CHINA	商 业 发 票 **COMMERCIAL INVOICE**	
To SKY INTERNATIONAL I/E LTD. 1000 ALGECIRAS STREET, SPAIN	No.: INV NO. 08FZ018	Date: NOV. 28, 2008
Transport Details FROM TIANJIN TO BARCELONA BY SEA	S/C No. SCN036	L/C No. LCN038
	Terms of payment L/C AT SIGHT	

Marks and numbers	Number and kind of packages, Description of goods	Quantity	Unit price	Amount
NAPKIN BARCELONA C/NO.1-722 MADE IN CHINA	NAPKIN MATERIAL: 50% COTTON, 50% POLYESTER SIZE:18*18CM PACKING: 100PCS/CARTON	72200(PCS)	USD1.8215	USD131512.30
		TOTAL: 72200PCS		USD131512.30

WE HEREBY CERTIFY THAT THE GOODS ARE OF CHINESE ORIGIN.

TIFERT TRADING CO., LTD
泰佛贸易有限公司
*

样例 13－2　发票

Shipper	B/L No. SINO081216
TIFERT TRADING CO., LTD NO.86, ZHUJIANG ROAD, TIANJIN,CHINA	SINOTRANS 中国外运天津公司 SINOTRANS TIANJIN COMPANY
Consignee or order TO ORDER OF SHIPPER	OCEAN BILL OF LADING
Notify address APPLICANT	SHIPPED on board in apparent good order and condition (unless otherwise indicated) the goods or packages specified herein and to be discharged at the mentioned port of discharge or as near thereto as the vessel may safely get and be always afloat. The weight, measure, marks and numbers, quality, contents and value, being particulars furnished by the Shipper, are not checked by the Carrier on loading. The Shipper, Consignee and the Holder of this Bill of Lading hereby expressly accept and agree to all printed, written or stamped provisions, exceptions and conditions of this Bill of Lading, including those on the back hereof. IN WITNESS whereof the number of original Bills of Lading stated below have been signed, one of which being accomplished the other(s) to be void.

Pre-carriage by	Port of loading
	TIANJIN, CHINA
Vessel: SHUNFENG V.0827	Port of transshipment
Port of discharge: BARCELONA, SPAIN	Final destination

Container. seal No. or marks and Nos.	Number and kind of package	Description of goods	Gross weight (kgs.)	Measurement (m^3)
NAPKIN BARCELONA C/NO.1-722 MADE IN CHINA	722 CARTONS SAY SEVEN HUNDRED AND TWENTY-TWO CARTONS ONLY	NAPKIN PREPAID FREIGHT	25992.00KGS	24.548CBM

Freight and charges			REGARDING TRANSSHIPMENT INFORMATION PLEASE CONTACT
Ex. rate	Prepaid at	Freight payable at	Place and date of issue TIANJIN, CHINA, DEC. 8, 2008
	Total prepaid	Number of original Bs/L THREE	Signed for or on behalf of the Carrier SINOTRANS TIANJIN COMPANY 张涛 As Agent

样例 13－3 提单

中保财产保险有限公司

The People's Insurance (Property) Company of China, Ltd

发票号码 INVOICE NO. 08FZ018
Invoice No.

保险单号次
PICC08526
Policy No.

海洋货物运输保险单
MARINE CARGO TRANSPORTATION INSURANCE POLICY

被保险人:
Insured: TIFERT TRADING CO., LTD

中保财产保险有限公司(以下简称本公司)根据被保险人的要求,及其所缴付约定的保险费,按照本保险单承担险别和背面所载条款与下列特别条款承保下列货物运输保险,特签发本保险单。

This policy of Insurance witnesses that the People's Insurance (Property) Company of China, Ltd. (hereinafter called "The Company"), at the request of the Insured and in consideration of the agreed premium paid by the Insured, undertakes to insure the undermentioned goods in transportation subject to conditions of the Policy as per the Clauses printed overleaf and other special clauses attached hereon.

唛头(6) Shipping Marks	保险货物项目(7) Descriptions of Goods	数量(8) Quantity	保险金额(9) Amount Insured
AS PER INV. NO. 123456	NAPKIN	722CARTONS (72200PCS)	USD144664.00

总保险金额:
Total Amount Insured: SAY U. S. DOLLARS ONE HUNDRED FORTY - FOUR THOUSAND SIX HUNDRED SIXTY - FOUR ONLY

承保险别
Conditions

COVERING ALL RISKS AND WAR RISK AS PER OCEAN MARINE CARGO TRANSPORTATION CLAUSES OF C. I. C. DATEED 1/1/1981.

保费(12) 载运输工具(13) 开航日期(14)
Premium as arranged Per conveyance S. S SHUNFENG V. 0827 Slg. on or abt AS PER B/L

起运港(15) 目的港
From TIANJIN, CHINA To BARCELONA, SPAIN

所保货物,如发生本保险单项下可能引起索赔的损失或损坏,应立即通知本公司下述代理人查勘。如有索赔,应向本公司提交保险单正本(本保险单共有 2 份正本)及有关文件。如一份正本已用于索赔,其余正本则自动失效。(16)

In the event of loss or damage which may result in acclaim under this Policy, immediate notice must be given to the Company's Agent as mentioned hereunder. Claims, if any, one of the Original Policy which has been issued in 2 original (s) together with the relevant documents shall be surrendered to the Company. If one of the Original Policy has been accomplished, the others to be void.

PICC SPAIN BRANCH
RM101, 10TH FLOOR SUPER BUILDING, BARCELONA, SPAIN
TEL: 0034 - 61 - 2458 7531

赔款偿付地点
Claim payable at CHINA IN USD

The People's Insurance (Property)
Company of China, Ltd
蒋彩石

日期 在
Date(18) DEC. 9, 2008 At TIANJIN

样例 13-4 保险单

Issuer TIFERT TRADING CO., LTD. NO. 86, ZHUJIANG ROAD, TIANJIN, CHINA	装 箱 单 **PACKING LIST/WEIGHT MEMO**
To SKY INTERNATIONAL I/E LTD. 1000 ALGECIRAS STREET, SPAIN	Invoice No. INV NO. 08FZ018 / Date NOV. 28, 2008

Marks and Numbers	Number and kind of package Description of goods	G.W	N.W	Meas.
NAPKIN BARCELONA C/NO.1-722 MADE IN CHINA	NAPKIN MATERIAL: 50% COTTON, 50% POLYESTER SIZE:18*18CM PACKED IN CARTONS OF 10PCS EACH	25992.00KGS	24909.00KGS	24.548CBM

WE HEREBY CERTIFY THAT EACH ITEM HAS BEEN MARKED THE LABEL"MADE IN CHINA"

样例 13－5　装箱单

CIQ

中华人民共和国出入境检验检疫　　　　正　本

ENTRY-EXIT INSPECTION AND QUARANTITE　　ORIGINAL

OF THE PEOPLE'S REPUBLIC OF CHINA

编号 No.:08CIQ1187

QUALITY CERTIFICATE

发货人

Consignor　TIFERT TRADING CO., LTD

收货人

Consignee　* * * *

品名 Description of Goods　NAPKIN 报检数量/重量 Quantity/Weight Declared　72200PCS 包装种类及数量 Number and Type of Packages　722CARTONS 运输工具 Means of Conveyance　BY SEA	标记及号码(9) Mark & No. NAPKIN BARCELONA C/NO.1-722 MADE IN CHINA

检验结果

Result of inspection

SAMPLES WERE DRAWN AT RANDOM FROM THE WHOLE LOT OF GOODS AND INSPECTED STRICTLY ACCORDING TO THE S/C NO. SCN036

THE ABOVE RESULTS OF INSPECTION ARE IN CONFORMITY WITH THE REQUIREMENTS IN THE SAID CONTRACT.

印章:　　签证地点 Place of Issue TIANJIN 签证日期 Date of Issue DEC 9, 2008

Official Stamp

授权签字人 Authorized Officer ZHANG CHI 签名 Signature 张弛

我们已尽所知和最大能力实施上述检验,不能因我们签发本证书而免除卖方或其他方面根据合同和法律所承担的产品质量责任和其他责任。

All inspection are carried out conscientiously to the best of our knowledge and ability. This certificate dose not in any respect absolve the seller and other related parties from his contractual and legal obligations especially when product quality is concerned.

样例 13 -6　检验证书

ORIGINAL

1.Exporter

TIFERT TRADING CO., LTD.
NO. 86, ZHUJIANG ROAD, TIANJIN, CHINA

Certificate No. 061210

CERTIFICATE OF ORIGIN
OF
THE PEOPLE'S REPUBLIC OF CHINA

2.Consignee

SKY INTERNATIONAL I/E LTD.
1000 ALGECIRAS ST., SPAIN

3.Means of transport and route

SHIPMENT FROM TIANJIN TO BARCELONA BY SEA

5.For certifying authority use only

4.Country / region of destination

SPAIN

6.Marks and numbers	7.Number and kind of packages; description of goods	8.H.S.Code	9.Quantity	10.Number and date of invoices
NAPKIN BARCELONA C/NO.1-722 MADE IN CHINA	722（SEVEN HUNDRED AND TWENTY-TWO）CARTONS OF NAPKIN	4202	72200PCS	INV NO. 08FZ018 NOV. 28, 2008

11.Declaration by the exporter

The undersigned hereby declares that the above details and statements are correct, that all the goods were produced in China and that they comply with the Rules of Origin of the People's Republic of China.

TIFERT TRADING CO., LTD
泰佛贸易有限公司
*

TIANJIN DEC. 7, 2008　张芳

Place and date, signature and stamp of authorized signatory

12.Certification

It is hereby certified that the declaration by the exporter is correct.

中国国际贸易促进委员会
天津分会

TIANJIN DEC. 7, 2008　王刚

Place and date, signature and stamp of certifying authority

样例 13－7　原产地证书

TIANJIN TIFERT TRADING CO. , LTD

NO. 86, ZHUJIANG ROAD, TIANJIN, CHINA

CERTIFICATE

DATE: DEC. 8 , 2008

INVOICE NO: 08FZ018

TO: WHOM IT MAY CONCERN

WE CERTIFY THAT A SET OF NON – NEGOTIABLE DOCUMENT UNDER L/C NO. LCN038 INCLUDING A COPY OF B/L, A COPY OF INVOICE, A COPY OF PACKING LIST HAVE BEEN MAILED TO THE SKY INTERNATIONAL I/E LTD. WITHIN 48 HOURS AFTER SHIPMENT.

TIFERT TRADING CO., LTD
泰佛贸易有限公司

....

Authorized Signature

样例 13 –8 受益人证明

BILL OF EXCHANGE

No. INV NO. 08FZ018　　　　Tianjin, China. DEC 17,2008

Exchange for USD131512.30

At * * * sight of this FIRST of Exchange(SECOND of exchange being unpaid),pay to the order of BANK OF CHINA

the sum of

U.S. DOLLARS ONE HUNDRED AND THIRTY ONE THOUSAND FIVE HUNDRED AND TWELVE AND THIRTY CENTS ONLY

Drawn under CENTRAL BANK OF SPAIN

L/C No. LCN038

Date NOV.23, 2008

To: BANK OF CHINA

TIFERT TRADING CO., LTD

泰佛贸易有限公司

*

样例 13－9　汇票

发票号 INV NO. 08FZ018	船名 SHUNFENG V.0827	提单号 SINO081216
开证行 CENTRAL BANK OF SPAIN		装期 DEC.16, 2008
		效期 DEC.31, 2008
信用证号 LCN038	结汇金额 USD 131512.30	交单期 DEC. 29, 2008

单据名称	汇票	发票	装箱单	保险单	产地证	检验证	GSP产地证	海关发票	船行证明	受益人证明	电抄	提单	提单副本	其他	
应交份数	2	6	3	3	2	3				1		3	3		

存在问题及处理意见

发票：

①单价和金额处漏写贸易术语 CIF　BARCELONA

②装运港和目的港后漏加注 CHINA 和 SPAIN 国别

③多加注了 WE HEREBY CERTIFY THAT THE GOODS ARE OF CHINESE ORIGIN 应删除

海运提单：

①提单抬头应制成 TO ORDER 而不是 TO ORDER OF SHIPPER

②被通知人 APPLICANT 应具体写成 SKY INTERNATIONAL I/E LTD. 1000 ALGECIRAS ST., SPAIN

保险单：

①赔付地点应是 SPAIN 而不是 CHINA

②保险单日期应在装船前，如 DEC. 5 , 2008 而不是 DEC. 9, 2008

装箱单：

①包装应该是 100 条口布装一纸箱，而不是 10 条

②在加注了声明文句后应有出票人的签字

检验证书：

① 其签证日期应该早于提单日，如 DEC. 5 , 2008 而不是 DEC. 9, 2008 ② 漏盖CIQ印章

产地证：

①漏声明文句“THE GOODS ARE WHOLLY PRODUCED IN CHINA”

②货物描述最后漏填*　*　*　*　*以示结束

汇票：

①金额大写应该为 U.S.DOLLARS ONE HUNDRED AND THIRTY ONE THOUSAND FIVE HUNDRED AND TWELVE AND THIRTY CENTS ONLY.

②付款人应为 CENTRAL BANK OF SPAIN

其他应注意事项：

单证员 王芳	审单员 庞峻岭	银行复核	结汇日期

样例 13－10　审单记录表

上岗操作

任务栏

1. 通知:公司已有以下合同项下的货物装运出口,请根据有关资料审核全套单据。
2. 目的:本项任务的目的是熟悉并掌握审核单据的技巧。
3. 要求:下班前将审核好的全套单据交给师傅复核。

一、动脑思考

1. 泰佛贸易公司接到国外开来信用证规定:"…Hongkong Shun Tai Feeds Development Co. as shipper on Bill of Lading."(……以香港顺泰饲料发展公司作为提单发货人)。泰佛贸易公司进出口公司在装运时即按信用证上述规定以转口商香港顺泰饲料发展公司作为提单的发货人。但在向银行交单时单证人员才发现:该提单系空白抬头,须发货人背书。提单既以香港顺泰饲料发展公司作为发货人,则应以香港该公司盖章进行背书。但该公司在本地并无代表,结果只好往返联系,拖延了三个星期香港才派人来背书。后因信用证过期无法议付,造成损失。我们应该从该案例中吸取什么教训?

2. 泰佛贸易公司出口一批货物,信用证要求提交"Marine shipped on board Bill of Lading",但船方提供的提单属于"收妥备运提单"。为了符合信用证要求,所以在提单空白处用打字机加注"Shipped on board"字样,最后承运人在提单签发栏"As agent for the Carrier"处签字盖章。该出口公司交单议付后,单据到国外被开证行拒付货款,理由是单证不符,所提供的提单并非"Shipped on board"提单。你认为开证行拒付理由成立吗?如果成立,我们应该吸取什么教训?

3. 泰佛贸易公司收到国外开来不可撤销信用证一份,由设在我国境内的某外资银行通知并加以保兑。泰佛贸易公司在货物装运后,正拟将有关单据交银行议付时,忽接该外资银行通知,由于开证银行已宣布破产,该行不承担对该信用证的议付或付款责任,但可接受泰佛贸易公司委托向买方直接收取货款的业务。对此,你认为我方应如何处理?

二、动手操作

1. 初级训练

泰佛贸易公司与法国巴黎时装贸易公司就进口高档晚礼服达成一进口合同,合同号为 TFI08G0218(见样例 13-11),付款方式采用 30% T/T 预付,70% D/P 即期,法国客户如期将 600 套晚礼服装船,现接到中国银行天津分行单据已到的通知,请仔细审核单据并填写审单记录(见样例 13-12),无误后付款赎单并办理相关的进口提货手续。

泰佛贸易公司

TIFERT TRADING CO., LTD.

NO. 86, ZHUJIANG ROAD, TIANJIN, CHINA

订 购 合 同

PURCHASE CONTRACT

卖方： THE SELLERS： PARIS FASHION APPAREL S. A. P. O. BOX1236, PARIS, FRANCE	合同号码： CONTRACT NO.：TFI08G0218 日期： DATE：OCT 25, 2008

经同意按照下列条款由卖方出售，买方购进下列货物：
THE SELLER AGREES TO SELL AND THE BUYER AGREES TO BUY THE UNDERMENTIONED COMMODITY ACCORDING TO THE TERMS AND CONDITIONS STATED BELOW：

1. 商品名称及规格
NAME OF COMMODITY, SPECIFICATION：
EVENING DRESS
STYLE NO. 8898
100% POLYESTER
600SETS
AT USD55.60 PER SET FOB MARSEILLES

2. 总值
TOTAL VALUE：USD33360.00

3. 包装
PACKING：ONE SET IN A PLASTIC BAG AND 12SETS TO A CARTON

4. 付款条件
TERMS OF PAYMENT：30% BY T/T IN ADVANCE, 70% D/P AT SIGHT

6. 保险
INSURANCE：TO BE COVERED BY THE BUYER

7. 装运时间
TIME OF SHIPMENT：NOT LATER THAN NOV 25, 2008

8. 装运唛头
SHIPPING MARK：TIFERT/ TFI08G0218/TIANJIN/NO. 1 – UP

9. 装运口岸
PORT OF LOADING：MARSEILLES

10. 目的口岸
PORT OF DESTINATION：TIANJIN

卖方(THE SELLERS)	买方(THE BUYERS)
PARIS FASHION APPAREL S. A. 米歇尔	TIFERT TRADING CO., LTD. 王宏

样例 13 – 11 晚礼服购货合同

(1)发票

PARIS FASHION APPAREL S.A.

P.O.BOX 1236, PARIS, FRANCE

COMMERCIAL INVOICE

TO: TIFERT TRADING CO.,LTD
NO.86, ZHUJIANG ROAD, TIANJIN
CHINA

INVOICE NO. HYL-A008
DATE: NOV 15, 2008
DESTINATION:TIANJIN

MARKS & NOS.	COMMODITTY DESCRIPTION	QUANTITY	UNIT PRICE	AMOUNT
			FOB MARSEILLES	
TIFERT **TFI08G0128** **TIANJIN** **NO. 1-50**	**EVENING DRESS** **STYLE NO. 8988** **50% POLYESTER** **50% VISCOSE**	**600PCS**	**USD55.60**	**USD33360.00**

PACKED: 1SET IN A PLASTIC BAG, ONE DOZ TO A CARTON

TIFERT TRADING CO., LTD.
王宏

(2)装箱单

PARIS FASHION APPAREL S.A.

P.O.BOX 1236, PARIS, FRANCE

PACKING LIST AND WEIGHT NOTE

DATE: NOV 15, 2008

MARKS & NOS.	DESCRIPTION OF GOODS	
TIFERT **TFI08G0128** **TIANJIN** **NO. 1-500**	50 CARTONS	**EVENING DRESS PER DOZEN**

TOTAL G. W. 12000.00KGS(@24.00KGS)
N. W. 11000.00KGS(@22.00KGS)

PACKED IN CARTONS OF ONE DOZ EACH

TIFERT TRADING CO., LTD.
王宏

(3)提单

Shipper

PARIS FASHION APPAREL S.A.
P.O.BOX 1236, PARIS, FRANCE

B/L NO

中国远洋运输（集团）总公司

CHINA OCEAN SHIPPING（GROUP）CO
Combined Transport BILL OF LADING

Consignee

TO OXRDER

Notify Party

TIFERT TRADING CO., LTD
NO.86, ZHUJIANG ROAD, TIANJIN, CHINA

Pre-carriaged by	Place of receipt
Ocean Vessel Voy No **DONGFENG V.122**	Port of Loading **TIANJIN**

Port of Discharge	Place of Delivery	Final Destination
MARSEILLES		

Marks & Nos Container Seal No.	No.of Containers or P'kgs	Kind of Packages;Description of Goods	Gross Weight	Measurement
TIFERT **TFI08G0128** **TIANJIN** **NO.1-50**	**50 BAGS**	**EVENING CLOTHS** **FREIGHT PREPAID**	**12,00.00KGS**	**12.500M3**

TOTAL NUMBER OF CONTAINERS
OR PACKAGES（IN WORDS） **FIVE HUNDRED BAGS ONLY**

FREIGHT & CHARGES	Revenue Tons	Rate	Per	Prepaid	Collect

Ex Rate	Prepaid at	Payable at	Place and date of Issue **MARSEILLES NOV 26,2008**
	Total Prepaid	No. of Original B(S)/L **THREE(3)**	Signed for the Carrier

LADEN ON BOARD THE VESSEL

DATE **NOV 26,2008** BY (TERMS PLEASE FIND ON BACK OF ORIGINAL B/L)

(COSCO STANDARD FORM 11)

发票号		提单号	
船名航次		付款方式	
单据存在的问题及处理意见			

样例 13－12 审单记录表

2. 中级训练

泰佛贸易公司出口猪皮劳动手套(Pig Leather Work Gloves),货号 WP301C,共 5000 打,欧元 28.28 每打,CIFC5 汉堡,装于 100 个纸箱内,每箱 50 打,每箱毛重 55 公斤,净重 51 公斤,体积 0.075 立方米。此批货物装于一个 20 英尺集装箱内,货装"XINXING"轮自新港运至汉堡,现在货已出运,全套单据已经缮制妥当,请根据信用证(见样例 13 - 13)认真审核全套单据并填写审单记录表(见样例 13 - 14),保证货款安全。

VEREINS - UND WESTBANK　　Hamburg, 5th May 2008

IRREVOCABLE DOCUMENTARY CREDIT　　No. 08/37 - 267

Advising Bank: Bank of China, Tianjin, China

Applicant: Helmut Feld Co.
Billstr. 177
2000 Hamburg Germany

Beneficiary: Tifert Trading Co., LTD.
No. 86, Zhujiang Road, Tianjin, China

Amount: EUR136800.00 (European Dollars One Hundred Thirty Six Thousand and Eight Hundred Only)

Expiry date: 15th July 2008 in China

Dear Sir(s),

We hereby issue in your favor this documentary credit which is available by negotiation of your draft at sight drawn on VEREINS - UNDWESTBANK, Hamburg bearing the clause:

"Drawn under documentary credit No. 08/37.267 of VEREINS - UNDWESTBANK"

accompanied by the following documents:

1. Signed commercial invoice in three folds
2. Full set of clean on board ocean bills of lading, issued to order and blank endorsed, notify applicant
3. Insurance policy or certificate, covering All Risks and War Risk for 110% of invoice value
4. Packing list in two folds, showing gross/net weight, shipping mark
5. Certificate of Chinese origin, Form A

Covering shipment of: Pig Leather Work Gloves

5000 doz. Art. WP 301C at EUR28.80/doz. CIFC5 Hamburg

shipment from Chinese port to Hamburg

Partial shipment: Prohibited　　Transshipment: Permitted

Special Conditions: Shipment must be effected latest 30th June 2008

Documents have to be presented within 15 days after dale of shipment.

Shipping marks: H　　F
HAMBURG
No. 1 - UP

We hereby engage with drawers and/or bona fide holders that drafts drawn and negotiated in conformity with the terms of this credit will be duly honored on presentation and that drafts accepted within the terms of this credit will be duly honored at maturity.

The advising bank is requested to notify the beneficiary without adding their confirmation.

Except so far as otherwise expressly stated, this documentary credit is subject to the "Uniform Customs and Practice for Documentary Credits" (2007 Revision) in accordance with Publication No. 600 of the International Chamber of Commerce.

Yours faithfully

VEREINS - UND WESTBANK

样例 13 - 13　猪皮劳动手套信用证

(1)发票

<table>
<tr><td colspan="2">Issuer
TIFERT TRADING CO., LTD.
NO. 86, ZHUJIANG ROAD, TIANJIN, CHINA</td><td colspan="3">商 业 发 票
COMMERCIAL INVOICE</td></tr>
<tr><td colspan="2">To
HELMUT FELD CO.
BILLSTR. 177
2000 HAMBURG GERMANY</td><td colspan="2">No BP200430134</td><td>Date: 18th May, 2008</td></tr>
<tr><td colspan="2" rowspan="2">Transport details
FROM XINGANG TO HAMBURG
PER S.S "XINXING"
BY SEA</td><td colspan="2">S/C No 08 / ST-122</td><td>L/C No 08/37-267</td></tr>
<tr><td colspan="3">Terms of payment
SIGHT L/C</td></tr>
<tr><td>Marks and Number</td><td>Number and kind of packages
Description of goods</td><td>Quantity</td><td>Unit Qrice</td><td>Amount</td></tr>
<tr><td>H F
HAMBURG
No. 1-100</td><td>100 CARTONS
PIG LEATHER WORK GLOVES</td><td>5000 DOZ</td><td>EUR 28.80
PER DOZ
CIFC5 HAMBURG</td><td>EUR144000.00</td></tr>
<tr><td></td><td colspan="4">TIFERT TRADING CO., LTD.
王宏</td></tr>
</table>

（2）提单

Shipper

TIFERT TRADING CO., LTD.
NO. 86, ZHUJIANG ROAD, TIANJIN, CHINA

B/L NO **123**

中国远洋运输（集团）总公司

CHINA OCEAN SHIPPING（GROUP）CO

Combined Transport BILL OF LADING

Consignee

TO ORDER

Notify Party

HELMUT FELD CO.
BILLSTR. 177
2000 HAMBURG GERMANY

Pre-carriaged by	Place of receipt
Ocean Vessel Voy No **XINXING V-1320**	Port of Loading **CHINA**

Port of Discharge	Place of Delivery	Final Destination
HANBURG		

Marks & Nos Container Seal No.	No.of Containers or P'kgs	Kind of Packages;Description of Goods	Gross Weight	Measurement
H F **HAMBURG** **No. 1-100**	**100 CTNS**	**PIG LEATHER WORK GLOVES** **FREIGHT TO COLLECT**	**7860KGS**	**33.200M3**

TOTAL NUMBER OF CONTAINERS
OR PACKAGES（IN WORDS） **SAY ONE HUNDRED CARTONS ONLY**

FREIGHT & CHARGES	Revenue Tons	Rate	Per	Prepaid	Collect

Ex Rate	Prepaid at	Payable at	Place and date of Issue **TIANJIN,25TH MAY, 2008**
	Total Prepaid	No. Of Original B(S)/L	Signed for the Carrier

LADEN ON BOARD THE VESSEL

DATE BY (TERMS PLEASE FIND ON BACK OF ORIGINAL B/L)

(COSCO STANDARD FORM 11)

（3）保险单

PICC 中国人民保险公司天津分公司

The People' s Insurance Company of China, Tianjin Branch

货物运输保险单　　　　**ORINGINAL**

CARGO TRANSPORTATION INSURANCE POLICY

发票号(INVOICE NO.)　　BP200430137　　保单号次
合同号(CONTRACT NO.)　　08/ST－122　　POLICY NO NT0213908725594308216
信用证号(L/C NO.)　　08/37－267
被保险人:TIFERT TRADING CO., LTD.
Insured:

中国人民保险公司(以下简称本公司)根据被保险人的要求,由被保险人向本公司缴付约定的保险费,按照本保险单承保险别和背面所列条款与下列特款承保下述货物运输保险,特立本保险单。

THIS POLICY OF INSURANCE WITNESSES THAT THE PEOPLE' S INSURANCE COMPANY OF CHINA(HEREINAFTER CALLED "THE COMPANY") AT THE REQUEST OF INSURED AND IN CONSIDERATION OF THE AGREED PREMIUM PAID TO THE COMPANY BY THE INSURED, UNDERTAKES TO INSURE THE UNDERMENTIONED GOODS IN TRANSPORTATION SUBJECT TO THE CONDITIONS OF THIS POLICY AS PER THE CLAUSES PRINTED OVERLEAF AND OTHER SPECIAL CLAUSES ATTACHED HEREON

标　记 MARKS & NOS.	数量及包装 QUANTITY	保险货物项目 DESCRIPTION OF GOODS	保险金额 AMOUNT INSURED
H　F HAMBURG No. 1－100	100 CTNS	PIG LEATHER WORK GLOVES	EUR158400.00

总保险金额
TOTAL AMOUNT INSURED: EUROPEAN DOLLARS ONE HUNDRED FIFTY－EIGHT THOUSAND FOUR HUNDRED ONLY

保费　　**启运日期:**　　**装载运输工具:**
PREMIUM AS ARRANGED DATE OF COMMENCEMENT AS PER B/L PER CONVEYANCE: XINXING
自　　经　　至
FROM XINGANG VIA ________ TO HAMBURG
承保险别:
CONDITIONS:
ALL RISKS AND WAR RISKS AS PER CIC

所保货物,如发生保险单项下可能引起索赔的损失或损坏,应立即通知本公司下述代理人查勘。如有索赔,应向本公司提交保险单正本(共2份正本)及有关文件。如一份正本已用于索赔,其余正本自动失效。

IN THE EVENT OF LOSS DAMAGE WHICH MAY RESULT IN A CLAIM UNDER THIS POLICY, IMMEDIATE NOTICE MUST BE GIVEN TO THE COMPANY AGENT AS MENTIONED HEREUNDER CLAIMS IF ANY, ONE OF THE ORIGINAL POLICY WHICH HAS BEEN ISSUED IN 2 ORIGINAL TOGETHER WITH RELEVENT DOCUMENTS SHALL BE SURRENDRED TO THE COMPANY IF THE ORIGINAL POLICY HAS BEEN ACCOMPLISHED, THE OTHERS TO BE VOID

赔款偿付地点
CLAIM PAYABLE AT HAMBURG　　　　中国人民保险公司天津市分公司
出单日期　　　　The People' s Insurance Company of China
ISSUEING DATE　**MAY 28TH, 2008**　　　　Tianjin Branch

(4) 装箱单

Issuer TIFERT TRADING CO., LTD. 86, ZHUJIANG ROAD, TIANJIN, CHINA	装 箱 单 PACKING LIST
To HELMUT FELD CO. BILLSTR. 177 2000 HAMBURG GERMANY	Invoice No BP**200430137** Date: May **18th, 2008**

Marks and Number	Number and kind of packages; Description of goods
H F HAMBURG No. 1 – 100	100 CTNS 5000 DOZ. PIG LEATHER WORK GLOVES TOTAL GROSS WEIGHT 5500KGS(@55KGS) NET WEIGHT 5200KGS(52KGS) PACKED IN CARTONS OF 50DOZ EACH TIFERT TRADING CO., LTD. 王宏

(5) 汇票

No. BP**200430137**

Exchange for EUR**136800.00**   Tianjin, MAY **26TH, 2008**

At ________ sight of this First of Exchange (Second of exchange being unpaid)

Pay to the order of BANK OF CHINA, TIANJIN, CHINA

The sum of EUROPEAN DOLLARS ONE HUNDRED THIRTY SIX THOUSAND AND EIGHT HUNDRED ONLY

Drawn under DOCUMENTARY CREDIT NO. **08/37 – 267** OF VEREINS – UNDWESTBANK

TO VEREINS – UNDWESTBANK
HAMBURG

TIFERT TRADING CO., LTD.
(signed)

（6）普惠制原产地证书

1. Goods consigned from (Export's name, Address, country) TIFERT TRADING CO., LTD. NO. 86, ZHUJIANG ROAD, TIANJIN, CHINA	Reference No. **GENERALIZED SYSTEM OF PREFERANCES** **CERTIFICATE OF ORIGIN** (Combined declaration and certificate) FORM A Issued in THE PEOPLE'S REPUBLIC OF CHINA (country)
2. Goods consigned to (Consignee's name, Address, country) HELMUT FELD CO. BILLSTR. 177 2000 HAMBURG GERMANY	
3. Means of transport and route (as far as known) FROM XINGANG TO HAMBURG PER S. S "XINXING" BY SEA	4. For official use

5. Item number	6. Marks and numbers of packages	7. Number and kind of packages; description of goods	8. Origin criterion	9. Gross weight or other quantity	10. Number and date of invoice
	H F HAMBURG No. 1 - 100	ONE HUDNRED (100) CTNS PIG LEATHER WORK GLOVES * * * * * * * * * * *	"P"	**5000** DOZ	BP**200430137** May **18th, 2008**

11. Certification It is hereby certified, on the basis of control Carried out, that the declaration by the exporter is correct. TIANJIN, MAY 21ST, 2008 Place and date, signature and stamp of certifying authority	12. Declaration by the exporter The undersigned hereby declares that the above details and statements are correct; that all the goods were produced in CHINA (country) And that they comply with the origin requirements specified for those goods in the Generalized System of Preferences for goods exported to E U (importing country) TIANJIN, MAY 21ST, 2008 Place and date, signature of authorized signatory

发票号		船名		提单号
开证行				装期
				效期
信用证号		结汇金额		交单期

单据名称	汇票	发票	装箱单	保险单	产地证	检验证	GSP产地证	海关发票	船行证明	受益人证明	电抄	提单	提单副本	其他	
应交份数															

存在问题及处理意见	
其他应注意事项：	

单证员	审单员	银行复核	结汇日期

样例 13 – 14　审单记录表

3. 高级训练

泰佛贸易公司与意大利 UNIWORLD 公司就出口中国大米达成一出口合同,400 公吨大米已装长江轮 V9437 航次运发往意大利威尼斯港,现全套单据已经缮制妥,请在送银行议付货款前依据信用证(见样例 13 - 15)仔细审核全套单据,填写审单记录表(见样例 13 - 16)力争做到单证相符、单单相符,保证安全收汇。

LETTER OF CREDIT

Sequence Total	* 27	1/1
Form of Doc Credit	* 40A	IRREVOCABLE
Applicable Rules	* 40E	UCP LATEST VERSION
Doc Credit Num	* 20	MLC9067
Date of Issue	31C	080916
Date/Place Exp	* 31D	Date 081115 Place CHINA
Applicant	* 50	UNIWORLD S. R. L VIA ARZAGA 28 20185 MILANO ITALY
Beneficiary	* 59	TIFERT TRADING CO., LTD NO. 85, ZHUJIANG ROAD, TIANJIN, CHINA
DC Amt	* 32B	USD Amount 24000. 00
Credit Amt	39B	NOT EXCEEDING
Avail With By	* 41D	ANY BANK BY NEGOTIATION
Drafts At	42C	SIGHT
Drawee	42D	ISSUING BANK
Partial Shipmts	43P	NOT ALLOWED
Transshipment	43T	ALLOWED
Loading on Brd	44E	TIANJIN, CHINA
Transport to	44F	VENICE, ITALY
Latest Shipment	44C	081030

Description of Goods

40MT OF CHINESE RICE AT A PRICE OF USD600 PER MT CIF VENICE, ITALY

SPECIFICATION: BROKEN GRAINS (MAX.) 20%

ADMIXTURE (MAX.) 0.2%

MOISTURE (MAX.) 10 %

PACKED IN BAGS OF 25KGS NET EACH

Docs Required 46A

+ SIGNED COMMERCIAL INVOICE IN QUADRUPLICATE + PACKING LIST IN QUADRUPLICATE
+ FULL SET OF CLEAN ON BOARD MARINE BILLS OF LADING (BEARING CONTAINER NUMBERS) CONSIGNED TO ORDER, ENDORSED IN BLANK, MARKED FREIGHT PREPAID NOTIFY APPLICANT.
+ CERTIFICATE OF ORIGIN ISSUED BY THE CHINA COUNCIL FOR THE PROMOTION OF INTERNATIONAL

TRADE AND BEARING L/C NO.

+ INSURANCE CERTIFICATE FOR 110 PERCENT OF INVOICE VALUE COVERING ALL RISKS AND WAR RISK AS PER AND SUBJECT TO OCEAN MARINE CARGO CLAUSES AND OCEAN MARINE CARGO WAR RISK CLAUSES OF P. I. C. C. DATED 1/1/1981
+ ORIGINAL BENEFICIARY'S CERTIFICATE STATING THAT ONE FULL SET OF ALL COPY DOCUMENTS HAVE BEEN SENT TO UNIWORLD S. R. L. BY COURIER BEFORE ETA OF SHIPMENT.

Conditions 47A

ALL PRESENTATIONS CONTAINING DISCREPANCIES WILL ATTRACT A DISCREPANCY FEE OF GBP40. 00 OR EQUIVALENT. THIS CHARGE WILL BE LEVIED WHETHER OR NOT WE ELECT TO CONSULT THE APPLICANT FOR A WAIVER IN ACCORDANCE WITH UCP600. AN ADDITIONAL FEE OF GBP 25. 00 PER MONTH WILL BE PAYABLE IF THE DOCUMENTS REMAIN UNPAID/UNACCEPTED FOR MORE THAN ONE MONTH AFTER PRESENTATION TO US. ALL CHARGES ARE FOR THE BENEFICIARY'S ACCOUNT.

Charges 71B ALL CHGS OUTSIDE COUNTRY OF ISSUE FOR ACCOUNT OF BENEFICIARY/EXPORTER TRANSIT INTEREST CHARGES ARE PAYABLE BY BENEFICIARY/EXPORTER

Period for Pres 48 WITHIN 15 DAYS AFTER THE DATE OF SHIPMENT BUT WITHIN THE VALIDITY OF THE CREDIT

Confirmation instructions *49 WITHOUT

Paying Bank 78 UPON RECEIPT OF DOCUMENTS PRESENTED IN ACCORDANCE WITH THE DOCUMENTARY CREDIT TERMS AND CONDITIONS WE WILL REMIT PROCEEDS AT MATURITY IN ACCORDANCE WITH YOUR INSTRUCTIONS.

Send Rec Info 72 DOCUMENTS TO BE DESPATCHED BY COURIER IN ONE LOT TO: HSBC BANK PLC, TRADE SERVICES, VENICE, INTERNATIONAL BRANCH, PO BOX 585, 4TM FLOOR, 6 ARTHUR STREET, VENICE, ITALY.

样例 13-15 大米信用证

(1) 发票

TIFERT TRADING CO., LTD
NO.86, ZHUJIANG ROAD, TIANJIN, CHINA

商 业 发 票

COMMERCIAL INVOICE

TO UNIWORLD S. R. L.
VIA ARZAGA 28
20185 MILANO
ITALY
FROM: TIANJIN, CHINA

INVOICE NO: JFC3721
DATE: OCT 4 2008
L/C NO: MLC9067
S/C NO: ZCM9368
TO: VENICE, ITALY

MARKS & NUMBERS	QUANTITIES AND DESCRIPTION S OF GOODS	UNIT PRICE	AMOUNT
UNIWORLD ZCM9368 MILANO NO.1-1600	**1600BAGS - 40 MT OF CHINESE RICE SPECIFICATION: BROKEN GRAINS (MAX.) 20% ADMIXTURE (MAX.) 0.2% MOISTURE (MAX.) 10 % PACKED IN BAGS OF 25KGS NET EACH**	**USD600/MT**	**USD24000.00**

(2) 装箱单

TIFERT TRADING CO., LTD
NO. 86, ZHUJIANG ROAD, TIANJIN, CHINA

装 箱 单

PACKING LIST

No. JFC3721
DATE: OCT 6 2008

MARKS & NUMBERS	QUANTITIES AND DESCRIPTION S OF GOODS
UNIWORLD ZCM6398 MILANO NO.1-1600	**1600BAGS - 40MT CHINESE RICE TOTAL GROSS WEIGHT 40500KGS NET WEIGHT 40000KGS PACKED IN BAGS OF 25KGS NET EACH** TIFERT TRADING CO., LTD 王宏

（3）产地证

<table>
<tr><td colspan="2">1.Exporter（full name and address）
TIFERT TRADING CO., LTD
NO.86, ZHUJIANG ROAD, TIANJIN, CHINA</td><td colspan="3" rowspan="2">CERTIFICATE No.

CERTIFICATE OF ORIGIN
OF
THE PEOPLE'S REPUBLIC OF CHINA</td></tr>
<tr><td colspan="2">2.Consignee（full name and adress）
UNIWORLD S. R. L.
VIA ARZAGA 28,20185 MILANO, ITALY</td></tr>
<tr><td colspan="2">3.Means of transport and route
FROM TIANJIN TO VENICE , ITALY BY SEA</td><td colspan="3" rowspan="2">5 For certifying authority use only</td></tr>
<tr><td colspan="2">4. Country / region of destination
VENICE , ITALY</td></tr>
<tr><td>6.Marks and numbers of packages</td><td>7.Description of goods; Number and kind of packages;</td><td>8. HS CODE</td><td>9.Quantity or weight</td><td>10.Number and date of invoices</td></tr>
<tr><td>**UNIWORLD**
ZCM9368
MILANO
NO.1-1600</td><td>**ONE THOUSAND SIX HUNDRED (1600) BAGS OF CHINESE RICE**
* * * *</td><td></td><td>**GROSS WEIGHT: 40500KGS**</td><td>**JFC3721**
OCT 4, 2002</td></tr>
<tr><td colspan="2">11. Declaration by the exporter
The undersigned hereby declares that the above details and statements are correct; that all the goods were produced in China and that they comply with the Rules of Origin of the People's Republic of China

TIANJIN,CHINA OCT 29, 2008

Place and date,signature and stamp of authorized signatory</td><td colspan="3">12. Certification
It is hereby certified that the declaration by the exporter is correct

TIANJIN,CHINA OCT 29, 2008

Place and date,signature and stamp of certifying authority</td></tr>
</table>

（4）提单

Shipper **TIFERT TRADING CO., LTD** **NO. 86, ZHUJIANG ROAD, TIANJIN, CHINA**		B/L NO 中国远洋运输（集团）总公司 CHINA OCEAN SHIPPING（GROUP）CO Combined Transport BILL OF LADING		
Consignee **TO ORDER**				
Notify Party **APPLICANT**				
Pre-carriaged by	Place of receipt			
Ocean Vessel　Voy No **CHANGJIANG V9437**	Port of Loading **TIANJIN,CHINA**			
Port of Discharge **VENICE, ITALY**	Place of Delivery	Final Destination		

Marks & Nos Container Seal No.	No.of Containers or P'kgs	Kind of Packages;Description of Goods	Gross Weight	Measurement
UNIWORLD **ZCM9368** **MILANO** **NO.1-1600**	**1600BAGS**	**CHINESE RICE** **TTNU7038062/54501** **TTNU7439205/54502** **FCL/FCL 2X20'CY/CY**	**40500KGS**	**54.000CBM**

TOTAL NUMBER OF CONTAINERS OR PACKAGES（IN WORDS）　**SAY TWO TWENTY FEET CONTAINER(2X20') ONLY**

FREIGHT & CHARGES	Revenue Tons	Rate	Per	Prepaid	Collect

Ex Rate	Prepaid at	Payable at	Place and date of Issue TIANJIN **OCT 28, 2008**
	Total Prepaid	No. Of Original B(S)/L **THREE(3)**	Signed for the Carrier

LADEN ON BOARD THE VESSEL

DATE　**OCT 28,2008**　　BY　　(TERMS PLEASE FIND ON BACK OF ORIGINAL B/L)

(COSCO STANDARD FORM 11)

（5）保险单

PICC 中国人民保险公司天津分公司

The People's Insurance Company of China, Tianjin Branch

货物运输保险单 **ORIGINAL**

CARGO TRANSPORTATION INSURANCE POLICY

发票号(INVOICE NO.) **JFC3721** 保单号次

合同号(CONTRACT NO.) **CHJ01-01** POLICY NO **PYCA20486750006745**

信用证号(L/C NO.) M521588

被保险人：**TIFERT TRADING CO., LTD**

Insured：

中国人民保险公司（以下简称本公司）根据被保险人的要求，由被保险人向本公司缴付约定的保险费，按照本保险单承保险别和背面所列条款与下列特款承保下述货物运输保险，特立本保险单。

THIS POLICY OF INSURANCE WITNESSES THAT THE PEOPLE S INSURANCE COMPANY OF CHINA（HEREINAFTER CALLED "THE COMPANY"）AT THE REQUEST OF INSURED AND IN CONSIDERATION OF THE AGREED PREMIUM PAID TO THE COMPANY BY THE INSURED，UNDERTAKES TO INSURE THE UNDERMENTIONED GOODS IN TRANSPORTATION SUBJECT TO THE CONDITIONS OF THIS POLICY AS PER THE CLAUSES PRINTED OVERLEAF AND OTHER SPECIAL CLAUSES ATTACHED HEREON

标　记 MARKS & NOS.	数量及包装 QUANTITY	保险货物项目 DESCRIPTION OF GOODS	保险金额 AMOUNT INSURED
AS PER INVOICE NO JFC3721	**1600 BAGS**	**CHINESE RICE**	**USD24,000.00**

总保险金额

TOTAL AMOUNT INSURED：**US DOLLARS TWENTY FOUT THOUSAND ONLY**

保费 启运日期： 装载运输工具：

PREMIUM **AS ARRANGED** DATE OF COMMENCEMENT **AS PER B/L** PER CONVEYANCE: **CHANGJIANG V9437**

自 经 至

FROM **TIANJIN,CHINA** VIA TO **VENICE,ITALY**

承保险别：

CONDITIONS：

ALL RISKS AND WAR RISK AS PER AND SUBJECT TO OCEAN MARINE CARGO CLAUSES AND OCEAN MARINE CARGO WAR RISK CLAUSES OF THE PEOPLE'S INSURANCE COMPANY OF CHINA DATED 1/1/1981.

所保货物，如发生保险单项下可能引起索赔的损失或损坏，应立即通知本公司下述代理人查勘。如有索赔应向本公司提交保险单正本（共 2 份正本）及有关文件。如一份正本已用于索赔，其余正本自动失效。

IN THE EVENT OF LOSS DAMAGE WHICH MAY RESULT IN A CLAIM UNDER THIS POLICY, IMMEDIATE NOTICE MUST BE GIVEN TO THE COMPANY AGENT AS MENTIONED HEREUNDER CLAIMS IF ANY, ONE OF THE ORIGINAL POLICY WHICH HAS BEEN ISSUED IN 2 ORIGINAL TOGETHER WITH RELEVENT DOCUMENTS SHALL BE SURRENDRED TO THE COMPANY IF THE ORIGINAL POLICY HAS BEEN ACCOMPLISHED， THE OTHERS TO BE VOID

赔款偿付地点

CLAIM PAYABLE AT ____________

中国人民保险公司天津市分公司

The People's Insurance Company of China

Tianjin Branch

出单日期

ISSUEING DATE **OCT 26,2008**

(6)受益人证明

TIFERT TRADING GO.,LTD

NO.86, ZHUJIANG ROAD, TIANJIN, CHINA

受益人证明

BENEFICIARY'S CERTIFICATE

OCT 29, 2008

RE: INVOICE NO.JFC3721

L/C NO: MLC9067

WE HEREBY STATE THAT ONE FULL SET OF ALL COPY DOCUMENTS HAVE BEEN SENT TO UNIWORLD S.R.L. BY COURIER BEFORE ETA OF SHIPMENT.

TIFERT TRADING CO., LTD

(7)受益人证明

No. JFC3721

Exchange for USD2400.00 TIANJIN, China

At * * * * * sight of this First of Exchange (Second of exchange being unpaid) Pay to the order of TIFERT TRADING CO., LTD

The sum of

SAY UNITED STATES DOLLARS ONE THOUSAND FOUR HUNDRED ONLY

Drawn under MILAND BANK PLC ITALY L/C NO MLC9067 DATED 080916

TO UNIWORLD S. R. L

VIA ARZAGA 28 20185 MILANO

ITALY

发票号		船名		提单号
开证行				装期
				效期
信用证号		结汇金额		
				交单期

单据名称	汇票	发票	装箱单	保险单	产地证	检验证	GSP产地证	海关发票	船行证明	受益人证明	电抄	提单	提单副本	其他	
应交份数															
存在问题及处理意见															

其他应注意事项：

单证员	审单员	银行复核	结汇日期

样例 13 – 16　审单记录表

附录一

世界主要港口一览表
（中英文对照）

港口名称	中译名	所属国家或地区	所属航线
以(A)开头的世界港口			
Aarhus	奥尔胡斯	丹麦	西北欧
Abadan	阿巴丹	伊朗	波斯湾
Abidjan	阿比让	科特迪瓦	西非
Abu Dhabi	阿布扎比	阿联酋	波斯湾
Acajutla	阿卡胡特拉	萨尔瓦多	中南美
Acapulco	阿卡普尔科	墨西哥	中南美
Accra	阿克拉	加纳	西非
Adelaide	阿得雷德	澳大利亚	澳新
Aden	亚丁	也门	红海
Alexandria	亚历山大	埃及	地中海
Algiers	阿尔及尔	阿尔及利亚	地中海
Amsterdam	阿姆斯特丹	荷兰	西北欧
Ancona	安科纳	意大利	地中海
Annaba	安纳巴	阿尔及利亚	地中海
Antofagasta	安托法加斯塔	智利	中南美
Antwerp	安特卫普	比利时	西北欧
Apapa	阿帕帕	尼日利亚	西非
Apia	阿皮亚	西萨摩亚	澳新
Aqaba	亚喀巴	约旦	红海
Arica	阿里卡	智利	中南美
Assab	阿萨布	埃塞俄比亚	红海
Athens	雅典	希腊	地中海
Auckland	奥克兰	新西兰	澳新
Avonmouth	阿芬默思	英国	西北欧
以(B)开头的世界港口			
Bahia Blanca	布兰卡港	阿根廷	中南美

Bahrain	巴林	巴林	波斯湾
Baltimore	巴尔的摩	美国(爱尔兰有同名港)	美国东岸
Banana	巴纳纳	扎伊尔	西非
Bandar Abbas	阿巴斯港	伊朗	波斯湾
Bandar Shahpour (Bandar Khomeini)	沙赫普尔港 (霍梅尼港)	伊朗	波斯湾
Bangkok	曼谷	泰国	泰国
Banjul(Bathurst)	班珠尔	冈比亚	西非
Barcelona	巴塞罗那	西班牙	地中海
Barranquilla	巴兰基利亚	哥伦比亚	中南美
Basra	巴士拉	伊拉克	波斯湾
Bassein	勃生	缅甸	孟加拉湾
Bata	巴塔	赤道几内亚	西非
Beira	贝拉	莫桑比克	东非
Beirut	帆鲁特	黎巴嫩	地中海
Belawan	勿拉沙璜湾	印度尼西亚	印尼
Belfast	贝尔法斯特	英国	西北欧
Belize	伯利兹	伯利兹	中南美
Benghazi	班加西	利比亚	地中海
Berbera	伯贝拉	索马里	东非
Bergen	卑尔根	挪威	西北欧
Bilbao	毕尔巴鄂	西班牙	西北欧
Blrkenhead	伯肯黑德	英国	西北欧
Bissau	比绍	几内亚比绍	西非
Bizerta	比塞大	突尼斯	地中海
Boma	博马	扎伊尔	西非
Bombay	孟买	印度	波斯湾
Bordeaux	波尔多	法国	西北欧
Boston	波士顿	美国(英国有同名港)	美国东岸
Bourgas (Burghaz 或 Burgas)	布尔加斯	保加利亚	地中海
Bremen	不来梅	德国	西北欧
Bremerhaven	不来梅哈芬	德国	西北欧
Brest	布雷斯特	法国	西北欧

Bridgetown	布里奇顿	巴巴多斯	中南美
Brighton	布赖顿	特立尼达和多巴哥 (英国有同名港口)	中南美
Brindisi	布林迪西	意大利	地中海
Brisbane	布里斯班	澳大利亚	澳新
Bristol	布里斯托尔	英国	西北欧
Brunei (BandarSeri Begawan)	文莱 (斯里巴加湾)	文莱	北加里曼丹
Bruseels	布鲁塞尔	比利时	西北欧
Buenaventura	布埃纳文图拉	哥伦比亚	中南美
Buenos Aires	布宜诺斯艾利斯	阿根廷	中南美
Buffalo	布法罗	美国	美国东岸
Bunbury	邦伯里	澳大利亚	澳新
Bushire	布什尔	伊朗	波斯湾
Butterworth	巴特沃思	马来西亚	新马

以(C)开头的世界港口

Cabinda	卡宾达	安哥拉	西非
Cadiz	加的斯	西班牙(菲律宾有同名港)	西北欧
Caloutta	加尔各答	印度	孟加拉湾
Callao	卡亚俄	秘鲁	中南美
Cambrigde	坎布里奇	美国	美国东岸
Cape Town	开普敦	南非	西非
Casablanca	卡萨布兰卡	摩洛哥	西非
Charleston	查尔斯顿	美国	北美
Chiba	千叶	日本	日本
Chicago	芝加哥	美国	北美
Chittagong	吉大港	孟加拉	孟加拉湾
Colombo	科伦坡	斯里兰卡	孟加拉湾
Colon	科隆	巴拿马	中南美
Columbus	哥伦布	美国	北美
Copenhagen	哥本哈根	丹麦	西北欧
Cork	科克	爱尔兰	西北欧
Cotonou	科托努	贝宁	非洲

Cristobal	克里斯托巴尔	巴拿马	中南美

以(D)开头的世界港口

Dacca	达卡	孟加拉	孟加拉湾
Dakar	达喀尔	塞内加尔	西非
Damman	达曼	沙特阿拉伯	波斯湾
Da Nang	岘港	越南	越南
Dar es Salaam	达累斯萨拉姆	坦桑尼亚	东非
Darwin	达尔文	澳大利亚	澳新
Detroit	底特律	美国	美国东岸
Djakarta(Jakarta)	雅加达	印尼	印尼
Djibouti	吉布提	吉布提	红海
Doha	多哈	卡塔尔	波斯湾
Douala	杜阿拉	喀麦隆	西非
Dover	多佛尔	英国	西北欧
Dubai	迪拜	阿联酋	波斯湾
Dublin	都柏林	爱尔兰	西北欧
Dunedin	达尼丁	新西兰	澳新
Dunkirk	敦刻尔克	法国	西北欧
Durban	德班	南非	东非
Durres	都拉斯	阿尔巴尼亚	阿尔巴尼亚
Dusseldorf	杜塞尔多夫	德国	西北欧

以(E)开头的世界港口

East London	东伦敦	南非	东非
Ensenada	恩塞纳尔	墨西哥	中南美

以(F)开头的世界港口

Felixstowe	费力克斯托	英国	西北欧
Fort de France	法兰西堡	马提尼克岛	中南美
Frankfurt	法兰克福	德国	西北欧
Freeport	弗里波特	巴哈马 (美国、百慕大群岛有同名港)	中南美
Freetown	弗里敦	塞拉立昂	西非

Fremantle	弗里曼特尔	澳大利亚	澳新
Fukuo	福冈	日本	日本
Funafuti	富纳富提	图瓦卢	澳新
Funchal	丰沙尔	马德拉群岛	西非

以(G) 开头的世界港口

Gdansk	格但斯克	波兰	西北欧
Gdynia	格丁尼亚	波兰	西北欧
Gelaka	杰拉	意大利	地中海
Genoa	热那亚	意大利	地中海
Georgetown	乔治敦 （美、加拿大、圭亚那、马来西亚均有同名港口）	圣文森特和格林纳丁斯	中南美
Ghent	根特	比利时	西北欧
Gibraltar	直布罗陀	直布罗陀	西北欧
Glasgow	格拉斯哥	英国	西北欧
Gothenburg	哥德堡	瑞典	西北欧
Grangemouth	格兰杰默斯	英国	西北欧
Guayaquil	瓜亚基尔	厄瓜多尔	中南美
Gwadur	瓜达尔	巴基斯坦	波斯湾

以(H) 开头的世界港口

Haifa	海法	以色列	地中海
Haiphong	海防	越南	越南
Hakodate	函馆	日本	日本
Halifax	哈利法克斯	加拿大	加拿大东岸
Halmstad	哈尔姆斯塔	瑞典	西北欧
Hamburg	汉堡	德国	西北欧
Hamilton	汉密尔顿	百慕大群岛 （加拿大有同名港口）	中南美
Haugesund	豪格松	挪威	西北欧
Havana	哈瓦那	古巴	中南美
Helsingborg	赫尔辛堡	瑞典	西北欧
Helsingor	赫尔辛格	丹麦	西北欧
Helsinki	赫尔辛基	芬兰	西北欧

Hiroshima	广岛	日本	日本
Ho Chi Minh City	胡志明市(西贡)	越南	越南
Hobart	霍巴特	澳大利亚	澳新
Hodeida	荷台达	也门	红海
Hongay	鸿基	越南	越南
Hong Kong	香港	中国	港澳
Honiara	霍尼亚拉	所罗门群岛	澳新
Honolulu	火奴鲁鲁(檀香山)	美国	美国西岸
Horta	奥尔塔	亚速尔群岛(葡属)	西非
Houston	休斯敦	美国	美国东岸
Hull	赫尔	英国	西北欧

以(I) 开头的世界港口

Immingham	伊明翰姆	英国	西北欧
Iquique	伊基克	智利	中南美
Iskenderun (Alexandretta)	伊斯肯德伦	土耳其	地中海
Istanbul	伊斯坦布尔	土耳其	地中海
Izmir	伊兹密尔	土耳其	地中海

以(J) 开头的世界港口

Jamestown	詹姆斯顿	圣赫勒那岛	西非
Jidda(Jeddah)	吉达	沙特阿拉伯	红海
Jogjakarta	日惹	印尼	印尼
Johore Bahru	柔佛巴鲁(新山)	马来西亚	新马

以(K) 开头的世界港口

Kaliningrad	加里宁格勒	俄罗斯	西北欧
Karachi	卡拉奇	巴基斯坦	波斯湾
Kavieng	卡维恩	巴布亚新几内亚	澳新
Kawasaki	川崎	日本	日本
Kholmsk	霍尔姆斯克	俄罗斯	俄罗斯
Khorramshahr	霍拉姆沙赫尔	伊朗	波斯湾
Kiel	基尔	德国	西北欧

Kieta	基埃塔	所罗门群岛	澳新
Kingston	金斯敦	牙买加	中南美
	(加拿大、中南美、澳大利亚有同名港口)		
Kingstown	金斯敦	圣文森特和格林纳丁斯	中南美
Kismayu	基斯马尤	索马里	东非
Kobe	神户	日本	日本
Kompong Som	磅逊	柬埔寨	泰国
Kota Kinabalu	亚庇(哥打基纳巴卢)	马来西亚	北加里曼丹
Kotka	科特卡	芬兰	西北欧
Kuching	古晋	马来西亚	北加里曼丹
Kudat	库达特	马来西亚	北加里曼丹
Kure	吴港	日本	日本
Kuwait	科威特	科威特	波斯湾

以(L)开头的世界港口

Labuan	拉布安(纳闽)	马来西亚	北加里曼丹
Lae	莱城	巴布亚新几内亚	澳新
La Guaira	拉瓜伊拉	委内瑞拉	中南美
Lancaster	兰开斯特	英国	西北欧

以(M)开头的世界港口

Macao	澳门	中国	港澳
Madang	马丹	巴布亚新几内亚	澳新
Madras	马德拉斯	印度	孟加拉湾
Mahe	马埃	印度	波斯湾
Majunga	马任加	马达加斯加	东非
Makassar(Macassar)	望加锡	印尼	印尼
Malabo(SantaIsabel)	马拉博	赤道几内亚	西非
Malacca	马六甲	马来西亚	新马
Male	马累	马尔代夫	波斯湾
Malindi	马林迪	肯尼亚	东非
Malmo	马尔默	瑞典	西北欧
Malta	马耳他	马耳他	地中海
Manchester	曼彻斯特	英国	西北欧

Manila	马尼拉	菲律宾	菲律宾
Manzanillo	曼萨尼略	墨西哥 (古巴、多米尼加共和国有同名港)	中南美
Maracaibo	马拉开波	委内瑞拉	中南美

以(N)开头的世界港口

Nagasaki	长崎	日本	日本
Nagoya	名古屋	日本	日本
Nakhodka	纳霍德卡	俄罗斯	远东线
Nampo	南浦	朝鲜	朝鲜
Nantes	南特	法国	西北欧
Napier	纳皮尔	新西兰	澳新
Naples(Napoli)	那不勒斯(那波利)	意大利	地中海
Nassau	拿骚	巴哈马联邦	中南美
Nauru	瑙鲁	瑙鲁	澳新
New Amsterdam	新阿姆斯特丹	圭亚那	中南美
Newcastle	纽卡斯尔 (美、加拿大、澳大利亚有同名港口)	英国	西北欧
New Orleans	新奥尔良	美国	美国东岸

以(O)开头的世界港口

Oakland	奥克兰	美国	美国西岸
Odessa	敖德萨	乌克兰	地中海
Oran	奥兰	阿尔及利亚	地中海
Oranjestad	奥腊涅斯塔德	安的列斯(荷属)	中南美
Osaka	大阪	日本	日本
Oslo	奥斯陆	挪威	西北欧
Otaru	小樽	日本	日本
Owendo	奥文多	加蓬	西非

以(P)开头的世界港口

Padang	巴东	印尼	印尼
Pago Pago	帕果帕果	东萨摩亚(美属)	澳新
Palembang	巨港	印尼	印尼

Panama	巴拿马	巴拿马	中南美
Papeete	帕皮提	波利尼西亚(法属)	澳新
Paramaribo	帕拉马里博	苏里南	中南美
Paranagua	巴拉那瓜	巴西	中南美
Penang	槟城	马来西亚	新马
Perth	珀斯	澳大利亚(美国有同名港口)	澳新
Philadedlphia	费城	美国	美国东岸
Phom Penh	金边	柬埔寨	暹罗海
Piraeus	比雷埃夫斯	希腊	地中海
Plymouth	普列茅斯	蒙特塞拉特岛	中南美
	(英、美、新西兰、特立尼达和多巴哥均有同名港口)		
Pointe - a - Pitre	皮特尔角	瓜德罗普岛	中南美
Pointe des Galets	加莱角	留尼汪岛(法属)	东非
Pointe Noire	黑角	刚果	西非
Ponce	蓬塞	波多黎各(美属)	中南美
Pondicherry	本地治里	印度	孟加拉湾
Pontianak	坤甸	印尼	印尼
Port Adelaide	阿德雷德	澳大利亚	澳新
Porau Prince	太子港	海地	中南美
Port Castries	卡斯特里港	圣卢西亚	中南美
Port Elizabeth	伊丽莎白港	南非	东非
Port Harcourt	哈科特港	尼日利亚	西非
Port Kelang	巴生港	马来西亚	新马
Port Kembla	肯布兰	澳大利亚	澳新
Portland(Maine 洲)	波特兰	美国	美国东岸
Portland(Oregon 洲)	波特兰	美国	美国西岸
		(英国、澳大利亚有同名港口)	
Port Limon	利蒙港	哥斯达黎加	中南美
Port Louis	路易港	毛里求斯	东非
Port Moresby	莫尔兹比港	巴布亚新几内亚	澳新
Port of Spain	西班牙港	特立尼达和多巴哥	中南美
Porto Novo	波多诺伏	贝宁	西非
Port Said	塞得港	埃及	地中海
Portsmouth	朴次茅斯	英国(美国有同名港口)	西北欧

Port Stanley	斯坦利港	福克兰群岛	中南美
Port Sudan	苏丹港	苏丹	红海
Port Victoria	维多利亚港	塞舌尔群岛 （澳大利亚有同名港口）	东非
Port Vila	维拉港	瓦努阿图	澳新
Priolo	辟利洛(普里奥洛)	意大利	地中海
Puerto Cabello	卡贝略港	委内瑞拉	中南美
Punta Arenas	彭塔阿雷纳斯	智利	中南美
Puntarenas	彭塔雷纳斯	哥斯达黎加	中南美
Pusan(Busan)	釜山	韩国	韩国

以(Q) 开头的世界港口

Quebec	魁北克	加拿大	加拿大东岸

以(R) 开头的世界港口

Rabat	拉巴特	摩洛哥	西非
Rabaul	腊包尔港	巴布亚新几内亚	澳新
Rangoon	仰光	缅甸	孟加拉湾
Rarotonga	拉罗通加	库克群岛	澳新
Recife	累西菲	巴西	中南美
Reykjavik	雷克雅未克	冰岛	西北欧
Riga	里加	拉脱维亚	西北欧
Rijeka	里耶卡	克罗地亚	地中海
Rio de Janeiro	里约热内卢	巴西	中南美
Rio Grande	里奥格兰德	巴西	中南美
Rostock	罗斯托克	德国	西北欧
Rotterdam	鹿特丹	荷兰	西北欧

以(S) 开头的世界港口

Sabang	沙璜	印尼	印尼
Sandakan	山打根	马来西亚	北加里曼丹
San Diego	圣迭戈	美国	美国西岸
San Fernando	圣费尔南多	特立尼达和多巴哥 （西班牙、阿根廷、菲律宾有同名港口）	中南美

San Francisco	旧金山	美国(巴西有同名港口)	美国西岸
San Jose	圣何塞	危地马拉	中南美
San Juan	圣胡安	波多黎各 (秘鲁、阿根廷有同名港口)	中南美
San Juan del Sur	南圣胡安	尼加拉瓜	中南美
San Lorenzo	圣洛伦索	阿根廷	中南美
Santa Cruz del Sur	圣克鲁斯蒂尔苏	古巴	中南美
Santa Cruz	圣克鲁斯	加那利群岛 (亚速尔群岛、阿根廷、美国、菲律宾有同名港口)	西非
Santiago	圣地亚哥	佛得角(古巴有同名港口)	西非
Santo	圣吐(桑托)	瓦努阿图	澳新
Santo Domingo	圣多明各	多米尼加共和国	中南美
Santos	圣多斯	巴西	中南美
San Tome	圣多美	圣多美和普林西北 (巴西有同名港口)	西非
Savannah	萨凡纳	美国	美国东岸
Seattle	西雅图	美国	美国西岸
Semarang	三宝垄	印尼	印尼
Sete	塞特	法国	地中海
Sharjah	沙迦	阿联酋	波斯湾
Sibu	诗巫(泗务、西布)	马来西亚	北加里曼丹
Singapore	新加坡	新加坡	新马
Southampton	南安普敦	英国	西北欧
Split	斯普利特	波黑共和国	地中海
Stavanger	斯塔万格	挪威	西北欧
St. Denis	圣但尼	留尼汪岛	东非
St. Georges	圣乔治	百慕大群岛 (加拿大、格林纳达有同名港)	中南美
St. John	圣约翰	加拿大	加拿大东岸
St. Johns	圣约翰斯	安提瓜和巴布达 (加拿大、南非有同名港口)	中南美
St. Lawrence	圣劳伦斯	加拿大 (澳大利亚有同名港口)	加拿大东岸
Stockholm	斯德哥尔摩	瑞典	西北欧

St. Thomas	圣托马斯	维尔京群岛(美属)	中南美
Suez	苏伊士	埃及	红海
Sur	苏尔	黎巴嫩(阿曼有同名港口)	地中海
Surabaya	泗水	印尼	印尼
Suva	苏瓦	斐济	澳新
Swansea	斯旺西	英国	西北欧
Sydney	悉尼	澳大利亚 (加拿大有同名港口)	澳新
Szczecin	什切青	波兰	西北欧

以(T)开头的世界港口

Tabaco	塔巴科	菲律宾	菲律宾
Takoradi	塔科拉迪	加纳	西非
Tallin	塔林	爱沙尼亚	西北欧
Tamatave	塔马塔夫	马达加斯加	东非
Tampico	坦皮科	墨西哥	中南美
Tandjungpriok	丹戎不碌	印尼	印尼
Tanga	坦噶	坦桑尼亚	东非
Tangier	丹吉尔	摩洛哥	西非
Tarawa	塔拉瓦	基里巴斯	澳新
Tawau	斗湖	马来西亚	北加里曼丹
Tel Aviv	特拉维夫	以色列	地中海
Tema	特马	加纳	西非
Tjirebon	井里汶	印尼	印尼
Tokyo	东京	日本	日本
Toronto	多伦多	加拿大	加拿大东岸
Toulon	土伦	法国	地中海
Trieste	的里雅斯特	意大利	地中海
Trincomalee	亭可马里	斯里兰卡	斯里兰卡
Tripoli	的黎波里	比亚(黎巴嫩有同名港口)	地中海
Trujillo	特鲁希略	洪都拉斯(秘鲁有同名港)	中南美
Tumaco	图马科	哥伦比亚	中南美
Tunis	突尼斯	突尼斯	地中海
Turku	图尔库	芬兰	西北欧

以(U)开头的世界港口

Umm Said	乌姆赛义德	卡塔尔	波斯湾

以(V)开头的世界港口

Valletta	瓦莱塔	马耳他	地中海
Valona	发罗拉(法罗拉)	阿尔巴尼亚	阿尔巴尼亚
Valparaiso	瓦尔帕莱索	智利	中南美
Vancouver	温哥华	加拿大(美国有同名港口)	加拿大西岸
Varna	戊尔纳	保加利亚	地中海
Vasa	瓦沙	芬兰	西北欧
Venice	威尼斯	意大利	地中海
Victoria	维多利亚	喀麦隆	西非
(澳大利亚、加拿大、马来西亚、几内亚、马耳他、塞舌尔群岛均有同名港口)			
Vigo	维哥	西班牙	西北欧
Visby	维斯比	瑞典	西北欧
Vostochny	东方港	俄罗斯	远东线

以(W)开头的世界港口

Walvis Bay	沃尔维斯湾	纳米比亚(西南非洲)	西非
Wellington	惠灵顿	新西兰	澳新
Wewak	威瓦克	巴布亚新几内亚	澳新
Willemstad	威廉斯塔德	安的列斯(荷属)(荷兰有同名港口)	中南美
Wismar	维斯马	德国	西北欧

以(Y)开头的世界港口

Yalta	雅尔塔	俄罗斯	地中海
Yokohama	横滨	日本	日本

以(Z)开头的世界港口

Zanzibar	桑给巴尔	坦桑尼亚	东非

附录二

世界各国货币一览表
（中英文对照）

亚洲	货币名称		货币符号		辅币进位制
	中文	英文	原有旧符号	标准符号	
中国香港	港元	HongKong Dollars	HK $	HKD	1HKD = 100cents（分）
中国澳门	澳门元	Macao Pataca	PAT.；P.	MOP	1MOP = 100avos（分）
中国	人民币元	Renminbi Yuan	RMB ¥	CNY	1CNY = 10 jao（角） 1 jao = 10 fen（分）
朝鲜	圆	Korean Won		KPW	1KPW = 100 分
越南	越南盾	Vietnamese Dong	D.	VND	1VND = 10 角 = 100 分
日本	日圆	Japanese Yen	¥；J. ¥	JPY	1JPY = 100 sen（钱）
老挝	基普	Laotian Kip	K.	LAK	1LAK 1LAK = 100ats（阿特）
柬埔寨	瑞尔	Camboddian Riel	CR.；J Ri.	KHR	1KHR = 100 sen（仙）
菲律宾	菲律宾比索	Philippine Peso	Ph. Pes.；Phil. P.	PHP	1PHP = 100 centavos（分）
马来西亚	马元	Malaysian Dollar	M. $；Mal. $	MYR	1MYR = 100 cents（分）
新加坡	新加坡元	Singapore Dollar	S. $	SGD	1SGD = 100 cents（分）
泰国	泰铢	Thai Baht（Thai Tical）	BT.；Tc.	THP	1THP = 100 satang（萨当）
缅甸	缅元	Burmese Kyat	K.	BUK	1BUK = 100 pyas（分）
斯里兰卡	斯里兰卡卢比	Sri Lanka Rupee	S. Re. 复数：S. Rs.	LKR	1LKR = 100 cents（分）
马尔代夫	马尔代夫卢比	Maldives Rupee	M. R. R；MAL. Rs.	MVR	1MVR = 100 larees（拉雷）
印度尼西亚	盾	Indonesian Rupiah	Rps.	IDR	1IDR = 100 cents（分）

续表

亚　洲	货币名称		货币符号		辅币进位制
	中　文	英　文	原有旧符号	标准符号	
巴基斯坦	巴基斯坦卢比	Pakistan Rupee	Pak. Re.;P. Re. 复数:P. Rs.	PRK	1PRK = 100 paisa (派萨)
印度	卢比	Indian Rupee	Re. 复数:Rs.	INR	1INR = 100paise(派士)(单数:paisa)
尼泊尔	尼泊尔卢比	Nepalese Rupee	N. Re. 复数:N. Rs.	NPR	1NPR = 100 paise(派司)
阿富汗	阿富汗尼	Afghani	Af.	AFA	1AFA = 100 puls(普尔)
伊朗	伊朗里亚尔	Iranian Rial	RI.	IRR	1Irr = 100 dinars(第纳尔)
伊拉克	伊拉克第纳尔	Iraqi Dinar	ID	IQD	1IQD = 1000 fils(费尔)
叙利亚	叙利亚镑	Syrian Pound	£.Syr.;£.S.	SYP	1SYP = 100 piastres(皮阿斯特)
黎巴嫩	黎巴嫩镑	Lebanese Pound	£ L.	LBP	1LBP = 100 piastres(皮阿斯特)
约旦	约旦第纳尔	Jordanian Dinar	J. D.;J. Dr.	JOD	1JOD = 1,000 fils(费尔)
沙特阿拉伯	亚尔	Saudi Arabian Riyal	S. A. Rls.;S. R.	SAR	1SAR = 100qurush(库尔什) 1qurush = 5 halals(哈拉)沙特里
科威特	科威特第纳尔	Kuwaiti Dinar	K. D.	KWD	1KWD = 1,000 fils(费尔)
巴林	巴林第纳尔	Bahrain Dinar	BD.	BHD	1BHD = 1,000 fils(费尔)
卡塔尔	卡塔尔里亚尔	Qatar Riyal	QR.	QAR	1QAR = 100 dirhams(迪拉姆)
阿曼	阿曼里亚尔	Oman Riyal	RO.	OMR	1OMR = 1,000 baiza(派沙)

续表

亚洲	货币名称		货币符号		辅币进位制
	中文	英文	原有旧符号	标准符号	
阿拉伯也门共和国	也门里亚尔	Yemeni Riyal	YRL.	YER	1YER = 100 fils（费尔）
土耳其	土耳其镑	Turkish Pound (Turkish Lira)	£ T.（TL.）	TRL	1TRL = 100 kurus（库鲁）
塞浦路斯	塞浦路斯镑	Cyprus Pound	£ C.	CYP	1CYP = 1,000 mils（米尔）

大洋洲	货币名称		货币符号		辅币进位制
	中文	英文	原有旧符号	标准符号	
澳大利亚	澳大利亚元	Australian Dollar	$ A.	AUD	1AUD = 100 cents（分）
新西兰	新西兰元	New Zealand Dollar	$ NZ.	NZD	1NZD = 100 cents（分）
斐济	斐济元	Fiji Dollar	F. $	FJD	1FJD = 100 cents（分）
所罗门群岛	所罗门元	Solomon Dollar.	SL. $	SBD	1SBD = 100 cents（分）

欧洲	货币名称		货币符号		辅币进位制
	中文	英文	原有旧符号	标准符号	
欧洲货币联盟	欧元	Euro	EUR	EUR	1EUR = 100 euro cents（生丁）
冰岛	冰岛克朗	Icelandic Krona（复数：Kronur）	I. Kr.	ISK	1ISK = 100 aurar（奥拉）
丹麦	丹麦克朗	Danish Krona（复数：Kronur）	D. Kr.	DKK	1DKK = 100 ore（欧尔）
挪威	挪威克朗	Norwegian Krone（复数：Kronur）	N. Kr.	NOK	1NOK = 100 ore（欧尔）

续表

欧 洲	货币名称		货币符号		辅币进位制
	中 文	英 文	原有旧符号	标准符号	
瑞典	瑞典克朗	Swedish Krona(复数:Kronor)	S. Kr.	SEK	1SEK = 100 ore(欧尔)
俄罗斯	卢布	Russian Ruble (or Rouble)	Rbs. Rbl.	SUR	1SUR = 100 kopee(戈比)
波兰	兹罗提	Polish Zloty	ZL.	PLZ	1PLZ = 100 groszy(格罗希)
捷克斯洛伐克	捷克克朗	Czechish Koruna	Kcs. ; Cz. Kr.	CZK	1CZK = 100 Hellers(赫勒)
匈牙利	福林	Hungarian Forint	FT.	HUF	1HUF = 100 filler(菲勒)
瑞士	瑞士法郎	Swiss Franc	SF. ;SFR.	CHF	1CHF = 100 centimes(分)
英国	英镑	Pound, Sterling	£ ;£ Stg.	GBP	1GBP = 100 new pence(新便士)
马耳他	马耳他镑	Maltess Pound	£ . M.	MTP	1MTP = 100 cents(分)1cent = 10mils(米尔)
罗马尼亚	列伊	Rumanian Leu(复数:Leva)	L.	ROL	1ROL = 100 bani(巴尼)
保加利亚共和国	列弗	Bulgarian Lev(复数:Lei)	Lev.	BGL	1BGL = 100 stotinki(斯托丁基)
阿尔巴尼亚	列克	Albanian Lek	Af.	ALL	1All = 100 quintars(昆塔)
希腊	德拉马克	Greek Drachma	Dr.	GRD	1GRD = 100 lepton(雷普顿)or lepta(雷普塔)

续表

美洲	货币名称		货币符号		辅币进位制
	中文	英文	原有旧符号	标准符号	
加拿大	加元	Canadian Dollar	Can. $	CAD	1CAD = 100 cents (分)
美国	美元	U. S. Dollar	U. S. $	USD	1USD = 100 cent (分)
墨西哥	墨西哥比索	Mexican Peso	Mex. $	MXP	1MXP = 100 centavos (分)
危地马拉	格查尔	Quatemalan Quetzal	Q	GTQ	1GTQ = 100 centavos (分)
萨尔瓦多	萨尔瓦多科朗	Salvadoran Colon	¢	SVC	1SVC = 100 centavos (分)
洪都拉斯	伦皮拉	Honduran Lempira	L.	HNL	1HNL = 100 centavos (分)
尼加拉瓜	科多巴	Nicaraguan Cordoba	CS	NIC	1NIC = 100 centavos (分)
哥斯达黎加	哥斯达黎加科朗	Costa Rican Colon	¢	CRC	1CRC = 100 centavos(分)
巴拿马	巴拿马巴波亚	Panamanian Balboa	B.	PAB	1PAB = 100 centesimos (分)
古巴	古巴比索	Cuban Peso	Cu. Pes.	CUP	1CUP = 100 centavos (分)
巴哈马联邦	巴哈马元	Bahaman Dollar	B. $	BSD	1BSD = 100 cents (分)
牙买加	牙买加元	Jamaican Dollars	$. J.	JMD	1JMD = 100 cents (分)
海地	古德	Haitian Gourde	G. ;Gds.	HTG	1HTG = 100 centimes (分)
多米尼加	多米尼加比索	Dominican Peso	R. D. $	DOP	1DOP = 100 centavos (分)
特立尼达和多巴哥	特立尼达多巴哥元	Trinidad and Tobago Dollar	T. T. $	TTD	1TTD = 100 cents (分)

续表

美　洲	货币名称		货币符号		辅币进位制
	中　文	英　文	原有旧符号	标准符号	
巴巴多斯	巴巴多斯元	Barbados Dollar	BDS. $	BBD	1BBD = 100 cents (分)
哥伦比亚	哥伦比亚比索	Colombian Peso	Col $	COP	1COP = 100 centavos (分)
委内瑞拉	博利瓦	Venezuelan Bolivar	B	VEB	1VEB = 100 centimos (分)
圭亚那	圭亚那元	Guyanan Dollar	G. $	GYD	1GYD = 100 cents (分)
苏里南	苏里南元	Suriname Dollar	S. Fl.	SRD	1SRG = 100 分 1SRD = 1000florin
秘鲁	新索尔	Peruvian Sol	S/.	PES	1PES = 100 centavos (分)
厄瓜多尔	苏克雷	Ecuadoran Sucre	S/.	ECS	1ECS = 100 centavos (分)
巴西	雷亚尔	Real Brasileiro	Gr. $	BRL	1BRL = 100 centavos (分)
玻利维亚	玻利维亚比索	Bolivian Peso	Bol. P.	BOP	1BOP = 100 centavos (分)
智利	智利比索	Chilean Peso	P.	CLP	1CLP = 100 centesimos (分)
阿根廷	阿根廷比索	Argentine Peso	Arg. P.	ARP	1ARP = 100 centavos (分)
巴拉圭	巴拉圭瓜拉尼	Paraguayan Guarani	Guars.	PYG	1PYG = 100 centimes (分)
乌拉圭	乌拉圭比索	Uruguayan Peso	N. $	UYU	1UYU = 100 centesimos (分)

续表

非洲	货币名称		货币符号		辅币进位制
	中文	英文	原有旧符号	标准符号	
埃及	埃及镑	Egyptian Pound	£ E.;LF.	EGP	1EGP = 100 piastres(皮阿斯特) = 1,000 milliemes(米利姆)
利比亚	利比亚第纳尔	Libyan Dinar	LD.	LYD	1LYD = 100 piastres(皮阿斯特) = 1,000 milliemes(米利姆)
苏丹	苏丹镑	Sudanese Pound	£ S.	SDP	1SDP = 100 piastres(皮阿斯特) = 1,000 milliemes(米利姆)
突尼斯	突尼斯第纳尔	Tunisian Dinar	TD.	TND	1TND = 1,000 milliemes(米利姆)
阿尔及利亚	阿尔及利亚第纳尔	Algerian Dinar	AD.	DZD	1DZ = 100 centimes(分)
摩洛哥	摩洛哥迪拉姆	Moroccan Dirham	DH.	MAD	1MAD = 100 centimes(分)
毛里塔尼亚	乌吉亚	Mauritania Ouguiya	UM	MRO	1MRO = 5 khoums(库姆斯)
塞内加尔	非共体法郎	African Financial Community Franc	C. F. A. F.	XOF	1XOF = 100 centimes(分)
布基纳法索	非共体法郎	African Financial Community Franc	C. F. A. F.	XOF	1XOF = 100 centimes(分)
科特迪瓦	非共体法郎	African Financial Community Franc	C. F. A. F.	XOF	1XOF = 100 centimes(分)
多哥	非共体法郎	African Financial Community Franc	C. F. A. F.	XOF	1XOF = 100 centimes(分)
贝宁	非共体法郎	African Financial Community Franc	C. F. A. F.	XOF	1XOF = 100 centimes(分)
尼日尔	非共体法郎	African Financial Community Franc	C. F. A. F.	XOF	1XOF = 100 centimes(分)

续表

非　洲	货币名称		货币符号		辅币进位制
	中　文	英　文	原有旧符号	标准符号	
冈比亚	达拉西	Gambian Dalasi	D. G.	GMD	1GMD = 100 bututses（分）
几内亚比绍	几内亚比索	Guine – Bissau peso	PG.	GWP	1GWP = 100 centavos（分）
几内亚	几内亚西里	Guinean Syli	GS.	GNS	辅币为科里 cauri，但 50 科里以下舍掉不表示；50 科里以上进为一西里
塞拉利昂	利昂	Sierra Leone Le-one	Le.	SLL	1SLL = 100 cents（分）
利比里亚	利比里亚元	Liberian Dollar	L. $£ ;Lib. $	LRD	1LRD = 100 cents（分）
加纳	塞地	Ghanaian Cedi	¢	GHC	1GHC = 100 pesewas（比塞瓦）
尼日利亚	奈拉	Nigerian Naira	N	NGN	1NGN = 100 kobo（考包）
喀麦隆	中非金融合作法郎	Central African Finan – Coop Franc	CFAF	XAF	1XAF = 100 centimes（分）
乍得	中非金融合作法郎	Central African Finan – Coop Franc	CFAF	XAF	1XAF = 100 centimes（分）
刚果布	中非金融合作法郎	Central African Finan – Coop Franc	CFAF	XAF	1XAF = 100 centimes（分）
加蓬	中非金融合作法郎	Central African Finan – Coop Franc	CFAF	XAF	1XAF = 100 centimes（分）

续表

非洲	货币名称		货币符号		辅币进位制
	中文	英文	原有旧符号	标准符号	
中非	中非金融合作法郎	Central African Finan – Coop Franc	CFAF	XAF	1XAF = 100 centimes (分)
赤道几内亚	赤道几内亚埃奎勒	Equatorial Guinea Ekuele	EK.	GQE	1GQE = 100 centimes (分)
南非	兰特	South African Rand	R.	ZAR	1ZAR = 100 cents (分)
吉布提	吉布提法郎	Djibouti Franc	DJ. FS;DF	DJF	1DJF = 100 centimes (分)
索马里	索马里先令	Somali Shilling	Sh. So.	SOS	1SOS = 100 cents (分)
肯尼亚	肯尼亚先令	Kenya Shilling	K. Sh	KES	1KES = 100 cents (分)
乌干达	乌干达先令	Uganda Shilling	U. Sh.	UGS	1UGS = 100 cents (分)
坦桑尼亚	坦桑尼亚先令	Tanzania Shilling	T. Sh.	TZS	1TZS = 100 cents (分)
卢旺达	卢旺达法郎	Rwanda Franc	RF.	RWF	1RWF = 100 cents (分)
布隆迪	布隆迪法郎	Burnudi Franc	F. Bu	BIF	1BIF = 100 cents(分)
刚果金	刚果法郎	Franc Congolais	Z.	CDF	1CDF = 100 cents (分)
赞比亚	赞比亚克瓦查	Zambian Kwacha	KW. ;K.	ZMK	1ZMK = 100 nywee (恩韦)
马达加斯加	马达加斯加法郎	Franc de Madagasca	F. Mg.	MCF	1MCF = 100 cents (分)
塞舌尔	塞舌尔卢比	Seychelles Rupee	S. RP(S)	SCR	1SCR = 100 cent (分)

续表

非 洲	货币名称		货币符号		辅币进位制
	中 文	英 文	原有旧符号	标准符号	
毛里求斯	毛里求斯卢比	Mauritius Rupee	Maur. Rp.	MUR	1MUR = 100 centimes (分)
津巴布韦	津巴布韦元	Zimbabwe Dollar	ZIM. $	ZWD	1ZWD = 100 cents (分)
科摩罗	科摩罗法郎	Comoros Franc	Com. F.	KMF	1KMF = 100 tambala (坦巴拉)

附录三

国际商务单证常用缩略语一览表
（中英文对照）

A

a(@)	at	按
A/B	Aktiebolaget	股份公司(瑞典文)
abt.	about	大约
A/C	for account of	代、代表
acct.	account	账(账户)
A. D.	Anno Domini(L)	公元(拉丁文)
ADB	Asia Development Bank	亚洲开发银行
add.	address	地址
Avdal	ad valorem	从值(从价)
A/G	Aktiengeselskabet	股份公司(德文)
a. m.	anno meridiem(L.)	上午
A/M	above mentioned	上述
amt.	amount	金额
A/O	account of...	入某人账户(由某人付账)
a. p. l.	as per list	按照列表
A. P. L.	American President Line	美国总统轮船公司
app.	appendix	附表
approx.	approximately	大约
A. R	All Risks	一切险
art.	article	条款、货款
A/S	Aktieselskabet	股份公司(丹麦文)
	AktieseLskapet	股份公司(挪威文)

	Akzijn Sabeedriba	股份公司(芬兰文)
A/S	after sight ＝at sight	见票后(即付)
asst.	assortment	搭配
Asst	Assistant	助理
A. T. L.	actual total loss	实际全损
Att.	attached	附
Attn.	Attention	请洽
Aug.	August	八月
A. V.	Ad Valorem	从值(从价)
AV	Average	海损
Ave.	Avenue	路、大道
AWB	air way bill	航空运单

B

b/ -	bale, bag	包、装
BAF	bunker adjustment factor	燃油附加费
bal.	balance	余额、平衡
B. B. Clause	both to blame collision clause	船舶互撞条款
B/C	bill for collection	托收汇票
B. C.	before Chirst	公元前
bdle.	bundle	把、捆
B/E	bill of exchange	汇票
BENELUX	Belgium, Netherland, Luxemburg	比、荷、卢(三国)
b/f	brought forward	承前页
bg	bag	袋
Bk.	bank	银行
bkt	basket	篮、筐

bl.	bale	包
B/L	bill of lading	提单
bldg	building	大厦
BOC	Bank of China	中国银行
B. O.	branch office	分公司
br	branch	分行、分支机构
brl	barrel	桶
Bros	brothers	兄弟(公司)
b/s	bales, bags	包、装(复数)
btl	bottle	瓶
BTN	Brussels Tariff Nomenclature	布鲁塞尔税则目录
bx(s)	box(es)	箱、盒

C

c/ -	case	箱
ca.	circa	大约
C/A	cable address	电挂
CAF	cost assurance freight	成本保险加运费价
CAF	currency adjustment factor	货币调整附加费
CAD	cash against delivery	货到付款
canc.	cancelled, cancellation	取消
Capt.	captain	船长
Caricom	Caribbean Community	加勒比海共同体
Cat.	catalogue	目录
	category	类别
C. C.	carbon copy	复写本
CCCN	Customs Co - operative Council Nomenclature	海关合作理事会税则目录

CCIB	China Commodity Inspection Bureau	中国商品检验局
CCIC	China Commodity Inspection Corporation	中国商品检验公司
CCPIT	China Council for Promotion of International Trade	中国国际贸易促进委员会
C. C. V. O	combined certificate of value and origin	价值、产地联合证明书（海关发票）
c/f	carried forward	续后页
C&F	cost and freight	成本加运费价
C&I	cost and insurance	成本加保险价
CFS	Container Freight Station	集装箱货物集散战
cft.	cubic feet	立方尺
ch.	cheque	支票
chg	charge	费用
Cia	Compania	公司（西班牙）
Cie	Compagnie	公司（法国）
C/I	certificate of inspection	检验证书
	certificate of insurance	保险证明书
CIC	China Insurance Clause	中国保险条款
CIF	cost, insurance, freight	成本、保险加运费价
CIFC	cost, insurance, freight, commission	成本保险运费加佣金价
C. I. O.	cash in order	订货时付款
CIP	carriage & insurance paid to	运费保险费付至……价
CISS	Comprehensive Import Supervision Scheme	进口商品全面监督计划
ck.	check	支票
CL	container load	集装箱装载

CLP	container load plan	集装箱装箱单
cm	centimetre	公分、厘米
C. M. T	cutting, making and trimming	裁剪、缝制、整烫(整理)
C/N	credit note	贷项账单
CNFTTC	China National Foreign Trade Transportation Corp	中国外贸运输公司
CNY	Chinese Yuan	中国元
Co.	Company	公司
C/O	certificate of origin	产地证书
	care of	转交
	cash order	本票
C. O. D	cash on delivery or collection on delivery	货到付款
comm.	commission	佣金
Cont.	contract	合同
contd.	continued	继续、未完
Co – op	co – operative	合作经营,合作社
Corp	Corporation	公司
COSCO	China Ocean Shipping Company	中国远洋运输公司
C/P	charter party	租船方
CPT	carriage paid to	运费付至……价
c. q. d	customary quick dispatch	习惯快速装卸
Cr.	credit	贷方
C/R	cargo receipt	货物承运收据
crt.	crate	板条箱
c/s	cases	箱
CTA	communicate to all address	分送电

C. T. B/L	combined transport bill of lading	联合运输提单
C. T. D	combined transport documents	联合运输单据
C. T. L	constructive total loss	推定全损
ctn.	carton	纸箱
C. T. O	combined transport operator	多式联运经营人
cu.	cubic	立方
c. u. ft.	cubic feet	立方尺
c. u. m	cubic metre	立方公尺
cur.	currency	币制
C. V. C.	Chief value of cotton	主要成分是棉制
C. V. S.	Chief value of synthetic	主要成分是人造纤维
C. W. O.	cash with order	订货时付款
CWT	hundred weight	亨特威(英制 100 镑)
CY	container yard	集装箱堆场
CY to CY	container yard/container yard	集装箱场地至集装箱场地
C. Z.	canal zone	运河地带

D

d.	denarius(L.) = penny or pence	便士
D/A	documents against acceptance	承兑交单
D/C	documentary credit	跟单信用证
D/D	demand draft	即期汇票
dd.	dated	日期
Dec.	December	十二月
Dept.	department	部、处、科
DEQ	deliver ex quay	码头交货价
DES	deliver ex ship	目的港船上交货价

D/F	dead freight	空舱费
DHL	DHL International Ltd	敦豪公司(信使传递)
diam	diameter	直径
disc	discount	折扣、贴现息
D/N.	debit note	借项账单
do.	ditto = the same	同上、同前
doc.	document	单据、单证
D/O, D. O.	delivery order	提货单
Dol.	dollar	元
Doz(Dz.)	dozen	打
D/P	documents against payment	付款交单
D/PT/R	documents against payment with trust receipt	付款交单可凭信托收据借贷
D. P. V.	duty paid value	完税价格
d/s	days	天数
Dr.	debit	借方
dup.	duplicate	副本

E

ea.	each	每
E. C. U	European Currency Unit	欧洲共同体货币单位
E/D	export declaration	出口申报书
E. E.	error excepted	错误当查
EEC	European Economic Community	欧洲经济共同体
e. g.	exempli gratia	例如
E/L	export license	出口许可证
EMP	European Main Ports	欧洲主要口岸

EMS	European Monetary System	欧洲共同市场货币体系
	Express Mail Service	特快专递
encl.	enclosure	附件
E. &. O. E	errors & omissions excepted	错漏当查
EPZ	export processing zone	出口加工区
equiv	equivalent	等于
Est	Establishment	机构、企业、商店
EAT	estimated time of arrival	预计到达时间
etc.	et cetera(and so on)	等等
ETCL	expected time of commencement of loading	预计开始装货时间
ETD	estimated time of departure	预计离港时间
ETFD	expected time of finishing discharging	预计卸完时间
ETFL	expected time of finishing	预计装完时间
ex.	example	举例
exc.	excepted	除外
exch.	exchange	兑换,汇票
Ex. Facie	in accordance with the documents	按照单证
exp.	export	出口
EXW	ex work	工厂交货价

F

F. A. Q.	fair average quality	大路货
F. A. S.	Free alongside ship	船边交货
F. B.	freight bill	运费账单
F. B/L	FIATA combined transport B/L	国际运输商协会联合会联合运输提单

Feb.	February	二月
FC&S	free of capture & seizure clause	战争险不保条款
Fch.	franchise	免赔率
F. C. L.	full container load	整箱货
F. C. L. B/L	FIATA combined transport B/L	国际运输商协会联合会 联合运输提单
FEFC	Far East Freight Conference	远东运费公会
FIATA	Federation Internationable des Associations de Transitaires et Assimeles	国际运输商协会联合会
F. I.	free in	船方不负担装货费用
F. I. O.	free in and out	船方不负担装卸费用
F. I. O. S.	free in and out and stowed	船方不负担装卸及积载费用
F. I. O. S. T.	free in and out and stowed and trimmed	船方不负担装卸及积载平舱费用
F. I. O. T.	free in and out and trimmed	船方不负担装卸及平舱费用
F. I. W.	free into wagons	车上交货
F. M. V.	fair market value	公平市场价
F. O.	free out	船方不负担卸货费用
F. O. B	free on board	离岸价
F. O. C	free on charge	免费
F. O. I	free on interest	免息
F. O. P	free on plane	飞机上交货价
F. O. Q.	free on quay	码头交货价
F. O. R.	free on rail	铁路交货价
F. O. T	free on truck	车上交货价
F. O. W.	free on wagon	火车交货价
F. P. A.	free of particular average	平安险

Franco	franco rendu (free delivered)	免费送货到指定地点价
F. R. E. C.	fire risks extension clauses	火险扩展条款
Fri.	Friday	星期五
frt.	freight	运费
FRWD	Fresh & Rain Water Damage	淡水雨淋险
F/T	freight ton	运费吨
Ft.	feet	英尺

G

GA	General Average	共同海损
gal.	gallon	加仑
GATT	General Agreement on Tariffs & Trade	关税及贸易总协定
gds.	goods	货物
Gent.	gentleman	先生、绅士
G. m. b. H	Gesellschaft mit beschrankter Haftung	有限公司
G. M. Q.	Good merchantable quality	上好可销品质
G. M. T.	Greenwich mean time	格林威治时间
G. P. O.	General Post Office	邮政总局
gr.	gross	罗
grm.	gram	克
G. R. T	gross registered tonnage	注册总吨
gr. wt.	gross weight	毛重
GSP	generalized system of preferences	普惠制
GSP C/O	generalized system of preferences certificate of origin	普惠制产地证
GSP Form A	generalized system of preferences Form A	普惠制格式 A

H

HAWB	house airway bill	航空分运单
H/H	house to house	集装箱门到门
H. O.	Head Office	总行
h. p.	horse power	马力
H/P	house to pier	从厂、库到码头
hrs.	hours	钟点
HSBC	Hongkong & Shanghai Banking Corporation	汇丰银行
ht.	height	高度
hund.	hundred	百

I

ICC	International Chamber of commerce	国际商会
	Institute Cargo Clause	伦敦保险学会条款
idem	(L.) = the same	同前
I/D	import declaration	进口申请书
i. e.	id est(L.) = that is	即是
I/E	import/export	进口/出口
I/L	import license	进口许可证
In.	inch	英寸
Inc.	Incorporated	有限公司
ind.	indent	委托代购单
incl.	including, inclusive	包括
INCOTERMS	International Rules for the Interpretation of Trade Terms	国际贸易术语解释通则
Ins.	insurance	保险

inst.	instant	本月
inv.	invoice	本票
I/O	instead of	代替
I/P	import permit	进口许可证
	insurance policy	保险单
I. O. P.	irrespective of percentage	不计免赔率
I. Q.	idem quod(the same as)	同
	import quota	进口配额
I. O. U.	I owe you	借据
ISO	International Standard Organization	国际标准化组织

J

Jan.	January	一月
Jul.	July	七月
Jun.	June	六月
JWOB	jettison &/or washing overboard	抛掷、海水冲击险

K

Kg.	kilogram	公斤
K. Line	Kawasaki Kisem Kaisha Ltd	川崎汽船株式会社
Km.	kilometer	千米、公里

L

LASH	lighter – aboard – ship	载驳船
lb(s)	pound(s)	磅
L/C	letter of credit	信用证
LCL	less(than) container load	拼装集装箱货

ldg	loading	装载
L/G	letter of guarantee	保函
LIBOR	London Interbank Offer Rate	伦敦银行同业拆放利率
L/T	long ton	长吨、英吨
Ltd.	Limited(company)	有限公司
ltg.	lighterage	驳船费

M

Mar.	March	三月
MAWB	master airway bill	总航空运单
max.	maximum	最大量、最高额
M. D.	malicious damage	恶意行为损坏
mdse	merchandise	货物、商品
med.	medium	中等
memo	memorandum	备忘录
mfg	manufacturing	制造中,生产
MFN	most favored nation	最惠国
mfr	manufacturer	制造商
min.	minimum	最小量
misc.	miscellaneous	其他
M. L. B.	Mini - Land - Bridge	小陆桥
M/L cls.	more or less clause	宽容条款
mm.	millimeter	毫米
Mon.	Monday	星期一
M. P. H	miles per hour	时速……里
M/R	mate's receipt	大副收据
M/S	motor ship	内燃机轮

M/T	mail transfer	信汇
	metric ton	公吨
M. V.	motor vessel	内燃机轮
M. T. O.	multi – modal transport operation	多式联运
M/W	measurement/weight	体积或重量

N

N/A	not applicable	不适用
N. B.	nota bene = note below	注意
N. C. V.	no commercial value	无商业价值
N/M	no mark	无唛头
N. N. B/L	non – negotiable, not negotiable B/L	副本提单
No.	number	号码
non. d	not delivery	提货不着
N. O. E.	not otherwise enumerated	除非另有列举
N. O. P. F.	not otherwise provided for	除非另有规定
N. O. S.	not otherwise specified	除非另有指定
Nov.	November	十一月
N. P.	notary public	公证人
N/S	not sufficient	不足
N. Wt.	net weight	净重

O

O/A	on account of	代表
O/B	on behalf of	代表
O/C	open cover	预约承保书
OC	ocean	海洋

OCP	Overland Common Point	内陆公共点
Oct	October	十月
OG(I)L	Open General(Import)License	开放配额
OK	corrected ,approved	已获批准
OMCC	Ocean Marine Cargo Clause	海洋运输货物保险条款
O/O	(by) order of	送交
Orig.	original	正本
oz(s)	ounce(s)	英两、盎司
OSS	ourselves	我们自己

P

P. A.	particular average	单独海损
p. a	per annum	按年(计息)
P. & I. Club	Protection & Indemnity Club	保障赔偿协会
payt	payment	付款
p. c.	percent	百分之
P/C	polyester/cotton	涤/棉
pcs	pieces	件、个、只、块、张
pct.	percent	百分之
pd.	paid	付讫
p. d.	per day	按日(计息)
PICC	The People's Insurance Company of China	中国人民保险公司
pkg.	package	件、包
pls.	please	请
p. m.	post meridiem(L.)	下午
	per month	按月计息

P. O.	post office	邮局
	purchase order	邮货订单
P. O. B.	Post Office Box	邮政信箱
P. O. D.	payment on delivery	付款交货
p. p.	per procuration	代表
pr(s)	pair(s)	双、付
pro rate	Proportionally	按比例
P. R. C	People's Republic of China	中华人民共和国
prem.	premium	保险费
prox.	proximo	下月
P. S.	postscript	附言
P. T. O	please turnover	请阅背面
pty	prioretary	企业公司
Pte.	private	私人
P/V	polyester/viscose	涤/粘
P. V. C	polyviny chloride	聚氯乙烯

Q

qr.	quarter	四分之一
Q. V.	quod vide(which see)	请查阅
qnty.	quantity	数量
qlty	quality	品质

R

Re	reference	参考
Ref. No.	reference number	参考号
Reg.	registered	注册

retd.	returned	退回
R. F. W. D	rain &/or fresh water damage	淡水雨淋险
Rm.	room	房间
RMB	Renminbi Yuan	人民币
R. S. V. P	repondezs'ill vous plait(Fr.) reply ,if you please	请复
Ry.	railway	铁路

T

T.	tare, ton	吨
T/A	transshipment allowed	允许转运
	transshipment additional	转船附加费
	train/air	陆/空
TAT	train - air - truck	陆空陆
T/C	trueran/cotton	涤/棉
tdg.	trading	贸易
TEU	twenty equivalent of unit	相当于20呎集装箱
Thur.	Thursday	星期四
Tlx	telex	电传
T. L. O.	total loss only	全损险
TM	telegram multiple	同文电
tonn	tonnage	吨位
T. P. N. D	theft ,pilferage & non - delivery	盗窃提货不着险
tr. wt	tare weight	皮重
T/R	trust receipt	信托收据
T. Q.	tale quale or tel quel	现状条件
T/T	telegraphic transfer	电汇

TTL	total	总计
Tues.	Tuesday	星期二

U

U. A. E	United Arab Emirates	阿拉伯联合酋长国
UCP	uniform customs & practice	统一惯例
U. K. Ports	United Kingdom Ports	英国港口
ult	Ultimo	上月
U/T	unlimited transshipment	无限制转船
U/M	under -mentioned	下述

V

V.	vide	参阅
val.	value	价值
viz.	videlicet namely	即是
voy.	voyage	航次
VV.	vice versa	反之亦然

W

W. A.	with average	水渍险
Wed.	Wednesday	星期三
whse	warehouse	仓库
W/M	weight/measurement	按重量或体积
W. O.	washing overboard	冲失
W. P. A	with particular average	水渍险
W. R.	war risks	战争险
Wt.	weight	重量

W/T	with transshipment	转船
wtd.	warranted	保证
wty.	warranty	保证条款
W/W	warehouse to warehouse clause	仓至仓条款

X

XL	Extra large	特大
XP	express paid	快信
xs.	excess	超过

Y

Y. A. R	York - Antwerp Rule	约克—安特卫普规定（国际共同海损规则）

附录四

常用单位换算一览表
（中英文对照）

长度

1 千米（km）=0.621 英里（mile）

1 米（m）=3.281 英尺（foot）=1.094 码（yard）

1 厘米（cm）=0.394 英寸（inch）

1 英里（mile）=1.609 千米（km）

1 英尺（ft）=0.304 8 米（m）

1 英寸（in）=2.54 厘米（cm）

1 海里（sea mile）=1.852 千米（km）

1 码（yd）=0.9144 米（m）

1 英尺（ft）=12 英寸（in）

1 码（yd）=3 英尺（ft）

1 英里（mile）=5280 英尺（ft）

1 海里（sea mile）=1.1516 英里（mile）

质量

1 吨（ton）=1 000 千克（kg）=2205 磅（pound/lb.）

=1.102 短吨（short ton）=0.934 长吨（long ton）

1 千克（kg）=2.205 磅（lb）

1 短吨（short. ton）=0.907 吨（t）=2000 磅（lb）

1 长吨（long. ton）=1.016 吨（t）=2240 磅（lb）

1 磅（lb）=0.454 千克（kg）

1 盎司（oz/ounce）=28.350 克（g）

密度

1 千克/米^3（kg/m^3）=0.001 克/厘米^3（g/cm^3）=0.0624 磅/英尺^3（lb/ft^3）

1 磅/英尺^3（lb/ft^3）=16.02 千克/米^3（kg/m^3）

1 磅/英寸^3（lb/in^3）=27 679.9 千克/米^3（kg/m^3）

1 磅/美加仑（lb/gal）=119.826 千克/米^3（kg/m^3）

1 磅/英加仑（lb/gal）=99.776 千克/米^3（kg/m^3）

1 磅/（石油）桶（lb/bbl）=2.853 千克/米^3（kg/m^3）

面积

1 平方公里(km^2) = 100 公顷(ha) = 247. 1 英亩(acre)
= 0. 386 平方英里($mile^2$)

1 平方米(m^2) = 10. 764 平方英尺(ft^2)

1 公亩(acre) = 100 平方米(m^2)

1 公顷(ha) = 10000 平方米(m^2) = 2. 471 英亩(acre)

1 平方英里($mile^2$) = 2. 590 平方公里(km^2)

1 英亩(acre) = 0. 4047 公顷(ha) = $40.47 * 10^{-3}$平方公里(km^2)
= 4047 平方米(m^2)

1 平方英尺(ft^2) = 0. 093 平方米(m^2)

1 平方英寸(in^2) = 6. 452 平方厘米(cm^2)

1 平方码(yd^2) = 0. 8361 平方米(m^2)

体积

1 立方米(m^3) = 1000 升(liter) = 35. 315 立方英尺(ft^3) = 6. 290 桶(bbl)

1 立方英尺(ft^3) = 0. 0283 立方米(m^3) = 28. 317 升(l)

1 千立方英尺(mcf) = 28. 317 立方米(m^3)

1 百万立方英尺(MMcf) = 2. 8317 万立方米(m^3)

10 亿立方英尺(bcf) = 2831. 7 万立方米(m^3)

1 万亿立方英尺(tcf) = 283. 17 亿立方米(m^3)

1 立方英寸(in^3) = 16. 3871 立方厘米(cm^3)

1 英亩 · 英尺 = 1234 立方米(m^3)

1 桶(bbl) = 0. 159 立方米(m^3) = 42 美加仑(gal)

1 美加仑(gal) = 3. 785 升(l)

1 美夸脱(qt) = 0. 946 升(l)

1 美品脱(pt) = 0. 473 升(l)

1 美吉耳(gi) = 0. 118 升(l)

1 英加仑(gal) = 4. 546 升(l)

参考文献

1. 孟祥年．国际贸易实务操作教程[M]．北京:对外经济贸易大学出版社,2005.
2. 张军．外贸单证实务[M]．南京:东南大学出版社,2004.
3. 杨金玲．国际商务单证实务[M]．北京:首都经济贸易大学出版社,2008.
4. 耿伟．出口贸易单证实务[M]．北京:首都经济贸易大学出版社,2005.
5. ICC 跟单信用证统一惯例 UCP600[M]．北京:中国民主法制出版社,2006.

图书在版编目(CIP)数据

国际商务单证操作实训/杨金玲,张建华主编.—北京:首都经济贸易大学出版社,2009.10

ISBN 978-7-5638-1740-5

Ⅰ.①国… Ⅱ.①杨…②张… Ⅲ.①国际贸易—票据—教材 Ⅳ.①F740.44

中国版本图书馆 CIP 数据核字(2009)第 172687 号

国际商务单证操作实训
杨金玲 张建华 主编

出版发行	首都经济贸易大学出版社
地　　址	北京市朝阳区红庙(邮编 100026)
电　　话	(010)65976483 65065761 65071505(传真)
网　　址	http://www.sjmcb.com
E-mail	publish@cueb.edu.cn
经　　销	全国新华书店
照　　排	北京砚祥志远激光照排技术有限公司
印　　刷	北京京华虎彩印刷有限公司
开　　本	787 毫米×980 毫米 1/16
字　　数	316 千字
印　　张	18.25
版　　次	2009 年 10 月第 1 版 2017 年 7 月第 1 版第 2 次印刷
书　　号	ISBN 978-7-5638-1740-5/F·994
定　　价	34.00 元